Urban Systems Development in Central Canada: Selected Papers

UNIVERSITY OF TORONTO DEPARTMENT
OF GEOGRAPHY RESEARCH PUBLICATIONS

1. THE HYDROLOGIC CYCLE AND THE WISDOM OF GOD: A THEME IN
   GEOTELEOLOGY by Yi-Tuan

2. RESIDENTIAL WATER DEMAND AND ECONOMIC DEVELOPMENT by
   Terence R. Lee

3. THE LOCATION OF SERVICE TOWNS by John U. Marshall

4. KANT'S CONCEPT OF GEOGRAPHY AND ITS RELATION TO RECENT
   GEOGRAPHICAL THOUGHT by J. A. May

5. THE SOVIET WOOD-PROCESSING INDUSTRY: A LINEAR PROGRAMMIN
   ANALYSIS OF THE ROLE OF TRANSPORTATION COSTS IN LOCATION
   AND FLOW PATTERNS by Brenton M. Barr

6. THE HAZARDOUSNESS OF A PLACE: A REGIONAL ECOLOGY OF
   DAMAGING,EVENTS by Kenneth Hewitt and Ian Burton

7. RESIDENTIAL WATER DEMAND: ALTERNATIVE CHOICES FOR MAN-
   AGEMENT by Angelo P. Grima

8. THE ATMOSPHERIC ENVIRONMENT: A STUDY OF COMFORT AND
   PERFORMANCE by Andris Auliciems

9. URBAN SYSTEMS DEVELOPMENT IN CENTRAL CANADA: SELECTED
   PAPERS edited by L. S. Bourne and R. D. MacKinnon

Urban Systems Development in Central Canada: Selected Papers

Edited by
L. S. Bourne
R. D. MacKinnon

Published for the University of Toronto
Department of Geography
by the University of Toronto Press

© University of Toronto Department of Geography
Published by University of Toronto Press
Toronto and Buffalo, 1972
Printed in Canada
ISBN 0-8020-3293-1
Microfiche ISBN 0-8020-0262-5

ENVIRONMENT STUDY

Preface

As a nation we are now faced with staggering urban problems, and
the prospect of mounting pressures by the end of the century. The
consequences of rapid urbanization, particularly in the last three
decades has accelerated interest in and the necessity for systematic research in Canada (Lithwick 1971). This anthology reflects
this need by collecting together a diverse set of research papers
concerned with the complex processes of urban growth and development. They offer one basis on which to assess the implications
of trends in urban growth for the changing environment of contemporary Canadian urban life, with a view to augmenting our ability
to anticipate and respond to the course of future events.

The focus of the following papers is confined to one aspect of
urban development--the growth and characteristics of the aggregate urban system in Ontario and Quebec, an area for which the
designation Central Canada is suggested. The research emphasizes those urban areas with populations over 10,000; their evolution, size distribution, cross-sectional characteristics and growth
performance, the interaction and flows which link these cities as
a system, the regional transportation network, and the resulting
impact of rapid urbanization on the rural economy and on urban
life styles and urban form. Most of the research papers selected
for inclusion derive from a project undertaken in the Centre for
Urban and Community Studies at the University of Toronto and supported by a grant from Bell Canada.[1]

---

[1] This project, entitled the Environment Study, has as its objective an examination of
evolutionary trends in the spatial form of urban development in Ontario and Quebec.
The interest of the Bell System in urban research is not recent. In his classic study
The City, originally published in 1925, Robert Park noted that the Bell Telephone
Company in the United States is "...now making, particularly in New York and Chicago,
elaborate investigations, the purpose of which is to determine, in advance of its actual
changes, the probable growth and distribution of the urban population..."

Objectives and Organization

The volume has two objectives. The first is simply to document some of the results of an extensive research project on urban development in Canada. There has not been systematic and continuous research on the Canadian urban system, or of any particular subregional system. Although the number and quality of contributions to the Canadian literature in urban studies has been increasing, most are of a more generalized nature (these are reviewed in several papers particularly those in Parts 1 and 2).[2] Few have attempted to incorporate empirical results and a range of analytical examples.

Most of the literature relating to urban growth and urban development utilized for research and teaching in Canada derive from studies in other countries, principally the United States (Berry and Horton 1970) and to a lesser extent from European and British sources (Cowan 1969). This literature is of course relevant to research in this country and is of critical importance both in the educational process and in providing comparative frameworks for the identification of urban policy (Miles 1970 and Wade 1969). But it lacks both empirical and theoretical reference to the Canadian urban situation as well as a sensitivity to unique Canadian problems and potentials.[3]

The second objective follows logically from the first. It is the desire to increase the flow of information and to stimulate student interest and research on urban development in Canada. Such interest both within and outside the university has grown immensely in recent years as the problems of planning, financing and environmental quality control which have been created, or at least compounded, by rapid urban growth become more critical and more apparent. The rationale for the orientation and sequence of studies in this volume therefore is an awareness of the necessity of providing a broad and thorough analysis of past trends and evolving structural interrelationships as a foundation for understanding urban development in this, the core area of the country. It is anticipated that students of urban affairs will find that the availability of empirical research material on Canadian

---

[2]Among the more substantial published works are Stone (1967), Lithwick and Paquet (1968), Plunkett (1968), Simmons and Simmons (1969), and Lithwick (1971).

[3]A comprehensive review of historical evolution and the present state of the art in urban geography in Canada is provided in Simmons (1967).

cities should complement existing texts,[4] and will be of considerable assistance in developing their own research interests and insights into aspects of the Canadian urban milieu, its development, problems, and futures.

Most of the papers included here, as a result of this premise, represent the extensive data manipulation and analysis which is a necessary prerequisite to analytical insight of present urban conditions, as well as to intelligent speculation on the future. An attempt is made, however, to minimize the unnecessary discussion of technique; although where the approaches are either crucial to the basic research ideas or controversial some discussion is considered warranted.

The volume itself is organized as a collection of individually-tailored research papers. Most of the papers first appeared as research reports, others are students' papers. Some are original papers drafted specifically for this volume. They have been revised at the discretion of the editors, but they have not been reoriented such that the unique contribution of each author in terms of strategies and procedures has been removed. Because of obvious limitations of length, most papers have also been shortened. That the papers selected for inclusion also vary markedly in style, scope and rigor, is to some degree inevitable in any collection of research papers on such wide and comprehensive issues as those under investigation here. Moreover, some redundancy between papers will be apparent and is in fact quite necessary in order to maintain the flow of ideas and reasoning in each study.

Contents

As noted above, the papers in this volume are concerned with analyzing the basic spatial, structural and growth characteristics of the urban system of Ontario and Quebec. The papers are divided into five parts, with each part organized around a central theme. These themes are: (1) the origin and definition of the urban system; (2) comparative structure and subdivisions of the system; (3) growth factors and characteristics; (4) transportation and interaction; and (5) the effects of growth on life styles and agriculture.

The first section treats the form, definition, and evolutionary behaviour of the aggregate of cities, and the process of urbanization in general, in the two provinces. In large part the papers

---

[4] There are, for example, a number of collections of readings available which are applicable to Canadian urban problems: see Feldman and Goldrick (1969), Putnam, Taylor and Kettle (1970), Bourne (1971) and Krueger (1971).

are descriptive, designed to provide a general overview in graphic and tabular form of the growth and distribution of urban population. The second part examines various aspects of the contemporary cross-sectional structure of the urban system, the underlying dimensions by which urban areas may be differentiated. Included here are two factor analytic studies, one of socioeconomic census data and the other of occupational data for Ontario-Quebec cities, both leading to the construction of a typology and grouping of cities on the basis of the dimensions obtained. Section three introduces the complex issue of growth in terms of the correlates between attributes of urban structure and the rate of growth; the contribution to each city's growth which results from regional advantages and differentials in local economic mix; and the variability in growth in small urban centres. The fourth section offers a broad introduction to the structure of transportation networks, interaction and flows among the cities and regions of the two provinces. It is these important flows and linkages which in fact give substance to the concept of a system of cities. The final section follows from the materials presented above in identifying two examples of the implications of urban growth in Ontario and Quebec on agricultural activities, and on the future form of metropolitan areas and the life styles of their residents.

Definitions
The label of Central Canada for Ontario and Quebec raises a minor but nevertheless interesting and controversial point. This title is primarily an attempt to suggest an appropriate regional context for the cities of these two provinces, particularly the southern areas, relative to the larger urban systems of Canada and the United States. Two points of disagreement may be raised; one is the label itself, and the second is the implicit assumption that this area, and the cities it contains, constitute a meaningful region and urban subsystem. The question of what label is appropriate for this area is in part a matter of convenience, but more importantly it reflects substantial perceptual differences resulting from diverse regional backgrounds in Canada. [5] To the Maritimer, Ontario and Quebec are frequently cited, often in a non-complimen tary fashion, as "Central" or "Upper" Canada. To a resident of

[5] Aspects of regional and cultural diversity in Canada are, for example, discussed from a traditional viewpoint in Clark (1962). Many of these interpretations are substantiated quantitatively in Ray and Murdie (1972).

the western provinces these older and more established areas of the country are described simply as the "East," particularly when the conversation concerns matters of politics and finance. [6] In Ontario and Quebec, neither the "Eastern" nor "Central" Canada label appears to be in widespread use, at least not consistently. Quite possibly Canada does not have a distinctively perceived central region or mid-west as exists in the United States, thanks to the severe barriers to development imposed by the Canadian Shield. [7]

The designation "Central" Canada therefore, in the absence of a more generally accepted description, represents a compromise to prevailing regional and historical attitudes. The term "Eastern" ignores the substantial area of the country east of Quebec City. "Central" on the other hand conveys the impression of a "core" area within the spatial structure of the Canadian national economy, which, although again open to some disagreement, is nevertheless a useful premise from which to begin this volume. "Central" also implies a close integration in historical development and economic fortunes with nearby areas in the United States, forming what is titled by some authors as the international Great Lakes Megalopolis. [8]

The second point open to question is the designation of the area as a separate region. Although most authors have tended to avoid semantic disagreements over what is and is not an appropriate region, there is substantial evidence to suggest that the southern and developed areas of the two provinces form a logical unit for study. The most important evidence perhaps is the physical separation of the area, in terms of continuous economic activity and integrated development, from the Maritimes by the Appalachians and from the beginnings of western agriculture in Manitoba by the Canadian Shield. [9] In addition, although this area is a functional part of the extensive Great Lakes metropolitan region, the international border does provide a meaningful subregional boundary as its impact on the behaviour of the urban system is considerable. The question that has been left open, however, is the extent to

[6] For example, the strength of financial dominance by the "East" is illustrated in Kerr (1965; 1968).

[7] This seems to be true even though rural southwestern Ontario does have a distinctive midwestern flavour.

[8] See for example Wade (1969) and Vournas and Drymiotis (1968).

[9] See for example Simmons (1970).

which the obvious cultural and historical contrasts between On-tario and Quebec cities produce distinctive differences in the structure and growth of the combined urban systems and the social systems which they reflect.[10] With these contrasts in mind, several papers attempt to contrast the characteristics of the Ontario and Quebec subsystems.

Similarly, the inclusion of cities in northern areas poses important definitional problems. It is clear that these towns and cities display somewhat different growth and structural patterns from those in southern areas of the provinces, given the obvious effects of their relatively isolated locations, specialized resource-based economies, and erratic growth performance. Although their significance in size is relatively small, their importance in numbers and thus in analyses based on all cities may in some instances be considerable. Most authors have considered the difficulties of interpretation to be sufficient to warrant the elimination of northern centres in their analyses.

Postscript

A final consideration must be recognized in treating urban development in Ontario and Quebec--the impact of recent political and social instability in Quebec. Isolationism in any form, in any major region, will most certainly have a substantial dampening and redistributive effect on the growth of the urban system, effects which will be most pronounced in the isolated region itself. Although the evidence is thin, preliminary population estimates indicate that Quebec's growth has slowed in concert with instability, and that Ontario has picked up the largest share of any redistributed growth.

However, as most of the following papers draw largely on data from the 1961 census, or in a few instances from the partial 1966 census, the analyses predate the recent tide of events. The initial effects of these events will not become apparent until the 1971 census is released. This volume then is timely, in a number of ways, by providing a set of basic analyses on which subsequent studies using the 1971 census may build.

---

[10] An interesting and relevant overview of contemporary Canadian Society is to be found in Mann (1968).

References

BOURNE, L. S., ed. 1971. Internal Structure of the City: Readings on Space and Environment. Toronto: Oxford University Press.

CLARK, A. H. 1962. Geographical diversity and the personality of Canada. In M. McCaskell, ed. Land and Livelihood: Geographical Essays in Honour of George Jobberns. Christchurch: New Zealand Geographical Society Miscellaneous Series, No. 4; reprinted in R. M. Irving, ed. Readings in Canadian Geography. Toronto: Holt, Rinehart, and Winston, 1968, pp. 3-16.

COWAN, P., ed. 1969. Developing patterns of urbanization. Special Issue of Urban Studies Vol. 6.

FELDMAN, L. D. and M. D. GOLDRICK, eds. 1969. Politics and Government of Urban Canada: Selected Readings. Toronto: Methuen.

FRIEDEN, B. J. and W. W. NASH, JR., eds. 1969. Shaping an Urban Future. Cambridge: M. I. T. Press.

GERTLER, L. O., ed. 1968. Planning the Canadian Environment. Montreal: Harvest House.

KERR, D. 1965. Some aspects of the geography of finance in Canada. Canadian Geographer 9:175-92.

--------. 1968. Metropolitan dominance in Canada. In J. Warkentin, ed. Canada: A Geographical Interpretation. Toronto: Methuen, pp. 531-55.

KRUEGER, R., ed. 1971. Urban Problems: A Canadian Reader. Toronto: Holt, Rinehart and Winston.

LITHWICK, N. H. 1971. Urban Canada: Problems and Prospects. A Report to Mr. R. Andras, Minister Responsible for Housing. Ottawa: Central Mortgage and Housing Corporation.

LITHWICK, N. H. and G. PAQUET. 1968. Urban Studies: A Canadian Perspective. Toronto: Methuen.

MANN, W. E., ed. 1968. Canada: A Sociological Profile. Toronto: Copp Clark.

MILES, S. R., ed. 1970. Metropolitan Problems: International Perspectives. Toronto: Methuen.

PARK, R. E. 1967. The city: suggestions for the investigation of human behavior in the urban environment. In R. E. Park and E. W. Burgess The City, reprinted with foreword by M. Janowitz. Chicago: University of Chicago Press.

PLUNKETT, T. J. 1968. Urban Canada and Its Government: A Study of Municipal Organization. Toronto: MacMillan.

PUTNAM, R. G.; F. J. TAYLOR; and P. G. KETTLE, eds. 1970. A Geography of Urban Places. Toronto: Methuen.

RAY, D. M. and R. A. MURDIE. 1971. Comparison of Canadian and American urban dimensions. In B. J. L. Berry, ed. Classification of Cities: New Methods and Evolving Uses. Washington: International City Managers Association.

SIMMONS, J. W. 1967. Urban geography in Canada. Canadian Geographer 11:341-56.

--------. 1970. Interprovincial interaction in Canada. Research Paper No. 24, Centre for Urban and Community Studies, University of Toronto.

SIMMONS, J. W. and R. SIMMONS. 1969. Urban Canada. Toronto: Copp Clark.

STONE, L. 1967. Urban Development in Canada: An Introduction to the Demographic Aspects. Ottawa: Queen's Printer, for the Dominion Bureau of Statistics.

VOURNAS, T. and A. DRYMIOTIS. 1968. The Great Lakes Megalopolis: principal component and similarity analyses. Ekistics 26: 152:60-82.

WADE, M., ed. 1969. The International Megalopolis Eighth Annual University of Windsor Seminar on Canadian-American Relations. Toronto: University of Toronto Press.

Acknowledgments

Many people have contributed to this book. The basic research project from which most of the papers derive, the Environment Study, was directed by the Centre for Urban and Community Studies at the University of Toronto and supported by a grant from Bell Canada. This generous support of academic research is gratefully acknowledged. The role of the former Director of the Centre, Professor J. Stefan Dupré,was of paramount importance in initiating and co-ordinating the early phases of the study.

The papers themselves are the result of contributions by several capable groups. The excellent cartographic displays were prepared by Jennifer Wilcox and Jane Ejima in the cartographic office of the Department of Geography, under the direction of Mr. Geoffrey Matthews. Extensive computer programming assistance was extended by Siegfried Schulte. Most important are the contributions of recent graduate students, some of which appear directly in the form of papers reproduced in this volume, others in supporting roles for various phases in the research program. These include: Gerald Barber, Trudi Bunting, George Bushell, Henry Chen, John Davies, Michael Doucet, Günter Gad, Stephen Golant, Frederick Hill, John Hodgson, Andrew Jacob, Robert Jones, Christopher Maher, Geoffrey McDonald, James Stark, and Robert van der Linde. Without their efforts this volume would not have been possible. We are also indebted to our colleagues, particularly Jim Simmons, for their contributed papers and for their helpful comments during preparation of the manuscript; and also to Miss Sheila Talley who turned our unintelligible revisions into a neatly typed final draft. We would like to thank Helga MacKinnon for her invaluable editorial assistance during the final stages of manuscript preparation.

Toronto   L. S. Bourne
March 1971   R. D. MacKinnon

Contents

Urban Systems Development in Central Canada: Selected Papers

I

Definition and Behaviour of the Urban System

1

Editors' comments

Systems are definitional rather than naively given constructs.[1]
In analyzing an urban system two definitional questions in particular are immediately apparent: first, whether the cities under
discussion constitute what might be termed a system; and second,
whether the spatial delimitations and member cities of that system
are appropriately specified. As the introductory section of this
volume, this chapter examines the recent path of development and
current state of urbanization in Ontario and Quebec in an attempt
to isolate the aggregate properties which define an urban system,
such as their distribution by size, and which illustrate the evolution of the form of that system over time.

Although no attempt is made in these introductory comments
or in the contributing papers to become involved in the semantics
of systems terminology, a few comments on the system concept
are relevant at this point. The word 'system' has many scientific as well as colloquial meanings. Hall and Fagen (1956), for
example, define a system as a "set of objects, together with
relationships between the objects and between their attributes."
Objects are simply the parts or components of the system, and

[1] The terminology of systems research is employed in its most general expression and
definition principally as a means of organizing different approaches to research into a
a more cohesive logical framework, rather than as an analytical construct. A most
useful collection of the classic articles on the development of systems theory is Buckley
(1968).

these components are unlimited in variety. For example, a city
may be considered an object. Its attributes may be physical size,
population, function, rate of growth, and distance from other
urban centres. The relationships which articulate the system by
linking its constituent objects are the concepts which give substance to the notion of a system. An analysis of an urban system
is an attempt to investigate the nature of these relationships not
only among urban places, such as accessibility links, but also
among the attributes of these places. Beer (1960) has suggested
that "system is one of the names of order, the antonym of chaos. "
The following papers are looking for order within a set of cities.

The question of what type of system model is applicable to
a set of cities is open to considerable disagreement. Buckley
(1967) argues strongly for the description of socio-cultural systems not in terms of analogies with mechanical systems, but
rather as complex adaptive systems. The important characteristic of an adaptive system is that it is open. As a result,
interrelationships both with the external environment and among
the components themselves may produce significant changes in
each of the components as well as in the system as a whole.
Clearly this characteristic is applicable to a set of cities in which
changes internal to a single city have important implications for
all cities with which it is linked. In general, interrelationships
within such adaptive systems are articulated by flows of information, flows which derive from both internal and external linkages.
These flows provide the means of self-regulation and self-
adaptation by which a system of cities may change or elaborate its
spatial structure in response to a changing environment in certain
specific and predictable directions (see Part 4 in this volume).

Acceptance of the concept of a set of cities as a directionally
adaptive system is at least a recognition on the part of the re-
searcher of its inherent complexity. Stimuli for growth and
adjustment within an urban system may derive from the external
components with which the cities are related; from changes in the
linkages between the cities, their attributes and information channels; from changes in the internal structure of each city; or from
a combination of such factors the origin of which it is difficult if
not impossible to trace. The openness of an urban system to
external pressures, and the complex adaptive mechanisms which
are acting within the system are basic premises on which the
following papers develop.

The introductory paper is a generalized overview of the form and distribution of urban development in the two provinces. Initially it summarizes the universal components of urbanization, as expressed in the growth of cities in Central Canada. The contemporary situation is introduced in terms of city-size distributions and rural-urban contrasts in the two provinces, and a series of illustrations document the form of urban development. Finally, a different and broader concept of an urban area is proposed to generate discussion on definitional problems in urbanization and to provide more meaningful estimates of the size and potential of urban population aggregates.

How are the cities of Ontario and Quebec ordered by size? How has this ranking changed over time, and what do these changes tell us about the way the urban system is evolving? The second paper tackles these questions in an attempt to document regularities in the urban system.

First, the paper examines the applicability of the rank-size rule to the size distribution of cities in Central Canada. The underlying theoretical arguments have been the subject of considerable debate in recent years. It is not the purpose of this paper, however, to debate these broader theoretical issues, but rather to isolate apparent empirical regularities in one expression of urban development. There is little question of the existence and relevance of regularities in a set of cities according to size of population if for no other reason than the fact that size is a dominant explanatory variable in the analysis of differences among urban centres.

The results indicate a definite consistency in the size ordering of cities in the two provinces suggesting the existence of similar system properties to those documented elsewhere. Of particular interest is the comparative examination of city-size distributions in Ontario and Quebec, the latter showing a "deficiency" in cities of medium-size. Moreover, a high degree of stability, and thus predictability, in the evolution of size distributions over time is also apparent in the results.

References

BEER, S. 1960. Below the twilight arch. General Systems 5:9-20.

BUCKLEY, W. 1967. Sociology and Modern Systems Theory. Englewood Cliffs, N.J.: Prentice-Hall.

--------, ed. 1968. Modern Systems Research for the Behavioral Scientist: A Sourcebook. Chicago: Aldine Publishing Co.

HALL, A. D. and R. F. FAGEN. 1956. Definition of a system. General Systems 1: 18-28.

2

Urbanization and urban growth in Ontario and Quebec: An overview

L.S. Bourne and G. Gad

The rapid urbanization in Canada during the last century, and particularly in the post-war years, has created an integrated and identifiable system of cities. Increasingly economic development is articulated through the urban system. Regional growth has become synonymous with the growth of cities in this system.[1] The core of the national system of cities is in Central Canada, the Ontario and Quebec subsystem (Figure 2.1). This subsystem, stretching in a linear form from Windsor to Quebec City, is rela-

---

[1] General overviews of urban characteristics and economic development patterns in Canada are provided in Ray (1970), Ray and Berry (1965), Paquet (1968), and the Economic Council of Canada (1965). Other references are provided in the following papers, particularly in Sections II and III.

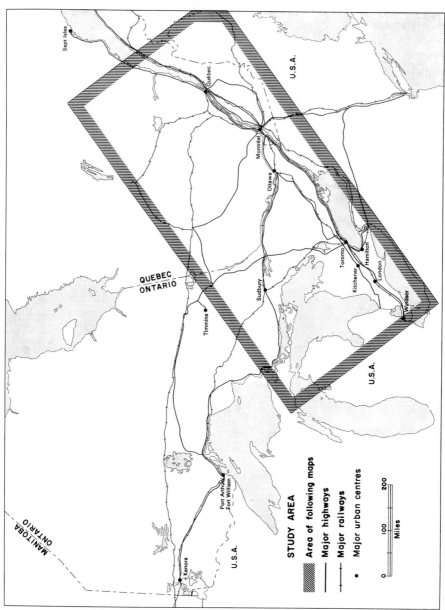

Figure 2.1 Map of study area

tively simply identified by its physical isolation from the Maritimes and West and by the international border.

This paper provides a descriptive overview of the urban system as an introduction to the volume. Drawing largely on graphic and tabular illustrations, it reviews the size and spatial distribution of cities, the components of population growth and the distribution of urban populations, and raises questions for subsequent analysis. The emphasis is largely contemporary as comprehensive census figures date only from 1951, and in light of the presence of parallel volumes on urban growth with substantial historical content (Stone 1967; Simmons and Simmons 1969; Easterbrook and Watkins 1967; and Spelt 1965). The paper concludes with a suggestion to expand our concepts of delimiting urban areas in response to rapid urbanization.

Components of Urban Growth
The recent and rapid growth of cities can be viewed simply as the result of three demographic processes: (1) urbanization--the movement of people from farm and village to city, with a consequent rise in the proportion of city dwellers (usually centres with over 1,000 population); (2) immigration--the movement of people into the cities directly from other regions or from foreign countries; and (3) natural increase--the surplus of births over deaths. The following paragraphs briefly summarize the implications of each of these components for the cities of Ontario and Quebec.

Urbanization: The process of urbanization, unlike the other two components of urban growth, does have an intrinsic limit which would be reached when 100 per cent of the population was urbanized. Recent experience in the highly urbanized countries suggests that a critical limit is reached when 80 to 90 per cent of the country becomes urbanized. Ontario and Quebec are beginning to approach this limit with 85 and 81 per cent of their populations respectively living in urban places (Table 2.1). The rate of urbanization in the two provinces has gradually decreased as the limit is approached. Future urban growth will as a result come mainly from the other two processes. Though the overall rate of increase in urbanization will continue to decline, a related process has increased sharply. This process is the movement of urban people upward through the urban size hierarchy into the larger centres and metropolitan regions--a process which some

9

TABLE 2.1 HISTORICAL GROWTH OF URBAN POPULATION
ONTARIO AND QUEBEC, 1851-1970

Year	ONTARIO		QUEBEC		CANADA	
	Total Population (000's)	Per Cent Urban*	Total Population (000's)	Per Cent Urban*	Total Population (000's)	Per Cent Urban*
1851	952	14.0	890	14.9	2,436	13.1
1861	1,396	18.5	1,112	16.6	3,230	15.8
1871	1,621	20.6	1,192	19.9	3,689	18.3
1881	1,917	27.1	1,359	23.8	4,325	23.3
1891	2,114	35.0	1,489	28.6	4,833	29.8
1901	2,183	40.3	1,649	36.1	5,371	34.9
1911	2,527	49.5	2,006	44.5	7,207	41.8
1921	2,934	58.8	2,361	51.8	8,788	47.4
1931	3,432	63.1	2,875	59.5	10,377	52.5
1941	3,788	67.5	3,332	61.2	11,506	55.7
1951	4,598	72.5	4,056	66.8	14,009	62.4**
1961	6,236	77.3	5,259	74.3	18,201	69.7
1966	6,961	83.5	5,781	78.3	20,015	74.5
1970 (est.)	7,652	85.0	6,016	81.0	21,406	77.5

SOURCE: Census of Canada and Stone (1967).
     * Defined as those living in cities and towns of 1,000 population and over.
    ** Includes Newfoundland.

authors have rather awkwardly called metropolitanization.[2] This trend is clearly evident in the tables that follow (see Table 2.2).

In association with the urbanization process and paralleling the increasing share of the population in metropolitan centres, there are other subcomponents of change, which influence the form of urban development. One is the suburbanization process. Cities reach out into the countryside urbanizing the rural and village population already in residence in these areas while adding a new population of "ex-urbanites." The latter may themselves be only one generation or one move from the farms.

The boundary between the rural and urban landscapes, which was more sharply defined in earlier periods, is now extremely blurred (see Paper 18). The commuting radius of major centres

[2] A variety of definitions are provided in Hauser and Schnore (1965).

10

TABLE 2.2 POPULATION DISTRIBUTION AND NUMBER OF CENTRES BY
SIZE CLASS IN THE URBAN HIERARCHY, ONTARIO-QUEBEC, 1941-1966

Population in 000's and Per Cent of Total Urban Population

Size Class	1941 No.	1941 Per Cent	1951 No.	1951 Per Cent	1956 No.	1956 Per Cent	1961 No.	1961 Per Cent	1966 No.	1966 Per Cent
250,000 and over	2055	44.2	3531	58.0	4242	57.8	5118	58.6	5953	58.9
100,000-249,999	773	16.6	400	6.6	469	6.4	745	8.5	1046	10.3
50,000- 99,999	272	5.9	506	8.3	772	10.5	901	10.3	840	8.3
30,000- 49,999	315	6.8	326	5.4	309	4.2	330	3.8	383	3.8
10,000- 29,999	410	8.8	482	7.9	520	7.1	511	5.9	650	6.4
5,000- 9,999	227	4.9	281	4.6	347	4.7	430	4.9	326	3.2
1,000- 4,999*	596	12.8	564	9.3	685	9.3	695	8.0	920	9.1
Total Urban Population	4648	100.0	6090	100.0	7344	100.0	8730	100.0	10118	100.0

* Estimated

Number of Centres

Size Class	1941	1951	1956	1961	1966
250,000 and over	2	5	5	5	5
100,000-249,999	4	3	3	5	7
50,000- 99,999	4	8	11	13	12
30,000- 49,999	9	8	8	9	10
10,000- 29,999	27	29	32	32	51
5,000- 9,999	36	45	53	64	49
1,000- 4,999	241	269	304	329	329
Totals	323	367	416	457	463

NOTES: 1. Total Urban Population based on Census Urban Totals.

2. Populations for size class 1,000-4,999 are calculated by the difference between the sum of all the larger size classes and Total Urban Population.

SOURCES: D.B.S. Census - 1966: 92-607 Table 10
D.B.S. Census - 1966: 92-608 Table 13
D.B.S. Census - 1961: 92-535 Table 9
D.B.S. Census - 1956: Tables 7 and 11
D.B.S. Census - 1951: Tables 9 and 14
D.B.S. Census - 1941: Table 14

now extends up to fifty miles and beyond. As urban development extends over larger and larger areas, some centres inevitably coalesce to form still larger metropolitan complexes. These complexes have gradually replaced their original parts--the old cities, villages, boroughs and townships--as the coherent, functioning units of the urban system.

Immigration: Urban growth attributable to foreign immigration has been particularly evident in Canada during the past two decades, more so than in most developed countries. The rate of immigration, however, has fluctuated markedly with changes in government policy, and in relation to political and economic conditions here as well as in the countries of immigrants' origins. In the period immediately after World War II the policy of the Canadian Government was to direct many foreign immigrants to rural areas. Despite such efforts many of them eventually found their way into cities, and the policy was subsequently changed. In more recent years the flow of immigrants has been increasingly to the major urban centres, particularly those of Ontario and Quebec, reinforced by government policies which renders entry into the country easier if the intended destination is a city with a growth economy and thus wide employment opportunities. This has had the obvious effect of further accelerating the growth of the already more economically favoured and larger centres.

Interregional migration also plays a major role in the distribution of urban growth (Anderson 1966 and Stone 1969). In central and eastern Canada, migration between provinces has been mainly westward from the Atlantic region to the provinces of Ontario and Quebec. Within both provinces, interregional migration has been primarily from the east and north to cities in the south and west. However, since data on such migrations are scarce for other than aggregate provincial movements, this component has to be ignored for most analytical purposes.

Natural Increase: Given that cities contain the largest proportion of the nation's population, their natural increase is obviously the major component of growth in the population as a whole and of growth in the cities themselves. Thus, to a greater extent than ever before, the future growth of the cities depends on what they are like now and have been like in the recent past, rather than on factors external to the urban system. Consequently, the initial focus of analysis in this volume must be on the population growth and character of the urban system itself.

The problem of differing rates of natural increase is a vexing one in any attempt to describe population growth. Previous attempts to project trends in birth rates have led to some embarrassment as passing years showed predicted rates of change to have not just the wrong magnitude, but even the wrong sign. More specifically, in the 1930's most scholars agreed that the populations of highly urbanized and industrialized countries would tend to stabilize and perhaps even to decline. Then the next two decades brought a sharp reversal of this trend in many countries,

12

with especially high birth rates in Canada. Throughout the 1960's birth rates have been falling in Canada and in both Ontario and Quebec. Natural increase has reached the lowest level recorded (less than 10 per thousand population) since the 1930's. Although there are many guesses about the underlying causes of these trends, few observers claim to understand them fully. Despite a very high degree of uncertainty about future rates of natural increase, it is possible to attribute the slowing rate of urbanization documented in Canada as elsewhere in recent years to falling levels of natural increase.

The Aggregate Urban System of Ontario and Quebec
What results have these processes of urban growth produced in Ontario and Quebec thus far? For the world as a whole the proportion of city-dwellers (taking only cities of over 100,000 people) is just over one-third, and is expected to reach one-half by 1990. By these standards Canada is a highly urbanized country. Canadian cities larger than 100,000 now contain about one-half of the population, and if smaller centres (over 1,000 population) are included about three-quarters of the population is considered to be urbanized. Within Canada, the Central region comprising the provinces of Ontario and Quebec and containing 64 per cent of the country's population, is even more highly urbanized; over half the population lives in cities larger than 100,000 and over four-fifths of the population is defined as "urban" by the Census (see Table 2.1). It would appear that in terms of the degree of urbanization Quebec lags about a decade behind Ontario.

    To express adequately the extent and form of the urbanization process, urban populations are initially arrayed on a scale based on size of city. Table 2.2 summarizes both the total urban population and the number of cities in Ontario and Quebec by city-size category for each census record since 1941. The size distributions displayed in the two parts of this table in themselves tell a great deal about the nature of the system and its recent history of growth. The total population resident in cities over 10,000 in the two provinces increased 134 per cent from 3.8 million in 1941 to 8.9 million in 1966 while the population of all cities and towns (over 1,000 population) increased 110 per cent from 4.6 to 10.1 million in the same period.

    To what extent has the process of metropolitanization increased the concentration of urban populations in the larger size categories? Such comparisons must be first tempered by an awareness of the

13

TABLE 2.3 CHANGES IN URBAN POPULATION DISTRIBUTION
ONTARIO-QUEBEC, 1941-1966

| Size Class | Per Cent Population Change | | | |
	1941-1951	1951-1956	1956-1961	1961-1966
Quebec				
100,000 and over	27.6	17.7	25.1	15.0
50,000 - 99,999	*	16.2	-22.0	6.7
30,000 - 49,999	-77.3	94.3	107.4	32.6
10,000 - 29,999	70.6	20.9	0.4	37.5
5,000 - 9,999	27.2	23.9	35.2	-15.8
1,000 - 4,999	12.1	20.1	20.5	18.6
Total Urban Population	32.0	19.4	20.5	15.8
Ontario				
100,000 and over	49.7	21.6	24.0	22.8
50,000 - 99,999	- 4.8	87.3	39.6	-11.2
30,000 - 49,999	80.7	-17.2	-21.6	3.7
10,000 - 29,999	- 6.0	- 2.6	- 3.8	16.4
5,000 - 9,999	24.9	23.3	15.8	-31.2
1,000 - 4,999	-33.2	23.7	-33.3	34.5
Total Urban Population	30.3	21.6	17.6	15.9

* Not calculated

effects of the size groupings employed. Table 2.3 for example, shows the extreme variability of population changes within size categories; changes which are as much a function of the number of cities shifting from one category to another as they are of different rates of growth for cities of differing size. Even so, returning to Table 2.2, certain trends are apparent. First, the proportion of urban populations residing in cities of metropolitan size (over 100,000 population) increased from 60.8 in 1941 to 69.2 in 1966. But the rate of increase has slowed and in fact the proportion in cities over 250,000 has remained essentially stable since 1951. At the same time, the proportion dwelling in small cities and towns (under 10,000) decreased from 17.7 to 12.3 in the same period. Yet the population in these smaller centres has progressively grown from 823,000 to 1,246,000 in the last 25 years. Since 1961 the proportion in the smallest size category actually increased slightly. Obviously the effects of forces leading to

metropolitanization are evident, but their impact is declining.
The small centres, typical suppliers of migrants moving upward
in the urban hierarchy have not declined in absolute size, but have
simply grown at a slower rate. More recent evidence suggests
that they are holding their own (see Part 3).

Cities as Elements of the Urban System

The elements in the urban size hierarchy are the individual cities.
However the question of how individual urban centres are defined
has been neglected thus far. The Dominion Bureau of Statistics
(D.B.S.) recognizes three classes of centres: first, the census
metropolitan area [3] (C.M.A.), generally those with over 100,000
population; second, an intermediate category referred to as major
urban area, [4] (M.U.A.), areas smaller than metropolitan status
but with substantial suburban development outside city boundaries;
and third, the city as a municipal or political unit. Table 2.4
lists the populations, according to these definitions, of all urban
areas in the two provinces from 1941 to 1966 which had 10,000
population or over at the time of the 1961 census. Figure 2.3
displays the locations of these cities by population size in 1966.
Using a population of 10,000 in 1961 as the minimum threshold
size for inclusion here, the urban system of Ontario and Quebec
contains 63 centres. A lower size threshold could have been
used but it would have presented serious problems in compiling
census figures for early time periods.

Although numerous sources provide statistics on one or other
of these areas, Table 2.4 is the first published attempt to place
population figures for all three types in relative context. This
task was not particularly easy. The "major urban area" category

[3] In 1961, the Census Metropolitan Area (C.M.A.) in Canada was defined as an
incorporated central city of at least 50,000 persons and a surrounding area which
together with the central city had a total population of 100,000 or more persons.
That part of the C.M.A. outside of the central city must have (1) at least 70 per
cent of its labour force engaged in non-agricultural acitivites, and (2) a minimum
population density of 1,000 persons per square mile. A criterion of linkages among
the major parts of the C.M.A. was also formulated such that at least 40 per cent of
the non-agricultural labour force in the municipalities adjacent to the central city
should commute to places of employment in the central city or its immediate suburban
fringe. Lack of data, however, made systematic application of the criterion impossible.

[4] The Major Urban Area (M.U.A.) definition arose to encompass the areas of suburban
development which sprang up around medium and small cities. These areas satisfy all
the criteria for C.M.A. status except that the minimum size of the central city (50,000
population) is not achieved, or the total population of the central city and suburbs is less
than 100,000 or both. Although there is no apparent minimum size for an M.U.A. the
smallest centres so designated are in the range of 40,000 total population. As yet scant
information is provided by the census for these areas.

TABLE 2.4 POPULATION OF MAJOR CENTRES: ONTARIO-QUEBEC, 1941-1966

Metropolitan Areas[b]	Census Population (in 000's)				
	1966	1961	1956	1951	1941[a]
1. Montreal	2,437	2,110	1,745	1,472	1,145
2. Toronto	2,159	1,825	1,502	1,210	910
3. Ottawa-Hull	495	430	345	293	226
4. Hamilton	449	395	338	280	198
5. Quebec City	413	358	312	276	225
6. London	207	181	154	129	91
7. Windsor	212	193	186	164	124
8. Kitchener-Waterloo	192	155	129	107	70
9. Sudbury	117	111	98	74	56
Major Urban Areas[b]					
10. St. Catharines	109	96	85	67	36
11. Chicoutimi-Jonquière	109	105	91	76	43
12. Oshawa-Whitby	100	81	63	50	33
13. Thunder Bay	98	92	80	68	55
14. Trois Rivières	94	88	75	66	42
15. Sherbrooke	80	70	62	55	38
16. Sault Ste. Marie	75	65	46	38	26
17. Kingston	72	63	56	48	30
18. Sarnia	67	61	51	40	30
19. Shawinigan	65	66	59	50	31
20. Brantford	62	56	52	47	32
21. Niagara Falls	61	57	49	41	22
22. Welland	59	54	30	23	20
23. Peterborough	56	52	44	40	25
24. Guelph	51	44	35	29	23
25. Brampton	45	20	13	8	6
26. Cornwall	46	44	18	17	14
27. Drummondville	43	39	37	35	11
28. St. Jean	43	39	31	25	17
29. Timmins	40	40	37	37	29
30. Valleyfield	34	32	26	24	17
31. Granby	34	31	27	22	14
32. St. Jérôme	33	29	21	18	11
Other Major Centres					
33. Belleville	33	31	21	20	16
34. Chatham	32	30	22	21	17
35. Woodstock	24	20	18	16	12
36. Barrie	24	21	17	13	10
37. St. Hyacinthe	24	22	20	20	18
38. North Bay	24	24	21	18	16
39. Stratford	23	20	20	19	17
40. St. Thomas	23	22	19	18	17

TABLE 2.4 — (continued)

Metropolitan Areas[b]	Census/Population (in 000's)				
	1966	1961	1956	1951	1941[a]
41. Alma	22	13	11	8	6
42. Thetford Mines	22	22	20	15	13
43. Victoriaville	21	19	16	13	9
44. Rimouski	20	18	15	12	7
45. Brockville	19	18	14	12	11
46. Joliette	19	18	17	16	13
47. Sorel	19	17	16	15	12
48. Sept Îles	19	14	6	2	1
49. Rouyn	19	19	17	15	9
50. Owen Sound	18	17	17	16	14
51. Pembroke	16	17	15	13	11
52. Orillia	15	15	14	12	10
53. Magog	14	13	13	12	9
54. Trenton	14	13	11	10	8
55. La Tuque	14	13	11	10	8
56. Val d'Or	12	11	10	9	4
57. Lindsay	12	11	10	10	8
58. Georgetown	12	10	6	3	3
59. Riviére–du-Loup	12	11	10	9	9
60. Cobourg	12	11	9	8	6
61. Noranda	12	11	10	10	5
62. Kenora	11	11	10	9	8
63. Asbestos	11	11	9	8	6

NOTES: Ranking is by 1966 population.

[a]1941 populations are estimates for most of the major urban areas.

[b]All metropolitan and major urban area populations have been adjusted to the 1961 census definition boundaries.

The total number of cities (63) compares to a census total of 73 separate municipalities when major urban area definitions are not employed. The cities included in the major urban areas are:
1. Chicoutimi North, Kenogami, Chicoutimi, Jonquière and Arvida are included in Chicoutimi-Jonquière M.U.A.
2. Grand'Mère and Shawinigan South are included in Shawinigan M.U.A.
3. Fort William and Port Arthur have been merged to form the Thunder Bay M.U.A.
4. Whitby is included in Oshawa M.U.A.
5. Trois Rivières M.U.A. includes Cap–de-la-Madeleine.
6. Welland M.U.A. includes Port Colborne.

SOURCES: Census of Canada, Dominion Bureau of Statistics. Central Mortgage and Housing Corporation.

for instance has been inconsistently applied over time and between cities. For census years prior to 1961 it was often necessary to estimate populations for most of these areas by means
of simple extrapolation. Equally difficult to assess are the effects of changing census boundary definitions for the larger
centres and the impact of annexations for the smaller municipalities (for example, Thunder Bay and North Bay). Here the
definitions of previous censuses have been adjusted, as the census
does itself, to the 1961 definiton to ensure compatibility. Whether
such adjustments are totally valid is open to question. The
reader interested in the problems of defining metropolitan areas
is referred to the growing literature on the subject (Berry 1968)
and to Part 5 of this volume.

Cities are clearly more than simple nodes in an urban system.
Figure 2.4 attempts to convey an impression of the spatial configuration of urban development. Surprisingly, an existing map
displaying the geographic limits of metropolitan areas, major
urban areas, as well as smaller municipalities in Ontario and
Quebec could not be found. On this map note that as these are
not the built-up areas of cities but the summation of existing
census definitions, the problems of overbounding and underbounding of certain cities have to be borne in mind. For example,
compare the similarity in size of the census metropolitan areas
of Hamilton and Ottawa with that of Montreal even though the latter is much larger in terms of population.

Despite these inconsistencies, this map does give some
indication of the spatial extent of urban development in Ontario
and Quebec. The dominant impression is one of concentration
within the few larger metropolitan areas and in two broad regional clusters around Montreal and the western end of Lake
Ontario. Thus, the linear form of development noted earlier
should be represented more accurately as an axis joining two
distinct poles of urban growth.

Profile of Change
Although population changes by city-size category may be relatively consistent over time, rates of growth for individual cities
are anything but consistent. Table 2.5 summarizes percentage
population change for cities in Ontario and Quebec, as given in
Table 2.4, for each of four census periods.

Two hypotheses are immediately apparent from this table,
both of which are discussed again by other essays in this volume.

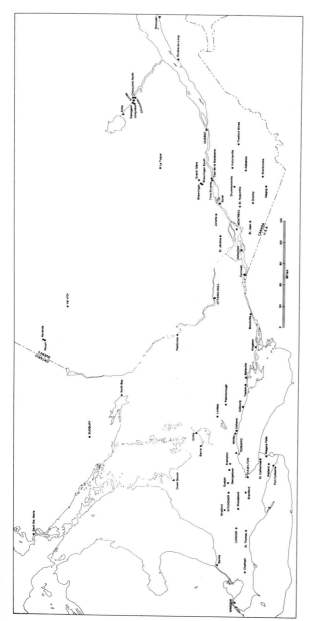

Figure 2.2 Reference map: names of urban centres

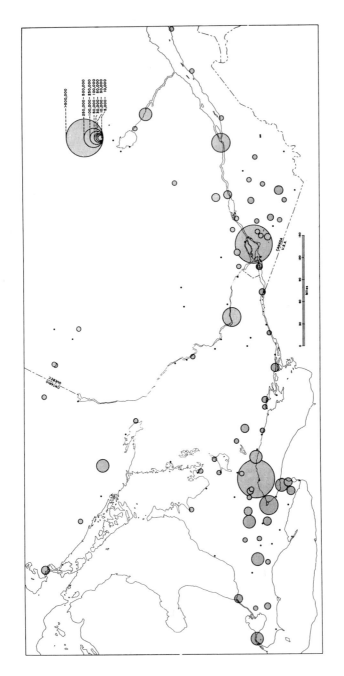

Figure 2.3   Population in urban centres, 1966:   Ontario and Quebec

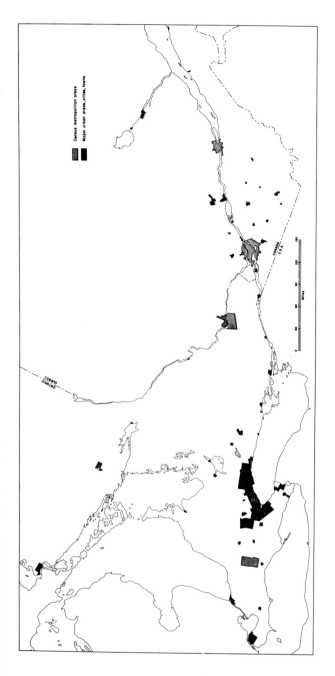

Figure 2.4 Urban areas with over 10,000 population in 1966

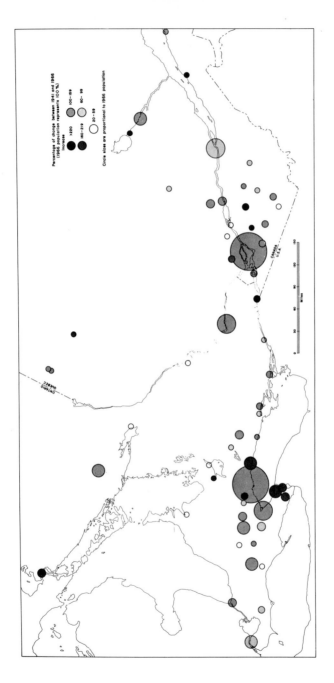

Figure 2.5 Population change by urban centres, 1941–1966: Ontario and Quebec

The first is that the distribution of urban population change shows wide fluctuations over time and across the urban size hierarchy. This variability is in part a function of the boundary definitions and changes noted above, but it is also a reflection of the from-rags-to-riches fortunes of many smaller communities. With no other information than the figures in this table one would conclude that predicting growth rates for individual cities is a difficult task at the best of times. Under these circumstances, the most productive analyses of urban growth may be those based on probabilistic techniques.

A second hypothesis suggests a cross-sectional relationship between variations in growth rates and the size of a city. For instance, note the generally consistent percentage population changes for metropolitan areas in comparison to those for the smaller cities and major urban areas. With two exceptions, metropolitan areas have been growing at much the same rate, at least in recent decades, a rate which closely approximates the average for the entire urban system. This is a well documented tendency, sometimes referred to as the urban ratchet effect (Thompson 1965), whereby the growth rates of larger centres converge on the national or regional average as these centres increase in size (see Part 3). The smaller the city, on the other hand, the more variable its growth may be, either upward or downward. No city over 40,000 population showed either a negative or zero growth rate in any of the census periods studied.

Other factors clearly influence these growth rates over and above city-size. Cities with specialized economies, and those in locations which are peripheral to the regional urban system usually exhibit slow rates of growth. For example, northern mining centres such as Timmins and Sudbury, and specialized manufacturing cities such as Windsor, Shawinigan, and Chicoutimi-Jonquière, have experienced only modest expansion in recent years. The spatial patterns displayed by these rates (Figure 2.5) are complex. Although detailed evaluations are left to subsequent chapters, it is apparent that the spatial variations in urban growth show the same polarity as noted above for the entire urban system. With few exceptions, rapidly growing cities are located within the sphere of metropolitan influence, particularly of Toronto and Montreal. The resulting picture is one of a dynamic and diversified urban system in which a large number of processes are operating to both entrench the present and thus to

TABLE 2.5   POPULATION CHANGES FOR MAJOR CENTRES: ONTARIO-QUEBEC, 1941-1966

Metropolitan Areas	PER CENT POPULATION CHANGE			
	1941-51	1951-56	1956-61	1961-66
1. Montreal	28.6	18.5	20.9	15.5
2. Toronto	33.0	24.1	21.5	18.3
3. Ottawa-Hull	29.6	17.7	24.6	15.1
4. Hamilton	41.4	20.7	16.9	16.9
5. Quebec City	22.7	13.0	14.7	15.4
6. London	41.8	19.4	17.5	14.4
7. Windsor	32.3	13.4	3.8	9.8
8. Kitchener	52.9	20.6	20.2	23.9
9. Sudbury	32.1	32.4	13.3	5.4
Major Urban Areas				
10. St. Catharines	36.1	26.9	12.9	13.5
11. Chicoutimi-Jonquière	76.7	19.7	15.4	3.8
12. Oshawa-Whitby	51.5	26.0	28.6	23.5
13. Thunder Bay	23.6	17.6	15.0	6.5
14. Trois Rivières	57.1	13.6	17.3	6.8
15. Sherbrooke	44.7	12.7	12.9	14.3
16. Sault Ste. Marie	46.2	21.1	41.3	15.4
17. Kingston	60.0	16.7	12.5	14.3
18. Sarnia	33.3	27.5	19.6	9.8
19. Shawinigan	61.3	18.0	11.9	1.5
20. Brantford	46.9	10.6	7.7	10.7
21. Niagara Falls	86.4	19.5	16.3	7.0
22. Welland	15.0	30.4	80.0	9.3
23. Peterborough	60.0	10.0	18.2	7.7
24. Guelph	26.1	20.7	25.7	15.9
25. Brampton	33.4	16.3	53.8	125.0
26. Cornwall	21.4	5.9	144.4	4.5
27. Drummondville	218.2	5.7	5.4	10.3
28. St. Jean	47.1	24.0	25.8	10.3
29. Timmins	27.6	0.0	8.1	0.0
30. Valleyfield	41.2	8.3	23.1	6.3
31. Granby	57.1	22.7	14.8	9.7
32. St. Jérôme	63.6	16.7	38.1	13.8
Other Major Centres				
33. Belleville	25.0	5.0	47.6	6.5
34. Chatham	23.5	4.8	36.4	6.7
35. Woodstock	33.3	12.5	11.1	20.0
36. Barrie	30.0	30.8	23.5	14.3
37. St. Hyacinthe	11.1	0.0	10.0	9.1
38. North Bay	12.5	16.7	14.3	0.0
39. Stratford	11.8	5.3	0.0	15.0
40. St. Thomas	5.9	5.6	15.8	4.5
41. Alma	33.3	37.5	18.2	69.2
42. Thetford Mines	15.4	33.3	10.0	0.0
43. Victoriaville	44.4	23.1	18.8	10.5
44. Rimouski	71.4	25.0	20.0	11.1

	1945-51	1951-56	1956-61	1961-66
45. Brockville	9.1	16.7	28.6	10.6
46. Joliette	23.1	6.3	5.9	10.6
47. Sorel	20.0	6.7	6.3	11.8
48. Sept-Îles	100.0	200.0	133.3	35.7
49. Rouyn	66.7	13.3	11.8	0.0
50. Owen Sound	14.3	6.3	0.0	5.9
51. Pembroke	18.2	15.4	13.3	-5.9
52. Orillia	20.0	16.7	7.1	0.0
53. Magog	33.3	8.3	0.0	7.7
54. ·Trenton	25.0	10.0	18.2	7.7
55. La Tuque	25.0	10.0	18.2	7.7
56. Val d'Or	125.0	11.1	10.0	9.1
57. Lindsay	25.0	0.0	10.0	9.1
58. Georgetown	0.0	100.0	66.7	20.0
59. Rivière-du-Loup	0.0	11.1	10.0	9.1
60. Cobourg	33.3	12.5	22.2	9.1
61. Noranda	100.0	0.0	10.0	9.1
62. Kenora	12.5	11.1	10.0	0.0
63. Asbestos	33.3	12.5	22.2	0.0

TABLE 2.6 PROBABILITY MATRICES FOR THE GROWTH
OF CITY-SIZE DISTRIBUTIONS, ONTARIO-QUEBEC

Population Size (000's)	1951-1961 Period					
5- 10	0.88	0.12	0	0	0	0
10- 30	0	0.87	0.13	0	0	0
30- 50	0	0	0.60	0.40	0	0
50-100	0	0	0	0.89	0.11	0
100-250	0	0	0	0	1.00	0
> 250	0	0	0	0	0	1.00

Population Size (000's)	1941-1951 Period					
5- 10	0.69	0.31	0	0	0	0
10- 30	0	0.81	0.19	0	0	0
30- 50	0	0	0.33	0.67	0	0
50-100	0	0	0	0.50	0.50	0
100-250	0	0	0	0	0.80	.20
> 250	0	0	0	0	0	1.00

mould the system of the future. This system may necessitate
new urban definitions and concepts.

Probabilities of City Growth
Urban growth may also be viewed, as noted above, as a probability process. For example, by observing changes in the number
(and relative frequency) of cities in each size category over each
census period we can construct probability matrices describing
regularities in the evolution of the urban system.

 Table 2.6, as one illustration, summarizes changes in city size
for all centres in Ontario and Quebec for two ten-year census
periods from 1941 to 1951 and 1951 to 1961. Each value measures
the probability of a city moving from one size category to another
in one census period. For example, in 1951 a city in the 10-30,000
population range had a 0.13 probability of moving into the 30-50,000
class by 1961, and a zero or insignificant probability of moving
over the boundaries into any class over 50,000.

 These transition matrices tell a lot about aggregate city size
changes in Ontario and Quebec. Proportions in the main diagonal
of the matrix (cities which did not change size category) are
measures of system stability; entries in the upper-right triangle
indicate growth, and those in the lower-left triangle measure the
probability of decline. The high proportions along the main diagonal suggest how slowly the urban system evolves, at least when
considered at this highly generalized level. The two matrices are
relatively similar in both scale and distribution, although the proportions in some cells vary markedly due largely to the small
sample of cities in certain size categories. Similar matrices were
also derived for each 5 year census period from 1941 to 1966, but
these showed even greater variability. While numerous arguments
could be advanced for probabilistic interpretations of urban growth,
they are beyond the scope of the present paper.

 In summary, the more obvious aspects of the evolution of an
urban system evident in these matrices may be re-iterated as
follows:

  1) that urban areas of the size range represented here seldom
     exhibit drastic shifts in their positions in the size hier-
     archy over any meaningful time period. The probability of
     decline has in all cases been either zero or insignifi-
     cantly small.

26

2) that transition matrices for ten-year periods reveal considerable instability. This is due in part to the limited sample size and the infrequency of positional changes in the urban hierarchy, but also to the tendency apparent in this analysis toward a definite clustering of cities of similar size in terms of growth performance.

3) that interpretations of urban growth, and the rates of change on which they are based, depend heavily on the number and size of aggregations (intervals) of size categories employed, as well as on spatial boundary conditions.

4) that a sequence of such matrices smoothed over different census periods offers one excellent basis for extrapolating the growth of an urban system without identifying every component of the growth process.

The Identification of Regional Urban Complexes

Thus far we have been dependent solely on published data sources and thus on municipal units or aggregates of such units. This inevitably limits the scope of the research and the quality of the results and the insights obtained. Also our images of what constitutes a city have changed (Part 5), and urban development has spread beyond most census boundaries rendering existing definitions increasingly inadequate.

There are of course other ways to view the distribution of urban population and to describe the relative importance of cities and clusters of cities in an urban system. One concept introduced here is that of regional urban growth complexes. Their definition has two basic components: it reflects the diversity of urban infrastructure which is the basis of economic growth in any area, and it encompasses the spatial confines within which location decisions tend to be essentially indifferent as to regional considerations. Infrastructure is a nebulous concept. It encompasses the full range of community support facilities, the existing economic structure and public services, as well as the potential these provide for sustained economic growth. Specific elements of infrastructure include a minimum population size, the range and diversity of the local employment mix, public utilities and amenities, social attributes of the population, historical persistencies, and even images pertaining to socio-economic opportunities. In this sense, the factor analysis results in Part 2 provide one indication of the common denominators of that part of the existing

27

urban infrastructure of Ontario and Quebec for which data are available.

Current census reporting units tend to underestimate the size of the urban region which provides this infrastructure. This underbounding may result either through strict adherence to municipal, township or county boundaries, or through an insufficient degree of interaction (commuting) between contiguous parts of the region to warrant their inclusion in the census metropolitan area.. Introduction of the designation "major urban area" (M. U. A.) for cities below metropolitan size, but with large suburban populations, reflects one attempt to broaden census definitions of urban areas and to more accurately measure their actual size.

In some instances, several centres may form a single complex (see Figure 2. 4). For example, of the three largest centres in close proximity in the Niagara area, St. Catharines with an estimated M. U. A. population of 116, 000 in 1970, Niagara Falls (M. U. A. population 62, 000) and Welland (including Port Colborne, M. U. A. population 60, 000), none approached the threshold population for a metropolitan area in the 1961 census (although St. Catharines will likely be so designated in the 1971 census). Combined as a regional cluster of cities, however, the population of the Niagara urban region totals about 240, 000, or about the level that some researchers have argued constitutes a minimum size for metropolitan status (Thompson 1965). These cities may not at present be contiguous nor even highly integrated in economic terms, and thus would not qualify as a metropolitan area by current census definitions, but the possibility for greater integration is present. Commuting to work, for instance, is generally practical throughout the area. Also cities in this area are attractive for new development over and above what is evidenced by their individual populations. Although commuting data are not yet available in Canada on a sufficiently systematic basis, they would greatly facilitate the identification of these complexes.

In cases where interacting complexes have not yet emerged, potential becomes important. It is not particularly relevant that cities may lie in close proximity through historical accident of location, or that their economies may be distinctly different and largely unrelated at present. The concept of a regional urban complex is valid as one which delimits "environmental" units or areas of future growth potential through close geographic proximity, complementary functions, and a common attraction for investment decisions.

Table 2.7 illustrates the relative sizes of regional urban complexes in Ontario and Quebec in 1970. In most instances, the core of each complex is a major urban area or census metropolitan area, to which adjacent unincorporated areas and urban centres in close proximity have been added. Although differences from census definitions are in some cases minimal, the results in total are revealing. The new centres fall rather neatly into three distinct size groups. The first group, the metropolitan centres, also may be divided into three subgroups. Obviously, Montreal and Toronto stand out as national as well as regional metropolises in Central Canada, of approximately the same size. The expanded Toronto metropolitan area, stretching north to Aurora and along the lakeshore from Oshawa to Oakville, has a 1970 estimated population of over 2,500,000. Combined with the adjacent Hamilton-Burlington metropolitan area (Burlington is a commuter suburb of both Toronto and Hamilton) the population of the Lake Ontario complex rises to over 3.0 million. This larger area is still much smaller than the urban region employed in the Metropolitan Toronto and Region Transportation Study.[5] The structural relationships of the two metropolitan areas in the Lake Ontario complex also bear a striking similarity to those of the Chicago-Gary consolidated S.M.S.A. (Standard Metropolitan Statistical Area) around Lake Michigan, adding further justification for their aggregation.

In the second subgroup within the metropolitan level are Ottawa-Hull and Quebec City, each with populations of about one-half million and with relatively similar economies and spatial juxtapositions. In the third subgroup are four cities all located in the southwestern part of the province of Ontario. These are the Kitchener-Waterloo-Galt-Guelph cluster of cities (1970 population 275,000), London-St. Thomas (population 255,000), metropolitan Essex-Windsor (250,000), and the Niagara regional cluster of cities described above. Although as a service centre, London ranks considerably above the others, in terms of growth potential the ordering of these four cities follows their ranking in the table.[6] The latter centre, Niagara, which combines three census major urban areas is at present the weakest cluster, partly because of its location between Toronto-Hamilton and Buffalo and partly

[5]See Metropolitan Toronto and Region Transportation Study (1963).

[6]This ordering is quite different from the central place hierarchy in Ontario identified by Carol (1969).

TABLE 2.7 REGIONAL URBAN GROWTH COMPLEXES:
ONTARIO–QUEBEC, 1970

ONTARIO		QUEBEC	
Urban Complex	Population 1970 (est.)	Urban Complex	Population 1970 (est.)
Metropolitan:			
1. Toronto (a)	2,500,000	1. Montreal (f)	2,800,000
2. Hamilton	500,000		
Lake Ontario	3,000,000		
3. Ottawa-Hull	540,000	2. Quebec City	440,000
4. Kitchener-Guelph (b)	275,000		
5. London-St. Thomas	255,000		
6. Essex (Windsor)	250,000		
7. Niagara (c)	240,000		
Emerging:			
8. Sudbury	125,000	3. Saguenay (g)	125,000
9. Thunder Bay	110,000	4. Trois Rivières	100,000
10. Kingston (d)	85,000	5. Sherbrooke	90,000
11. Sault Ste. Marie	80,000		
Potential:			
12. Sarnia	70,000	6. Shawinigan	70,000
13. Peterborough-Lindsay	70,000		
14. Brantford-Paris	70,000		
15. Mariposa-Lake Simcoe (e)	50,000		
16. Cornwall	50,000		
17. Belleville-Trenton	50,000		

NOTES: (a) Toronto C.M.A., Oshawa-Whitby, Brampton, Aurora
　　　　(b) Kitchener C.M.A., Guelph
　　　　(c) St. Catharines, Thorold, Niagara Falls, Welland, Port Colborne
　　　　(d) Kingston, Gananoque
　　　　(e) Barrie, Simcoe, Midland
　　　　(f) Montreal C.M.A., St. Jean, Beauharnois, St. Thérèse
　　　　(g) Chicoutimi-Jonquière M.U.A., Bagotville, Port Alfred

because a strong regional core has yet to develop. It is a striking feature that there are no centres in the province of Quebec of
a similar order. (Other studies which point to structural differences of Quebec cities are Denis [1963]; Trotier [1959]; and
Higgins; Martin; and Raynault [1970]).

The second level in the hierarchy (emerging centres) contains seven urban areas ranging in size from 80,000 to 125,000

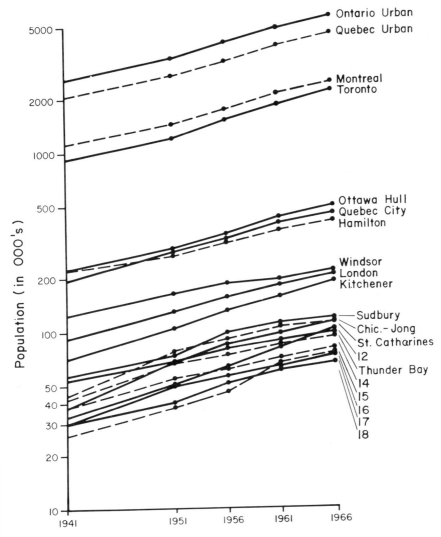

Figure 2.6 Population growth of major centres: Ontario – Quebec, 1941–1966

population, including the Sudbury metropolitan area, Thunder Bay (Fort William-Port Arthur) and the cluster of smaller cities along the Saguenay River centred on Chicoutimi-Jonquière. These centres, because of their size and economy and frequently their peripheral location, rank far below the metropolitan group in services and in growth rate, although all are approaching the threshold of metropolitan size and several may be classified accordingly in the 1971 census (Figure 2.6).

31

Cities in the third group (potential centres), range in size from 50,000 for Belleville-Trenton to 70,000 for Sarnia, Peterborough-Lindsay, and the Shawinigan-Grand'Mère major urban area. These centres are presently well below the minimum size necessary to provide a metropolitan infrastructure, and will remain so in the immediate future. With the possible exception of Sarnia and Peterborough these centres have tended to be slow-growing, or even stagnant. Some, particularly Cornwall and the centres of the Lake Simcoe region have been the recipients of government development assistance in order to augment their industrial structure (see for example Yeates and Lloyd [1969]).

In total, the 23 regional urban complexes listed above contained about 9,000,000 persons or nearly 70 per cent of the provincial totals in 1970. These seem to cover most existing centres of metropolitan development in Central Canada, and to provide a more realistic view of the spatial distribution of existing urban infrastructure, and thus of the potential for urban growth, than present census areas. The concept is also helpful initially in suggesting reasons for differentials in growth between Ontario and Quebec urban systems, and for the recent growth performance of particular cities (see Part 3).

The sharp contrast in the structure of urban development as it is presently occurring in Ontario and Quebec is basically one of alternative growth complexes to the greater Toronto and Montreal metropolitan areas. Outside of the economic region of the expanded Toronto metropolitan area (2,500,000), new investment has nearly half a dozen alternative centres in which to locate. These include the Kitchener-Guelph cluster, the Niagara regional cluster, and the London and Essex (Windsor) metropolitan areas. Each of these clusters represents a viable locational alternative to the Oshawa-Toronto-Hamilton area, in part because of relative location within the heartland of Ontario's space economy and in part through the attainment of a sufficient size to ensure sustained growth. [7] They have the infrastructure for growth at present as well as the potential for broadening this infrastructure.

In Quebec similar growth alternatives do not exist. The Montreal urban complex, considered here to include the census metropolitan area (1970 population 2,570,000) and surrounding

_____

[7] The application of heartland-hinterland concepts to southern Ontario is developed in Ray (1970b).

environs extending to St. Jean, Beauharnois and Ste. Thérèse, has an aggregate population of approximately 2,800,000 or nearly 50 per cent of the provincial total. Next to Montreal in the urban size scale is Quebec City, which holds a position relatively isolated from the spatial economy and transportation networks of the province of Quebec much as Ottawa does in Ontario. Both are dominated and will most likely continue to be dominated by governmental functions. The next set of urban clusters in Quebec: Saguenay, Trois Rivières-Cap de la Madeleine, Shawinigan-Grand'Mère, and Sherbrooke-Lennoxville, are smaller than the four parallel urban clusters in Table 2.7 for Ontario, they are also more peripheral and they have been growing at a slower rate. Moreover, all four lack a strong central focus such as in the Windsor, London, and Kitchener-Waterloo regions in Ontario. As a result, the growth potential for Quebec urban centres outside of the Montreal region, appears to be substantially less than that for Ontario outside of the Toronto region. This may be one of the most substantial conclusions to derive from this preliminary comparison of the urban systems of the two provinces.

It is also interesting to note that sharp differences exist in recent growth performance among the different size groups (see Tables 2.3 and 2.5). All of the major centres, with the possible exception of the Windsor metropolitan region, have exhibited rapid rates of population growth in recent census periods. Without exception, the medium size centres have been areas of relatively slow growth. Smaller centres on the average exhibit modest rates of population expansion, but the variability in growth rates is that much higher. Centres of a similar size to those in the latter two categories which are experiencing rapid growth, such as Oshawa, Brampton, Guelph, Burlington, and Oakville in Ontario, are all in close proximity to, and are thus included within the broader definition of, a metropolitan urban complex employed here. The point is clear, there are no major urban centres in Ontario and Quebec undergoing rapid growth, outside of the large metropolitan regions.

This conclusion emphasizes the necessity to complement studies which are based strictly on census and municipal reporting units, with analyses drawing on broader spatial concepts. One such concept is the urban growth complex and another to be discussed subsequently is the formulation of a field of urban interaction. Both of these are worthy of further investigation.

References

ANDERSON, I. B. 1966. Internal Migration in Canada: 1921-1961. Ottawa: Queen's Printer.

BERRY, B. J. L., et al. 1968. Metropolitan Area Definition A Re-Evaluation of Concept and Statistical Practice, Working Paper No. 28, U.S. Department of Commerce. Washington: Bureau of the Census.

CAROL, H. 1969. Development regions in southern Ontario based on city centred regions. Ontario Geographer 4:13-29.

DENIS, P.-Y. 1963. La présence urbaine au Québec et dans l'Ontario. Revue Canadienne de Géographie 18:3-8.

EASTERBROOK, W. T. and M. H. WATKINS, eds. 1967. Approaches to Canadian Economic History. Toronto: MacClelland and Stewart.

ECONOMIC COUNCIL OF CANADA. 1965. Second Annual Review Towards Sustained and Balanced Economic Growth. Ottawa: Queen's Printer.

HAUSER, P. M. and L. F. SCHNORE. 1965. The Study of Urbanization. New York: Wiley.

HIGGINS, B.; F. MARTIN; and A. RAYNAULD. 1970. Les orientations du développement économique régional dans la Province de Québec. Report of the Department of Regional Economic Expansion. Ottawa: Queen's Printer.

METROPOLITAN TORONTO AND REGION TRANSPORTATION STUDY. 1963. Transportation Study Prospectus. Toronto: MTRTS.

PAQUET, G. 1968. Some views on the pattern of Canadian economic development. In T. N. Brewis, ed. Growth and the Canadian Economy. Toronto: McClelland and Stewart.

RAY, D. M. 1970a. A factorial ecology of Canada. Papers and Proceedings of the Regional Science Association 23:7-23.

--------. 1970b. The growth and form of urban centres in southwestern Ontario. Trends, Issues and Possibilities for Urban Development in Central and Southern Ontario. Toronto: Ontario Economic Council, pp. 1-22.

RAY, D. M. and B. J. L. BERRY. 1965. Multivariate socio-economic regionalization: A pilot study in Central Canada. In S. Ostry and T. K. Rymes, eds. Papers on Regional Statistical Studies. Toronto: University of Toronto Press, pp. 75-122.

SIMMONS, J. W. and R. SIMMONS. 1969. Urban Canada. Toronto: Copp Clark.

SPELT, J. 1955. The Urban Development in South-Central Ontario. Assen: Van Gorcum.

STONE, L. 1967. Urban Development in Canada: An Introduction to the Demographic Aspects. D.B.S. Census Monograph. Ottawa: Queen's Printer.

--------. 1969. Migration in Canada Regional Aspects. D.B.S. Census Monograph. Ottawa: Queen's Printer.

34

THOMPSON, W. 1965. Preface to Urban Economics. Baltimore: Johns Hopkins Press, for Resources for the Future, Inc.

TROTIER, L. 1959. Some functional characteristics of the main service centres of the Province of Quebec. Cahiers de Géographie de Québec, April-September, pp. 243-59.

YEATES, M. H. and P. E. LLOYD. 1969. Impact of Industrial Incentives. Southern Georgian Bay Region, Ontario. Geographical Paper No. 44, Department of Energy, Mines and Resources. Ottawa: Queen's Printer.

3

Behaviour of the Ontario-Quebec urban system by size distribution[1]

J. B. Davies

In any political or economic region urban centres tend to behave in differing degrees as an integrated system. The extent of this integration, the form in which it is expressed, and the way in which it has changed over time provides useful insights into the nature of urban growth and its regularities. The most obvious point of departure is the distribution of cities by population size over time for a given region with a view to establishing a consistent structure in the urban hierarchy.

One means of examining regularities in the distribution of urban growth, and subsequently of the application of a systems context, is the rank-size rule of city-size distributions. This paper examines the distributional regularities for all cities in Ontario and Quebec from 1941 to 1966 which had populations over 10,000 in 1961. The analysis has the following objectives: first to provide one general definitional framework and a point of departure for subsequent studies of the structural characteristics of Ontario-Quebec cities, particularly in the following chapter; second, to compare aggregate city-size trends in the two provinces; and, finally, through an examination of changes over time in the rank-size regularity to discuss growth trends and contribute one highly generalized but relevant approach to understanding the distribution of urban growth. One advantage of examining

[1] This paper has been adapted from Davies and Bourne (1968) and Davies (1969).

regularities in city-size distributions is that they convey impressions of changes within an urban system on the basis of relative position in a size continuum, rather than by reference to any particular city thus incorporating an explicit probabilistic element in the conceptual framework of urban growth.

City-Size Distributions: Theoretical Basis

Urban researchers have tended to lean heavily upon two theoretical bases when concerned, as in this study, with size distributions in a system of cities; namely the central place formulations of Christaller (1933) and Lösch (1954), and the rank-size rule of Zipf (1949). These formulations are sufficiently well known and documented that only limited reference need be made here to critical points of interpretation. Christaller and Lösch hypothesize hierarchical structures of urban centres as central places, and Zipf postulates a continuum of city sizes. Although apparently contradictory, the two theories have been neatly rationalized by Berry (1964), who points out that they are not in conflict, but rather are concerned with different sub-systems. He comments that:

> In a systems framework we should no longer worry about apparent contradictions between the kinds of conclusions reached for different subsystems, that is, between the distribution of city sizes and the functional arrangements of market centers in a hierarchy... for the difference is understood to be one of the relative balance of entropy – approximating or order-generating processes in various parts of the system.

This study is concerned with that particular characteristic of the total urban system which relates to city-size distributions (Fig. 3.1).

The Rank-Size Relationship

The rank-size rule states that for a group of cities in a given country or economic region, the population of any individual city bears a direct relationship to its rank by size and to the population of the largest city. The relationship is such that:

$$P_r^q = P_1/r$$

where P_1 is the population of the largest or first ranking city
P_r is the population of the city of rank r
r is the rank of the city in descending order of size, and
q is an empirically derived constant.
Hence, under transformation the relationship becomes:

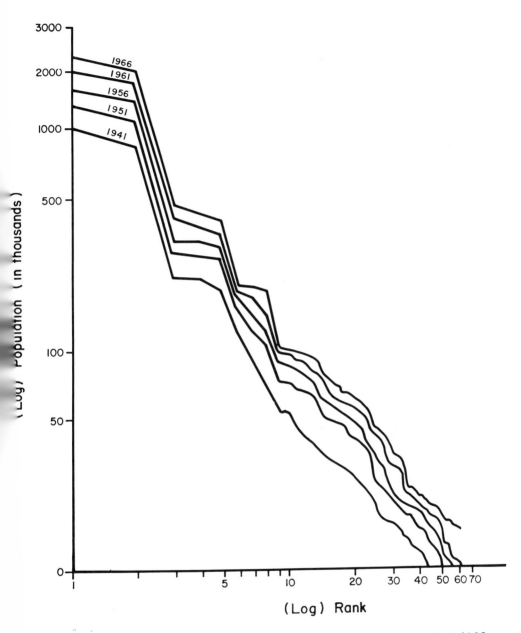

Figure 3.1   Rank-size distributions: Ontario and Quebec, 1941-1966

$$\text{Log } r = \text{Log } P_1 - q \text{ Log } P_r, \qquad (1)$$

such that a plot of rank against size on double logarithmic paper should give a straight line with a slope of -q. This slope coefficient expresses the degree of concentration or dispersion of population within the urban system. The rationale for such a relationship has been discussed by Zipf (1949), Lukerman (1961), Berry and Garrison (1958), Berry (1964), Curry (1964), Beckmann (1958) and Simon (1955).

The Regression Results: Ontario Urban System

Initially, regression equations were derived for each of the 73 cities and metropolitan areas, 40 in Ontario and 33 in Quebec, with populations over 10,000 listed in the principal data inventory. For this study, several smaller cities were combined into major urban areas conforming to the figures and number of cities previously given in Table 2.4. Given that the definition of major urban areas more realistically reflects the distribution of urban population than do figures for individual municipalities, the hypothesized rank-size relationship should improve substantially. In Ontario, this meant reducing the sample size from 40 to 37 by merging Fort William and Port Arthur (now combined as Thunder Bay), Welland and Port Colborne, and Whitby and Oshawa. The regression results for Ontario cities are summarized in Table 3.1.

Since 1941 the Ontario system of cities has shown remarkable distributional stability by size. In all time periods the relationship hypothesized by Zipf successfully "explains" more than 96 per cent of the variance (as expressed in the coefficient of determination R^2). It must be noted again, however, that a considerable degree of the fit between theoretical and actual values is inevitable due to the ranking procedure. The explanatory power of the model must be extremely high to be meaningful.

Equally interesting are the changes in the regression parameters. The Y intercept value, denoting the theoretical size (in logarithms) of the largest city, has increased steadily and consistently over the period of study. There has also been modest growth in the regression coefficient (b) particularly between 1941 and 1951. The general conclusion is that although the total system has experienced steady growth, the larger cities have been increasing at a greater rate than the smaller centres

TABLE 3.1 REGRESSION EQUATIONS, 1941-1966: ONTARIO CITIES

Year	Y intercept	b	R	R^2
1966	$\log P_r = 6.28612 - 1.353 \log r$		.987	.974
1961	$\log P_r = 6.20979 - 1.331 \log r$		.990	.978
1956	$\log P_r = 6.14896 - 1.353 \log r$		.990	.979
1951	$\log P_r = 6.07351 - 1.352 \log r$		.983	.965
1941	$\log P_r = 5.88319 - 1.293 \log r$		.981	.963

P_r = population of city of rank r

r = population rank of city

R = correlation coefficient

R^2 = coefficient of determination

n = 37

TABLE 3.2 REGRESSION EQUATIONS, 1941-1966: QUEBEC CITIES

Year	Y intercept	b	R	R^2
1966	$\log P_r = 5.97817 - 1.411 \log r$		.973	.946
1961	$\log P_r = 5.92187 - 1.401 \log r$		.975	.950
1956	$\log P_r = 5.88413 - 1.433 \log r$		.978	.965
1951	$\log P_r = 5.85425 - 1.476 \log r$		.964	.929
1941	$\log P_r = 5.75181 - 1.570 \log r$		.943	.889

n = 26

compared with their respective ranks between 1941 and 1951, but that urban growth has been evenly distributed along the size continuum since then.

Because the theoretical basis of rank-size is a probability distribution, it becomes difficult to interpret the residuals as they refer to particular observations or cities in the original

39

data. The rank-size rule, because it is a probability model for a set of cities differentiated only by size, should not be employed to estimate the population of any one particular city.

The pattern of residuals exhibits considerable stability. Cities over 100,000 population tend to have mixed residuals mainly due to the fact that the secondary position is shared by Hamilton and Ottawa, and that the latter's planned political function distorts the expected distributional pattern of urban development. Throughout the period cities between 20,000 and 100,000 tend to be underestimated by the linear regression model, and it is within this range that the larger residuals occur. Ontario it seems is relatively well endowed with cities of this size. Below the 20,000 threshold negative residuals are the order, and the reverse conclusion applies.

Regression Results: Quebec Urban System
Table 3.2 shows parallel results for the regression of city population on rank for 26 cities in Quebec from 1941 to 1966. The resulting coefficients of determination and the trend of the regression lines since 1941 remain much the same as in Ontario. From 1941 to 1956 the total system has moved toward the theoretical rank-size relationship, but since that date there has been a slight movement away. An analysis of the regression residuals indicates that the obvious position of the Montreal metropolitan area has a substantial effect on the overall relationship. As in other instances, Montreal dominates the urban population distribution of the province of Quebec to a far greater extend than the Toronto metropolitan area does in Ontario.

Since 1941 the residual attributable to Montreal has been steadily increasing (the regression considerably underestimated the size of this city) so that from 1941 to 1956 the growth of other centres, notably Chicoutimi-Jonquière and Trois Rivières offset the growth of Montreal. Since 1956 the dominance of Montreal has overcome this counterbalance. It is unlikely that the Quebec system will, in the foreseeable future, move any closer to the theoretical rank-size relationship because of the continued growth of the Montreal urbanized area.

The steady increase in the Y intercept value indicates an overall growth of the system since 1941, with the largest increase occurring in the period 1961-1966. The increase in the regression coefficient points out that the smaller centres grew

40

more rapidly than the larger centres relative to their respective ranks, although since 1961 there has been a slight reversal of this tendency.

It may seem peculiar that a distribution of cities such as in Quebec with a dominant primate city and a relatively weak secondary city should demonstrate such a good fit to the theoretical rank-size relation. This is essentially a function of the large number of smaller cities in the sample. An analysis of the residual pattern in 1966 shows that by far the major part of the variance from linearity is concentrated in the top few cities indicating that the linear relationship provides a better fit for smaller centres. This is in contrast to the residual pattern for Ontario cities, where with the exception of Ottawa the residuals are evenly distributed throughout the range. In this respect then the set of Quebec cities operate as much less of a system than do the Ontario cities. The structure of the Quebec system is that of a surfeit of smaller centres and a deficit of the larger cities whose functions have been centralized in Montreal.

The Combined Ontario-Quebec System

The combined Ontario-Quebec system of 63 cities displays even greater regularity. The R^2 value increased from 92.9 per cent variance explained in 1941 to 98.5 per cent in 1966 (see Table 3.3). In common with both previous analyses the intercept value steadily increased with the total overall growth that has occurred, the largest increase being that between 1961 and 1966. Up to 1961 the regression coefficient decreased indicating the effect of the large number of small Quebec centres upon the distribution, but this trend has also reversed since 1961.

Not surprisingly, metropolitan Toronto has a consistently high positive residual indicating that its size is underpredicted by the rank-size model. Given the existence of two primate cities, Montreal and Toronto, it is surprising that such a good fit to the hypothesized relationship exists within the combined system. The adverse effect of the high residual in the second rank seems to be offset by an extremely efficient fit at all other ranks. The cultural and historic differences between the provinces can be seen as one barrier which has disturbed the operation of the system and allowed the development of these distinct dual primate cities.

The residuals are mixed for cities above 250,000, whereas negative residuals indicating overestimation predominate in the

41

TABLE 3.3 REGRESSION EQUATIONS, 1941-1966: THE COMBINED
SYSTEM OF CITIES

Year	Y intercept b	R	R^2
1966	$\log P_r = 6.47370 - 1.326 \log r$	.992	.985
1961	$\log P_r = 6.40046 - 1.309 \log r$	.994	.988
1956	$\log P_r = 6.34351 - 1.324 \log r$	.992	.985
1951	$\log P_r = 6.28751 - 1.338 \log r$	.980	.960
1941	$\log P_r = 6.15731 - 1.354 \log r$	.964	.929

n = 63

TABLE 3.4 AVERAGE CHANGES IN RANK-SIZE REGRESSION VALUES, 1941-1966

	Changes in Y (intercept)				Changes in b (regression coefficients)		
Time Period	Ontario-Quebec System	Ontario System	Quebec System	Time Period	Ontario-Quebec System	Ontario System	Quebec System
1941-1951*	.065	.095	.051	1941-1951*	-.008	.030	-.047
1951-1956	.056	.065	.030	1951-1956	-.014	.001	-.043
1956-1961	.057	.061	.038	1956-1961	-.015	-.022	-.032
1961-1966	.073	.076	.056	1961-1966	.017	.022	.010

*   This value represents 1/2 of the 1941-1951 change to make it compatible
within the series.

70,000 to 250,000 population range. No particular significance
should be attached to this pattern, however, because the position
of the line has been strongly affected by the obvious positive
influence of Toronto as the second city in the combined analysis.
Below the 70,000 level the residuals are extremely small and
show no systematic pattern except for the negative residuals in
all centres below 15,000 population.

Overall, the rank-size regularity offers an interesting
representation of the distribution of cities by size in Ontario and

42

Quebec. To illustrate the accuracy of the linear fit, and the apparent stability of change in the regression equations over time, Table 3.4 summarizes average changes in the slope of the rank-size regressions for each of the three systems. Note that the slope of the regression line indicates incremental changes in the relationship between a city's size and its relative ranked position in the urban system.

An Alternative Formulation: Yule Distribution

Unlike many rank-size studies that have concerned themselves only with the major cities within a given county or region, usually with a threshold minimum of 100,000 population, this study has included cities that vary in size from over two million to 10,000. It seems reasonable to suggest that the possibilities for random error decrease as the number of observations within a given size range increases if a ranking procedure is adopted. For example, simply by ranking 10 cities whose populations vary from 10,000 to 50,000 it would seem likely that a greater variance from a linear relationship is possible, than in a system that has 100 cities within the same population range. It is argued that as the smaller centres represent a large number of cities within a relatively narrow population range that they can have a positive influence on the degree of the fit due simply to the ranking procedure.

Unfortunately the extent to which these arguments have affected the conclusions is unknown, and for this reason the following section adopting the formulation of Simon (1955) has been included, not because it provides a direct comparison with the preceding regression analysis, but because it provides a method of comparing actual and theoretical city-size distributions without recourse to the ranking procedure.

The Yule distribution is an exponential function that closely approximates the rank-size relationship of Zipf (1949). Berry and Garrison (1958) have adapted Simon's original formulation so that a theoretical distribution of city sizes can be formulated. This theoretical distribution can then be tested against the actual distribution using X^2 (chi-square) as a test statistic of goodness of fit.

It should be noted that two differences occur between this analysis and the previous regression study that render the conclusions incompatible in any strict sense. The two differences are: one, the theoretical distribution of Simon is on a class basis,

and two, it has been found necessary here to include cities between 5,000 and 10,000 population because of the nature of
Berry's and Garrison's formulation as well as the small sample
size. [2]

The distribution of cities by size can be approximated by a
theoretical Yule distribution. Table 3.5 shows the example of
the Ontario-Quebec urban system in 1961 compared with such a
theoretical Yule distribution. It can been seen from the table
that the distribution is constructed using the original 73 cities
with populations over 10,000 in 1961. The major urban area
category has been omitted because the larger sample thus provided improves the degree of accuracy in the computation of a
continuous theoretical distribution. Table 3.5 suggests that in
1961 there was no significant difference between the actual and
theoretical distributions indicating that the size distribution of
cities in Ontario and Quebec in that year can be approximated
by a Yule distribution.

Quebec cities can been seen from Table 3.6 to have shown
instability over the period since 1941 in terms of the fit to the
Yule distribution, although there has been an overall trend away
from this theoretical distribution.

An analysis of the residuals from the theoretical shows that
the X^2 values for Quebec are highest for cities above 35,000 and
between 10,000 and 15,000. As has been noted previously Quebec
is overendowed with small size centres, but has few large centres
probably due to the dominance of Montreal in all facets of the
urban realm. The fact that the Quebec cities no longer conform
to the Yule distribution suggests that the fit of .946 in the regression analysis of the preceding section was overly influenced by
the ranking procedure and by the number of small sized centres
in the sample.

Similarly the fit to the theoretical Yule is now significantly
different from zero in the Ontario system (Table 3.7), indicating
again that the ranking procedure in the preceding section exaggerated the rank-size relationship as it actually exists.

In contrast, the fit of the total combined system has in fact
remained close to the Yule distribution at all time periods since
1941 (see Table 3.8), although there has been a marked trend
away from this theoretical distribution.

[2] Because the Yule distribution is open, that is, it incorporates all cities over 5,000
population including new additions in each selected year, the sample size will vary
from year to year.

TABLE 3.5 A STATISTICAL COMPARISON OF THE ONTARIO-QUEBEC
URBAN SYSTEMS IN 1961 WITH A THEORETICAL YULE DISTRIBUTION

City Size	Expected Number E	Actual Number A	$\frac{(E-A)^2}{E}$
5,000-10,000	80	96	3.2
10,000-20,000	40	30	2.5
20,000-30,000	13	16	0.7
30,000-50,000	8	11	1.1
50,000-100,000	9	7	0.4
100,000 +	11	9	0.3
			$\chi^2 = \overline{8.2}^*$

* Not significantly different from zero at the 95 per cent level

TABLE 3.6 THE QUEBEC URBAN SYSTEM: SIGNIFICANCE TESTS
OF GOODNESS OF FIT TO A THEORETICAL YULE DISTRIBUTION,
1941-1966

Year	χ^2	Test*
1966	25.9	Significant
1961	10.9	Not Significant
1956	13.5	Significant
1951	7.0	Not Significant
1941	7.4	Not Significant

* 95 per cent confidence level

Analysis of Residuals

An analysis of the Ontario-Quebec residuals shows that there has
been very little in the way of any strong trend since 1941, which
is not surprising considering the contrasting nature of the separate provincial cities. For example the rapid growth of several
smaller mining towns in Quebec has to an extent offset the decline
of similar centres in Ontario, and the relative sparsity of, and
lack of growth in, the cities in the 100,000+ range in Quebec is

45

TABLE 3.7 THE ONTARIO URBAN SYSTEM: SIGNIFICANCE TESTS
OF GOODNESS OF FIT TO A THEORETICAL YULE DISTRIBUTION,
1941-1966

Year	x^2	Test*
1966	16.0	Significant
1961	13.4	Significant
1956	7.2	Not Significant
1951	13.9	Significant
1941	8.3	Not Significant

* 95 per cent confidence level

TABLE 3.8 THE ONTARIO-QUEBEC URBAN SYSTEM: SIGNIFICANCE
TESTS OF GOODNESS OF FIT TO A THEORETICAL YULE
DISTRIBUTION, 1941-1966

Year	x^2	Test*
1966	10.2	Not Significant
1961	8.2	Not Significant
1956	4.4	Not Significant
1951	6.7	Not Significant
1941	3.1	Not Significant

* 95 per cent confidence level

counteracted by the number and growth of those cities in Ontario.
In terms of numbers of cities in the given size groups two trends
can be identified. First, the number of cities in the size group
5,000-10,000 has been increasing, and despite the fact that the
Yule distribution is an open distribution which would theoretically
incorporate growth there has been an increase in the positive
residual for this category (there being more cities within this
category than predicted). Secondly, the residual for the 10,000
to 20,000 size group has remained high and negative with the
Yule distribution overpredicting in this particular class. If system is defined as order in terms of a theoretical Yule distribution
then only the combined Ontario-Quebec cities operate as a system,

a result which adds further substance to the original regression analysis results. Although the χ^2 test has limitations especially with regard to the effect of the class groupings selected, it is argued that this limitation is less serious than the ranking procedure of the previous analysis, and hence the results are more meaningful. Simon contends that if a system of cities exhibits a Yule distribution of sizes then its development can be understood as the result of growth being solely due to the excess of births over deaths, with net growth proportional to present population.

Conclusions and Implications

This paper has provided some insight into the nature and behaviour of the urban system in Ontario and Quebec. In all cases the fit between actual city-size and the theoretical rank-size continuum improved with the two groups merged. But several problems have been left unanswered. Most critical are questions concerning the relationship between the ranking system and the regression analysis, and whether rank and size may be considered as two distinct variables. Also, the explicit effects of including centres as small as 10,000 population have not been assessed, other than to emphasize the tendency for this inclusion to greatly increase the degree of fit on the regression line. For this reason, more importance should be attached to differences in the parameters of the equations over time and between the two sets of cities than to the absolute level of variance explained or degree of fit.

The questions should also be raised here as to whether the cities of Ontario and Quebec constitute a logical basis for this kind of analysis. The degree of fit in the equations suggests that they do. More convincing, however, is the argument that Ontario and Quebec, neatly divided as they are from the Atlantic provinces and western Canada by largely undeveloped areas, and from the United States by the Great Lakes and an international boundary, form a logical regional subsystem of North American cities.

Despite these difficulties, it may be concluded that the distribution of cities by size in Ontario and Quebec follows the form of a lognormal distribution. Each time period analysed represents one stage in the outcome of growth processes in the urban system. Until 1956 the rank-size equations increasingly approached lognormality, indicating more uniform distribution of growth by size within the system. Since 1956 there has been a modest tendency away from the lognormal with proportionately higher growth rates among the very large and the relatively small (10,000 to 20,000 population) centres.

The comparative analysis of Ontario and Quebec size distributions provides additional evidence of basic contrasts in the size distributions resulting from urban development. The most important of these contrasts, and one that is fundamental in understanding urban growth in these regions, is the dominance of Montreal and the relative absence of cities in the middle size range in Quebec.[3] Equally important is the fact that over time this relative deficiency has not improved. Although the exact effects of this pattern on urban and economic development in Quebec have not been measured, it is likely that the effect has been negative on the rate of growth overall.

The reasons for this distributional pattern are equally difficult to assess. Berry (1964) argues that there is no direct relationship between the type of city-size distribution and the level of economic development or degree of urbanization, yet the tendency to lognormal distributions

.... is somehow tied to the number and complexity of forces affecting the urban structure of countries, such that when few strong forces obtain primacy results, and when many forces act in many ways with none predominant a lognormal distribution is found.

Lognormal distributions therefore are essentially the result of stochastic growth processes, with distortions from lognormality the result of barriers to the operation of many forces within the system.[4]

In Ontario and Quebec, these barriers are hypothesized to include the historical effects of colonial rule, which tended to produce dual primacy, such as that of Toronto and Montreal; the effects of an economic system which is partially protected from American competition and thus from certain institutional barriers; and the linguistic-cultural differences which have in the past encouraged separate development in the two provinces. Yet despite these barriers there is sufficient basis for expecting that the trends in city-size distribution documented here will persist for some time as the forces shaping the distribution expand and become more complex.

[3] This point is also emphasized in the discussion of alternative growth centres in paper 8 in this volume.

[4] See also Thomas (1967).

References

BECKMANN, M. J. 1958. City hierarchies and the distribution of city size. Economic Development and Cultural Change 6:243-48.

BERRY, B. J. L. 1964. Cities as systems within systems of cities. In J. Friedmann and W. Alonso, eds Regional Development and Planning. Cambridge, Mass.: M.I.T. Press, p. 132.

--------. 1969. City size and economic development: conceptual synthesis and policy problems, with special reference to South and South-East Asia. Paper presented at the International Geographical Union Commission on Quantitative Methods, Ann Arbor, Michigan.

BERRY, B. J. L. and W. L. GARRISON. 1958. Alternate explanations of urban rank-size relationships. Annals, Association of American Geographers 48:89-131.

CHRISTALLER, W. 1933. Die Zentralen Orte in Süddeutschland. Jena:Gustav Fischer. Translated in 1954 at the Bureau of Population and Urban Research, University of Virginia, by C. Baskin.

CURRY, L. 1964. Explorations in settlement theory: The random spatial economy, part I. Annals Association of American Geographers, Vol. 54.

DAVIES, J. B. 1969. The analysis of city-size distributions in the cities of Ontario and Quebec. Unpublished M.A. research paper. Department of Geography, University of Toronto.

DAVIES, J. B. and L. S. BOURNE. 1968. Behaviour of the Ontario-Quebec urban system: city size regularities. Research Paper No. 2, Centre for Urban and Community Studies, University of Toronto.

LÖSCH, A. 1954. The Economics of Location. Second Revised Edition. New Haven: Yale University Press.

LUKERMAN, F. 1961. The role theory in geographical inquiry. The Professional Geographer 13:1-5.

PARR, J. B. 1969. City hierarchies and the distribution of city size. A reconsideration of Beckmann's contribution. Journal of Regional Science 9 (1969):239-254.

ROSING, K. E. 1966. A rejection of the Zipf Model (rank-size rule) in relation to city size. The Professional Geographer 18:75-82.

SIMON, H. A. 1955. On a class of skewed distribution functions. Biometrika 42:425-440.

SIMON, H. A. and C. P. BONINI. 1958. The size distribution of business firms. American Economic Review 48:607-17.

THOMAS, E. N. 1967. Additional comments on population size relationships for sets of cities. In W. L. Garrison and D. F. Marble, eds Quantitative Geography, Northwestern University Studies in Geography No. 13. Evanston, Ill. pp. 167-90.

ZIPF, G. K. 1949. Human Behaviour and the Principle of Least Effort. Cambridge: Addison Wesley Press.

II

Structural Characteristics of the Urban System

4

Editors' comments

A study of a system of cities is often initiated by an examination
of the characteristics of that system at a single point in time
when data are most readily available. This cross-sectional structure, however, is logically viewed as the cumulative outcome of
a series of development processes up to that time. That is, structure is the cumulative inheritance of past periods, a horizontal
slice or snapshot through a vertical or time dimension of urban
growth and system evolution. Each period of growth superim-
poses a new structure on and selectively alters that provided by
previous periods. The papers in this section represent different
approaches to the examination of the aggregate system properties
of cities in southern Ontario and southern Quebec.

The first paper, by Bunting, represents a multivariate principal components analysis of a large data inventory for each of
67 cities in the two provinces with populations over 10,000 in
1961. The use of data from both 1951 and 1961 censuses permits
a comparative examination of the changing structure of the urban
system, albeit with considerable limitations, which represents
one major step in examining processes of change.

The question of the areal definitions of cities is equally
important. If our studies are intended to differentiate the underlying characteristics of the urban system, it is clear that data
should relate to the spatial unit which is the appropriate economic
and social area for each city in the system. In most instances

this is the census metropolitan area or, for smaller centres, the major urban area. In this study it has only been possible to assemble comprehensive data for the census metropolitan area.

The initial premise of the multivariate approach is two-fold. First, that cities are not unique in all of their structural characteristics, either at one point in time, or over time. Thus a logical approach to the complex dimensions of urban growth and development involves sorting out which characteristics are common to all cities, or a group of cities, from those which are unique. Second, the obvious complexity of urban areas and of any urban system negates the feasibility of a single-variable approach while the availability of multivariate computer programs facilitates the objective treatment of many characteristics without strict a priori assumptions of which variables are important.

The cities of Ontario and Quebec do exhibit common variance. There are systematic regularities in demographic, sociological, economic, physical, and locational attributes which enable the ordering of cities into similar structural and spatial clusters. The output of the principal components analysis is a set of statistically independent dimensions or factors representing combinations of structural characteristics. The most important factors that emerge relate to differences between cities in terms of cultural and linguistic contrasts; in the diversity of employment mix and general economic health; in the contrast between metropolitan status and the isolated smaller centres in peripheral areas of the two provinces; and between the highly specialized cities and towns such as residential satellites, institutional and resource-based centres, which have distinct characteristics as a result of their functional specialization.

The final step in the analysis involves a regionalization of the cities. The respective factor scores for each city on each of the important factors are subject to a grouping algorithm which produces independent city groups based on similar structural characteristics. These groups provide one basis for subsequent research on the growth of these same cities.

The second paper offers a different yet complementary approach to the classification of cities in Ontario and Quebec. Using occupational data, Britton attempts to measure more specific similarities and differences in the economic structure of these cities. Occupational characteristics are measured both in absolute terms (proportions) and in relative terms (location quotients). The application of factor analysis differs

52

from that above in that it is considered to be direct rather than indirect measure of structure. In this analysis, the cities themselves appear as variables while the characteristics appear as observations (Q-mode factor analysis), the reverse of the traditional (R-mode factor analysis) procedure employed by Bunting. The resulting groupings of cities, although not expected to be similar to those of Bunting because of different data sources and because they are based on the statistical distances between the cities rather than between the attributes, emphasizes the sharp functional contrasts between cities in Ontario and Quebec. In addition, by providing a discussion of differences in the economic (occupational) profiles of cities in Ontario and Quebec this analysis also offers a useful basis on which to shift to the analysis of growth in the next section.

5

Dimensions and groupings in the Ontario-Quebec urban system, 1951 and 1961

T. Bunting

The present study proposes to achieve a succinct yet realistic overview of cities in Ontario and Quebec in 1951 and 1961. Factorial analysis is used to reduce a wide array of descriptive measures of individual cities to a series of representative dimensions that elucidate the underlying structure of the urban system of the two provinces. In addition, a classification of different city types is produced by grouping urban places on the basis of their relative dimensionality. Overriding both aspects of the analysis is the question of change in the ten-year period under study.

Conceptual and Methodological Background

Recent systems modelling has facilitated our ability to conceptualize external urban structure. Berry (1964) emphasizes this fact. He points out that prior research consists of two polarized methodologies--(i) simple inductive statements of observable fact such as rank-size and population density studies, and (ii) abstract logical constructs such as central place theory. He suggests that a merging of the two approaches is a prerequisite to more sophisticated urban modelling. Systems theory and concomitant multivariate analysis provide one vehicle for the merger. In the present case, our focus is on the inductive and empirical approach. The aim is essentially that of eliminating the simple dichotomy of approaches from earlier type research.

As Smith (1965) has emphasized, it is impossible to justify a priori simplifications of complex urban phenomena. His review of the experience of urban functional classification isolates the fallacy in studies that rely on univariate indices to identify urban functional parameters. He maintains that multivariate statistical techniques--especially factor analysis--help to overcome the problem. In addition, we would add that such an approach yields results amenable to the systematic framework stressed by Berry. For example, a factor analysis of urban structural characteristics provides a basis for evaluating more abstract theoretical concepts (see Berry and Neils 1969). Berry's (1968) formulation of a "field theoretic" approach to urban regions further evidences the potential in preliminary factorial studies.

The application of factorial techniques to the study of urban system structure at a national or subnational level has developed rapidly over the last decade.[1] Existing research proves that large sets of interrelated urban characteristics can be reduced to a small number of independent dimensions which encompass the vast majority of the underlying variance. Further, the findings indicate basic similarities between different urban systems and provide a standardized basis for the comparison of such systems (Hodge 1971). For example, cultural, socioeconomic, locational, and age-size factors generally appear as major components. However, since we are interested in the

---

[1] See for example, Moser and Scott's (1961) analysis of British towns, Ahmad's (1965) research on Indian cities, and the work on American urban dimensions by Hadden and Borgatta (1965) and Harold Mayer. The latter has not yet been published, though it is summarized by Berry and Neils (1969).

specific structural composition of the Ontario-Quebec system, there is little to be gained from a detailed review. The following discussion is limited to evidence regarding Canadian urban dimensions.

Canadian Urban Dimensions

Among others, Simmons (1967) has decried the lack of urban research in Canada while stressing the inappropriateness of applying findings from the U.S. scene. Since 1965 the situation has improved markedly. We are able to reference several studies which provide background for the present research.

Two previous works have attempted to isolate major components of the total Canadian urban system. One conducted by Ray et al.(1968) relies on three types of data (economic, cultural, and locational) and applies factor analysis to reduce the redundancy inherent in the original data. The resulting factor structure comprises eight dimensions that retain 84 per cent of the original variance. In order of importance the dimensions are: French-English contrasts, the prairie type city, mining-service town contrasts, post-war growth centres, the British Columbia type city, specialized manufacturing centres, metropolitan growth centres, and centre-periphery contrasts. This factor structure gives a clear outline of both regional and national distinctions vis à vis the Canadian urban context.

Another Canadian study was undertaken by King (1966) and is perhaps most relevant to this paper. King factor analyzed over 50 economic, demographic, social, and locational characteristics at two points in time--the same two points as are used here, 1961 and 1951. In 1961, he found 11 components which accounted for over 83 per cent of the total variance. In 1951, the same proportion of variance was explained with 12 components. Both the components and subsequent city groupings (derived from multi-dimensional cluster analysis) were similar to Ray's in that regional contrasts in the Canadian urban system were emphasized. Especially important for the purposes of this research however, was the evidence of change in the system over the ten year period, particularly the increase in metropolitan areas and suggestions of stronger relationships among certain variables. Interestingly enough, the relative location of cities in multi-dimensional space remained stable over the period, undoubtedly as a result of strong regional similarities among the cities. We might question whether the same type of cross-sectional change will be found when Ontario and Quebec cities are examined separately.

Both of the above studies emphasize the disparate nature of Canadian urban phenomena. More specifically, they validate Maxwell's (1965) original thesis on the overwhelming influence of regional variations--especially the heartland-hinterland distinction. In this respect, they support our reduced focus on the provinces of Ontario and Quebec as representative of the Canadian heartland. The point is that an examination of the total national system allows obvious regional variations to obscure more subtle aspects of urban structure. While we retain a strong regional variation between the French- and English-speaking provinces, we have eliminated many additional regional derivatives. This type of focus is relatively unique to Canadian urban research.

The only direct precedent to the present focus is King's (1967) research on urban growth in Ontario and Quebec 1951-1961. King applied discriminant analysis to distinguish between 4 groups of cities--growing vs. declining places in Ontario and Quebec respectively. Regional differences explained over 80 per cent of the variance in urban growth rates. However, the negation of other attributes appears peculiar to King's particular study design. While we might anticipate a primary regional distinction, our broader empirical design should reveal a series of other independent dimensions.

Empirical Design

This study is basically similar to existing factorial (principal components) approaches to the analysis of urban system characteristics. The assumption is that the dimensions or factors extracted will reflect underlying structural parameters. It follows that these structural dimensions provide a useful basis for classifying the cities under study. Thus, cluster analysis is subsequently applied to build an urban taxonomy for Ontario and Quebec. The principal components and cluster analysis are run on both the 1951 and 1961 data. The results are interpreted separately for each time period. Our interpretation of change is set out alongside the 1951 findings.

Urban Places

Data were collected on all urban places with populations over 10,000--73 cities (40 Ontario, 33 Quebec) in 1961, and 56 cities (33 Ontario, 23 Quebec) in 1951. In the case of metropolitan area (places over 100,000), the Dominion Bureau of Statistics (D.B.S.) provides data on both the central city and the larger urban area. The latter was considered the more suitable unit since it more adequately reflects the city as a spatial and economic unit. Most previous studies have been based on municipal cities only and thus are somewhat distorted. Unfortunately, there are not similar details available for cities below this size range, and specifically for the census-defined major urban areas (30-100,000).[2] It should be noted that the units of measurement were kept consistent from 1951 to 1961.[3] The data inventory used here is the same as that utilized for other papers in this volume.

Variable Criteria

The choice of input data is a critical step in any type of factorial analysis since the nature and relative important of the dimensions extracted are directly dependent on the initial data set. However, since factorial designs for urban systems analysis are still in preliminary stages of investigation, there are no specific guidelines in this regard. In addition, both problem orientation and available data vary from study to study. Our aim is to provide a comprehensive description based on reliable measures of urban attributes for the selected cities. Variable input for each of the two time periods comprises five types of data--i) demographic, ii) socio-cultural, iii) economic, iv) locational, and v) physical characterisitcs.[4] A complete listing is provided alongside the first analytical results (Table 5.1). Note that with the exception of locational measures calculated specifically for this study, all variable criteria derive from Dominion Bureau of Statistics (D.B.S.) published statistics.

---

[2] Since cities in this size range with a few exceptions, do not exhibit extensive urban development outside the municipal boundary, the limitation imposed is not serious. Even so, the availability of data for these units, particularly in that this is the size category from which metropolitan areas derive, would be a considerable improvement on the present data base.

[3] There was only one serious complication — Kitchener-Waterloo. This city is classified as a metropolitan area only in 1961. The 1951 counter-part consists of the separate cities of Kitchener, Waterloo, Galt, Preston, and surrounding urbanized areas. The closest approximation that we could achieve involved aggregating data for the four cities into an urban complex for 1951.

[4] Again, we encountered some problems in attempting to provide comparative measures for 1961 and 1951. Many additional data were available in the 1961 census. Thus, 73 variables exist for 1961 but only 58 for 1951. Every attempt was made to keep the two data sets analogous without sacrificing relevant material. However, the differences that do exist are not to be negated in the interpretation of change from 1951-1961.

Statistical Models

Both factorial and cluster analysis are widely documented in the contemporary literature.[5] We will therefore dispense with a detailed account of the operational procedures. Essentially, all factorial models embody six general steps--i) an input matrix n x m (n= number of cities; m= number of variables), ii) an m x n intercorrelation matrix, iii) the calculation of a set of common roots (eigenvalues) and an associated set of vectors (eigenvectors), iv) an m x r factor matrix, v) rotation procedures to achieve simple structure (optional), and vi) an n x r matrix of factor scores--a score for each city on each factor (in standard form with mean zero and standard deviation of one). Of course, the results from any given factor analysis depend substantially on the particular type of model selected. There is no unique solution. The solution used here is principal components with varimax rotation. The advantage is that the factors constitute a set of variates measured along orthogonal axes in r-dimensional space and thus are independent and additive. Further, the solution is constrained so as to achieve a parsimonious description of the input data; that is, to account for most of the variance by only a few factors.

The basis of the cluster analysis is the n x r matrix derived from the principal components. As the factor scores indicate how each city ranks on each of the various dimensions, the purpose is to group together those places whose similarity is evidenced in the factor score matrix. The analysis proceeds in a stepwise fashion. Initially, each city represents a separate group. Each succeeding step combines the two most similar groups in such a way as to minimize within group variance. A complete series of reiterative groupings would produce a single group containing all the variance. Note that not all factors need be included--it is often most efficient, both for programming purposes and for subsequent interpretation, to rely on certain selected dimensions.

Interpretation of cluster analysis involves selecting a particular set of groups from the sets provided by the successive steps of the analysis. No unique solution exists; the two criteria most generally used for selecting a meaningful set of groups are the number of groups desired and the reduction in the ratio of between group variance to total variance at each step.

[5]The reader might refer to King (1969) for a general discussion of both techniques with geographic examples.

THE PRINCIPAL COMPONENTS OF ONTARIO AND QUEBEC CITIES

Urban Dimensions 1961

The 1961 analysis is based on an initial variable array of 71
attributes for all 73 cities. The factor loadings describing the
complete factor structure are summarized in Table 5.1. From
groupings of similar factor loadings we identify eight components
which include 56 of the input variables and retain 79 per cent of
the total variance. Highest explanations are given by dimensions
representing obsolescent centres (19.5 per cent) and cultural-
linguistic composition (18.5 per cent).

The first factor is titled the "obsolescent centre" (Figure
5.1). There are four main elements in this factor. The first
three variable loadings describe a population that is middle-aged
or elderly.[6] This corresponds closely with a second type of
variable describing characteristic household structure (high percentage "other"--i.e., widows, high percentage females, high
percentage women in the labour force, low on average household
size, and high labour force participation). A third type of loading pertains to the building stock. Like the population, it is
aging; a high proportion of dwelling units having been built prior
to 1920.[7]

Our interpretation of factor I is corroborated by the factor
scores. Cities with high positive loadings are: Brockville,
Jolliette, Kingston, Lindsay, Niagara Falls,[8] Owen Sound,
Orillia, Rivière du Loup, St. Hyacinthe, Stratford, and St.
Thomas. Conversely, those with high negative scores include:
Alma, Arvida, Asbestos, Chicoutimi North, Georgetown,
Jonquière, Kenogami, Noranda, Sept-Îles, Sudbury, and
Shawinigan South. With the exceptions of Sudbury and Kingston
all of the cities with high factor scores are relatively small
places (10-25,000 population). Thus, a positive score identifies
small cities which are aging economically, structurally, and
demographically. Opposed to these (negative scores) are the

---

[6]Had the middle-aged (15-65 years) category been dis-aggregated it would undoubtedly
have been more indicative of an aging population.

[7]The U.S. born factor loading is most interesting but would require additional historical
research for interpretation.

[8]It should also be noted that Niagara Falls annexed considerable areas of suburban
development so that this result may be misleading.

TABLE 5.1 DIMENSIONS OF URBAN DEVELOPMENT – FACTOR STRUCTURE, 1961

Variable Description	I Obsolescent Centre	II Cultural Linguistic Contrast	III Metropolitan Centre	IV Commercial Centre	V Peripheral Centre	VI Educational Occupational Structure	VII Fast Growing Centre	VIII Public Admin. and Defense Centre	TOTAL
	Factor Loadings								
1. Per cent population over 65 years	+0.793								
2. Per cent population under 15 years	-0.840								
3. Per cent population 15-64 years	+0.585								
4. Per cent population "single"		-0.810							
5. Per cent population "married"		+0.847							
6. Per cent population "other"	+0.777	+0.539							
7. Per cent population Jewish			+0.876						
8. Per cent population Catholic		-0.908							
9. Per cent population Protestant and other		+0.908							
10. Per cent immigration since 1945		+0.817							
11. Per cent English mother tongue		+0.901							
12. Per cent French mother tongue		-0.925							
13. Per cent born in U.S.	+0.566								
14. Per cent born in U.K.		+0.875							
15. Per cent born in Italy									
16. Per cent native born		-0.844							
17. Per cent born elsewhere		+0.767							
18. Per cent families earnings less than $3,000		-0.747							
19. Per cent of population with elementary education or less		-0.763							
20. Per cent of population with university education						-0.753			
21. Per cent of population in elementary school									
22. Per cent of population in university						-0.607			
23. Per cent full-time resident university students									
24. Per cent residential building permits in single family									
25. Per cent residential building permits in apartments									
26. Per cent value of residential building permits									
27. Per cent value of industrial building permits							+0.847		
28. Per cent value of commercial building permits							+0.812		
29. Per cent value of institutional building permits									
30. Value of building permits per capita									
31. Value of residential building permits per capita									
32. Per cent unemployment	+0.532								
33. Labour participation	+0.811								
34. Female labour participation		+0.595							

#	Variable	1	2	3	4	5	6	7	8
36.	Per cent professional occupations								
37.	Per cent clerical occupations		+0.507						
38.	Per cent sales occupations				+0.853				-0.706
39.	Per cent service occupations								
40.	Per cent in transport occupations								
41.	Per cent in crafts								
42.	Per cent labourers								
43.	Per cent in manufacturing industry					-0.731			
44.	Per cent in construction industry								
45.	Per cent in transportation industry					+0.768			
46.	Per cent in trade industry				+0.791				
47.	Per cent in finance, insurance, and real estate		+0.649				+0.519		
48.	Per cent in community, business and personal service						-0.804		-0.784
49.	Per cent in public administration and defense		+0.940						
50.	Per cent in single family dwelling units		-0.909						
51.	Per cent in apartments								
52.	Per cent dwelling units constructed prior to 1920	+0.749							
53.	Per cent dwelling units constructed since 1945	-0.627						+0.570	
54.	Per cent "owned" dwelling units		+0.889						
55.	Per cent "rented" dwelling units		-0.893						
56.	Per cent dwelling units in need of major repair								
57.	Per cent dwelling units occupied by one owner for ten years or more	+0.568			+0.913				
58.	Population 1961	-0.680							
59.	Sex ratio		-0.628						
60.	Average household size	-0.656	+0.673						
61.	Average family income								
62.	Annexation								
63.	Location relative to highway 401		+0.507			+0.799			
64.	Metropolitan accessibility			+0.683					
65.	Nodality index					-0.737			
66.	Situation								
67.	Proximity to nearest city of same or larger size			+0.709		-0.570			
68.	Urban population in commuting radius								
69.	Median value of dwelling units								
70.	Average contract rent		+0.655						
71.	Male labour participation	-0.811							

	1	2	3	4	5	6	7	8	Total
Number of Variables Loading	13	23	5	3	5	3	3	2	56 *
Eigenvalue	13.89	13.13	6.97	6.08	5.46	4.03	3.91	2.60	56.07
Percentage of Total Variance Explained	19.5	18.5	9.9	8.6	7.7	5.6	5.5	3.7	79.0

* Allow for rounding error

rapidly growing small centres, many of which possess natural resource bases or are dormitory towns. Interpretations of this factor can, in light of the findings, be broadened to encompass the theoretical postulates that have been made about the growth of smaller urban places. Wilbur Thompson (1965), for example, provides the concept of an urban size ratchet suggesting that cities beyond a certain threshold size grow almost automatically and their growth rates converge on the national average. The most variable growth rates occur in small cities.

The term "cultural-linguistic contrasts" is applied to the second factor because it contrasts the distinctive characteristics of English-speaking Ontario with French-speaking Quebec. Uniquely "French" variables have strong negative loadings--a high percentage of single persons (i.e., a youthful population), high percentage of Catholic and French-speaking inhabitants, a high percentage of persons with low educational achievement, a high percentage of "native" born, and a large proportion of apartments and "renters." Household size is large. In addition, the Quebec cities are characterized by low immigration rates, low incomes, low rates of labour force participation and low average rents. A bi-polar relationship exists between these characteristics and those of English-speaking cities. Factor scores serve to reinforce this interpretation, as illustrated in Figure 5.2. High positive scores are found for Ontario cities; high negative scores for Quebec cities. Low to insignificant factor scores indicate cities that have a balance of French and English populations-- Ottawa, Sudbury, and Sept-Îles for example. Further, it should be noted that very high scores are achieved by small to medium sized places indicating that cultural contrasts are most apparent in smaller, relatively homogeneous communities. In the aggregate this second factor is most interesting. It offers proof that purely cultural-linguistic differences relate closely to many other variables. In addition to the obvious contrasts, differences exist in demographic, socio-economic, and building stock characteristics as well. It must be emphasized that this factor is nearly as strong as the first one, but is of course in a statistical sense completely independent of it.

Factor III is readily identifiable. It loads variables that are distinctive attributes of large metropolitan centres; thus abstracting the metropolitan city type as a unique urban dimension (Figure 5.3). The factor scores are substantive. Except for Kitchener-

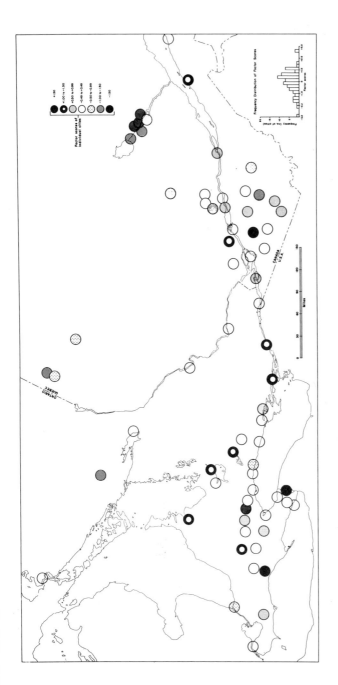

Figure 5.1   Structural dimensions of urban centres, 1961.   Factor 1: obsolescent centre

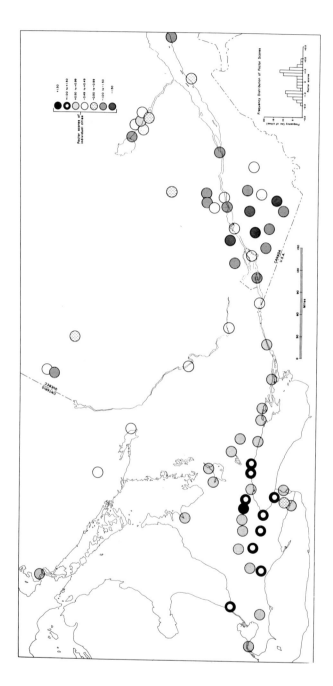

Figure 5.2   Structural dimensions of urban centres, 1961   Factor 2:   cultural-linguistic contrasts

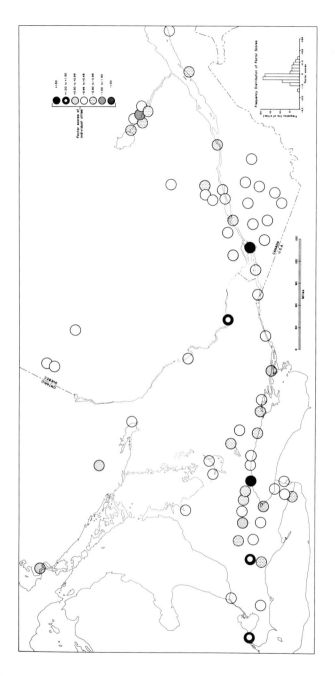

Figure 5.3   Structural dimensions of urban centres, 1961.   Factor 3:   metropolitan centre

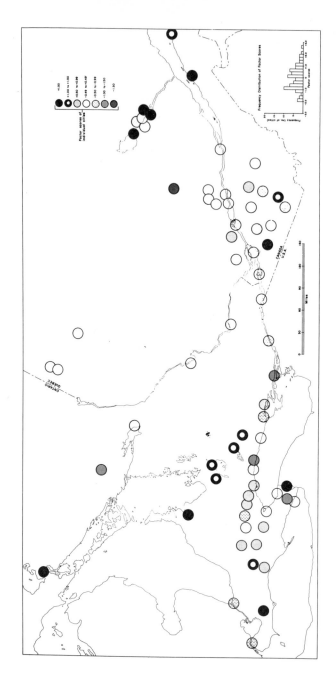

Figure 5.4   Structural dimensions of urban centres, 1961.   Factor 4:   commercial centre

Waterloo,[9] all of the 1961 metropolitan areas have high positive values. Their attributes comprise large Jewish populations, high proportions of employment in finance, insurance, and real estate, large total populations, a distant location from cities of the same or larger size, and high degrees of nodality.

Unlike previous dimensions, factor IV is entirely functional. It defines commercial centres in which the trade economy (managerial and sales occupations) is of major importance. The factor scores indicate that these are medium-sized regional centres, some distance from larger places, presumably far enough away to warrant the servicing of extensive hinterlands (Figure 5.4). In contrast, centres with high negative scores are specialized in some particular industry, such as iron and steel in Sault Ste. Marie and nickel in Sudbury.

Factor V is interesting as it draws out the employment and locational features of peripheral centres, or those places which are distant from the highly urbanized corridor in the central lowlands and which have relatively little urban development in their immediate environs. Employment in manufacturing is low, probably reflecting the remote locations, and employment in the transportation industry is quite high. The majority of cities characterized by this factor are located in the Canadian Shield. Not all of these are involved in mineral processing. However, they all specialize in bulk produce which incur high transportation inputs, as for example with grain at Port Arthur and Fort William (Thunder Bay). In contrast to these places are those showing high negative scores--cities located around Toronto and Montreal. These are cities specializing in light manufacturing such as Georgetown, Brampton, Magog, and Granby.

The sixth factor is best described as educational attainment. Variables loading highly on this factor are: percentage of population not presently in school but having had a university education, percentage of population attending university, and percentage of population in professional occupations. The variables isolate cities which employ specialized professional degree-holding people, that is, government cities (Quebec City and Ottawa), corporation towns (Arvida, Chicoutimi, Noranda, and Sarnia), and university and institutional administration cities (Kingston and London).

[9]Kitchener-Waterloo, as already has been mentioned, is somewhat unique in its form. In addition, growth of this area to metropolitan status has been very recent.

Factor VII is noteworthy with respect to a few cities, but is not definitive of the entire urban system. The factor describes rapidly growing centres which owe their high growth rates to very specific and recent occurrences. Growth is indexed by the percentage of dwelling units built since 1945 and by the percentage value of commercial and industrial building permits issued in the year previous to the census. Cities scoring high on this factor are Barrie and Brampton in Ontario, and Sept-Îles in Quebec. Barrie and Brampton owe their recent residential and industrial growth to a location close to Metropolitan Toronto. Sept-Îles is a specialized corporation town built in the 1950's as the port for iron ore from the Labrador mines to the north.

The eighth and final factor loads variables attributable to public administration and defense type centres. There are only two variable loadings--percentage of service occupations and percentage of public administration and defense employment. Yet the factor is quite explicit. It abstracts places whose economic base incorporates public administration and defense and which, as a result, also employ a high percentage of persons in service occupations (hotels, restaurants, entertainment, etc.). The majority of cities obtaining high factor scores have armed forces bases and research facilities--Barrie, Kingston, Pembroke, St. Jean, and Trenton.

Urban Dimensions 1951

It must be emphasized that the 1951 analysis is treated in a manner somewhat different from that for 1961. Interest is not focussed on the 1951 urban dimensions per se. Rather, it is proposed that the results be compared to those from 1961. The design is similar to that adopted by King (1966)--the analysis of elements of stability and change in the Ontario-Quebec urban system over the ten-year period. Yet caution must be exercised because of inherent limitations in the data. Most of the input variables are comparable. Both sets include demographic, socio-cultural, economic, locational, and physical-structural measures. However, as noted earlier, analysis of the 1951 system was constrained by a lack of certain data that were available for 1961. Thus, only substantial variations in the results are considered as indices of change.

Table 5.2 outlines the 1951 results. Table 5.3 provides a combined summary of these results and the 1961 analysis (com-

parable factors for 1951 are listed under the 1961 factor labels).
As with the 1961 analysis, eight factors were interpretable in
1951. The per cent of total variance explained is somewhat lower,
75.4 per cent, and with 52 of the 56 variables loading significantly
on the eight factors. The structural components are identified
as representative of cultural-linguistic contrasts, metropolitan
status, centre-peripheral contrasts, as well as educational-
occupational, stagnant (trade), institutional, public administration and defense, and transportation centres.

There are several obvious dissimilarities. One is the
appearance of two entirely new dimensions in 1951--institu-
tional and transportation centres--and the absence of the 1961
factor describing commercial and fast growing centres. The
latter was taken as being unique to the time and place. The
similarity in the other six dimensions would seem to reflect
stability over time. However, considerable change is apparent
in the ordering and strength of the various factors. In 1961,
the declining trade centre component is somewhat similar to the
obsolescent centre of 1961. In 1961 this was the first factor,
here it is the fifth. The cultural-linguistic dimension attains a
much higher proportion of the total variance (30 per cent) in the
1951 analysis. Note, however, that this dimension is not so
very much stronger than in 1961. (The high eigenvalue is undoubtedly relative to the fact that other dimensions are less distinctive
in 1951 and, of course, to the fact that the number of original
variables was lower). The education-occupation and public
administration and defense components both appear with slightly
higher explanations in the 1951 analysis. In all, the general
hypothesis suggested here is that the 1951 structure is less
distinctive, but that modifications in the variables included
should not produce the degree of difference that emerged.

The first and very outstanding factor in 1951 is the cultural-
linguistic contrast. Factor loadings are similar to 1961. (Birth-
place and income variables were not available for 1951). Only
two new variable types appear. One is age structure which
corresponds with household structure and the predominance of
young people in French-Canada. The other variable, per cent
in managerial occupations, joins with clerical occupations to
distinguish the occupational structure in Ontario towns. Factor
scores are rearranged somewhat from 1961. There are fewer
places with low factor scores indexing combined English-French
populations. The implication is that in the ten year period, cer-

TABLE 5.2 DIMENSIONS OF URBAN DEVELOPMENT – FACTOR STRUCTURE, 1951

Variable Description	I Cultural Linguistic Contrasts	II Metropolitan Centre	III Centre Peripheral Contrasts	IV Educational Occupational Structure	V Stagnant Trade Centre	VI Institutional Growth Centre	VII Public Admin. and Defense Centre	VIII Transportation Centre	TOTAL
	Factor Loadings								
1. Per cent population over 65 years	+0.841								
2. Per cent population under 15 years	-0.853								
3. Per cent population 15–64 years	+0.680								
4. Per cent population "single"	-0.964								
5. Per cent population "married"	+0.947								
6. Per cent population "other"	+0.869								
7. Per cent population Jewish		+0.924							
8. Per cent population Catholic	-0.962								
9. Per cent population Protestant and "other"	+0.963								
10. Per cent immigration since 1945	+0.728								
11. Per cent English mother tongue	+0.958								
12. Per cent French mother tongue	-0.963								
13. Per cent "other" mother tongue									
14. Per cent families earning less than $3,000	-0.846								
15. Per cent population with no schooling									
16. Per cent population with 13 yrs. or more of schooling	+0.792								
17. Per cent population in grades 9–12	+0.846								
18. Per cent population in grade 13 or more	+0.511			+0.563					
19. Per cent in single family dwelling units	+0.843								
20. Per cent in apartments	-0.859								
21. Per cent in "other" dwelling units									
22. Per cent dwelling units in need of major repair	-0.523								
23. Per cent dwelling units occupied by one owner for ten years or more	+0.710								
24. Per cent value of industrial building permits									
25. Per cent value of commercial building permits						+0.742			
26. Per cent value of institutional building permits						-0.777			
27. Per cent value of residential building permits						+0.730			
28. Value of building permits per capita									
29. Value of residential building permits per capita								-0.512	

	1	2	3	4	5	6	7	8	
30. Per cent unemployment					+0.789				
31. Labour participation	+0.707								
32. Female labour participation	+0.545			+0.658					
33. Per cent managerial occupations									
34. Per cent professional occupations				+0.829					
35. Per cent clerical occupations	+0.558	+0.535							
36. Per cent manufacturing occupations			-0.686						
37. Per cent in transportation occupations								+0.672	
38. Per cent in commercial and financial occupations					+0.735				
39. Per cent in service occupations							+0.862		
40. Per cent in labour									
41. Per cent in manufacturing industries			-0.613						
42. Per cent in construction industries						+0.503			
43. Per cent in transportation industries								+0.709	
44. Per cent in trade industries					+0.621				
45. Per cent in finance, insurance and real estate		+0.641							
46. Per cent in community, business, and personal service				+0.788					
47. Per cent in public administration and defense							+0.903		
48. Population in 1951		+0.935							
49. Average household size	-0.871								
50. Assessed land use		+0.746							
51. Sex ratio				-0.655	-0.528				
52. Metropolitan accessibility			+0.658						
53. Nodality index		+0.654							
54. Situation			-0.856						
55. Proximity to nearest city of same or larger size									
56. Urban population in commuting radius		+0.851	-0.812						
Number of Variables Loading	23	7	5	5	4	5	2	3	52 *
Eigenvalue	17.23	5.62	5.00	3.85	3.51	2.63	2.51	2.18	42.53
Percentage of Total Variance Explained	30.7	10.0	8.9	6.8	6.2	2.6	4.4	3.8	75.4

* Allow for rounding error

tain Ontario cities (Kingston and Sudbury) gained French-speaking elements while certain Quebec cities gained English-speaking inhabitants (Noranda, Sept-Îles, Shawinigan-South, and Thetford Mines). The latter are all corporation towns which employ large numbers of non-local skilled people. The 1951 cities attaining high factor scores are somewhat different but the major generalization made earlier appears to hold--that is, places which manifest the most marked French-English characteristics are small or medium-sized communities.

In 1951, the second most distinctive dimension represents metropolitan centres. This factor is very similar in loadings and percentage of total variance explained to the third factor in the 1961 analysis. In 1951, only Toronto, Montreal, and Ottawa have high factor scores. The government functions in Ottawa require a high proportion of clerical workers and may account for the introduction of this variable loading. This obvious growth of metropolitan areas from 1951-1961 by itself is a strong indication of the dynamic nature of the urban system.

Given such metropolitanization trends, the question arises as to the viability of smaller cities in the system. The comparative factor structures in Table 5.3 suggest decline or at least stagnation of certain small to medium-sized places. For 1961, the first factor is identified as obsolescence. Except perhaps for the fifth factor which interrelates a high percentage of unemployment and a high percentage of females, with large proportions of the population in commercial, financial, and trade occupations, there is little evidence of this obsolescence in 1951. Those 1951 cities having high factor scores on this component are found in 1961, either in the obsolescent or commercial centre component. A tentative interpretation and one which demands further consideration might be outlined briefly as follows:

1) Between 1951 and 1961 size-proportionate growth occurred only for centres with larger populations. Thus, by 1961, there are a number of distinctive metropolitan areas.

2) For smaller and medium-sized cities growth rates are variable. No one dimension of growth per se appears in 1961 and this can be taken as referencing the highly diversified growth rates therein. However, by 1961, there is obvious evidence of decline and stagnation.

72

TABLE 5.3 COMPARATIVE FACTOR STRUCTURE: URBAN DEVELOPMENT,
1951 and 1961

| Factors Identified | 1961 | | 1951 | |
	Rank	Variance Explained (Per Cent)	Rank	Variance Explained (Per Cent)
Obsolescent centre	1	19.5	5	6.2
Cultural-linguistic contrasts	2	18.5	1	30.7
Metropolitan centre	3	9.9	2	10.0
Commercial centre	4	8.6	-	-
Peripheral centre	5	7.7	3	8.9
Educational-occupational structure	6	5.6	4	6.8
Fast growing centre	7	5.5	-	-
Public administration and defense centre	8	3.7	7	4.4
Institutional growth centre	-	-	6	4.6
Transportation centre	-	-	8	3.8
TOTAL		79.0		75.4

3) In 1951, there is a not very distinctive group of small
places which lacks a specialized economic base (commercial trade centres) and which shows some initial signs of
decline. By 1961, the decline increased to the extent that
the most emphatic dimension describes the obsolescent
centre.

The above assertions concur with Thompson's size ratchet
ideas. In small places, growth fluctuates and is highly variable --
the centres are certainly not self-sustaining. To reiterate, in
1951, many small Ontario and Quebec cities were in a transition
stage. By 1961, the aging population and physical structure begin
to appear as dominant growth factors. Conversely, a few places
show increased growth in the service sector.

Other temporal variations in the Central Canadian urban
system are not as outstanding as the above but still deserve mention. In 1951, the third component describes the peripheral or

73

northern centre. Loadings, and the per cent variance accounted
for, are comparable to 1961 except that transportation variables
appear as a separate factor in 1951. There is some change in
the cities isolated by the factor but this is largely indicative of
new resource-based Shield communities (Sept-Îles, Val d'Or,
Kenora). The fourth factor--educational and occupational structure, is also directly comparable to a similar 1961 dimension.
The diluted quality of the "university" characteristic is an obvious function of the existence of fewer degree-holding people in
1951.

Consideration has already been given to the declining trade
centre component. The next factor, "institutional growth centre,"
need not be discussed at length. It is analogous to the growth
factor (no. 7) derived from the 1961 analysis in that it presents
a specific time-place component isolating rapid institutional
growth for certain centres in 1951. Note that the factor identified
as a public administration and defense centre is almost identical
to the 1961 component with the same name. In 1961, more places
are characterized by the dimension as a result of an increase in
these functions over the ten year period.

The final factor identifies a transportation function that does
not appear in 1961. Variables loading encompass transportation
employment and occupations and a low value for residential building permits per capita. The latter variable might represent an
index of decline helping to account for the deletion of this factor
in 1961. Cities abstracted are railroad centres which even in
1951 showed signs of stagnation. By 1961, the importance of the
railroad centre in the Ontario-Quebec urban system is negligible.
A centre such as St. Thomas (factor score of 3.01), whose major
economic base is depended on railroads, is by 1961 characterized
as an obsolescent centre.

The Classification of Ontario and Quebec Cities

The principal components analysis indicates that major discriminants between cities in Ontario and Quebec are representative
of size, age, function, culture and location. While we have
identified the relative dimensionality of each city through its
factor scores, we are nonetheless dealing with independent measures. Each city has a unique position on each factor. In order
to achieve a comprehensive overview of the attributes of any one
city relative to the total system, it is necessary to examine the
multidimensional attributes of each urban place against all other

74

places. Multidimensional grouping, what is commonly described as cluster analysis, may be used to classify all cities on the basis of their factor scores on all major factors. Given the relatively small number of observation units, only four factors are considered here. Further, the cultural-linguistic factor was deleted for both 1961 and 1951--the premise being that the relative location of cities with respect to this dimension is well known. Its inclusion would complicate groups unnecessarily and hinder the comparison of other structural differences in the 1961 and 1951 findings.

The 1961 cluster analysis is based on the factors previously identified as obsolescent centre, metropolitan centre, commercial centre, and peripheral centre. After 60 steps, the analysis yielded a 13-group classification which is outlined in Table 5.4 and plotted in Figure 5.5. At this point, between group variance reduction was 76 per cent. The first and largest group comprises a series of diversified places, that is, communities which have multi-functional bases and/or do not manifest a dominant characteristic urban structure. St. Catharines, St. Jérôme, Cobourg, Valleyfield, Sherbrooke, and Kitchener are examples. The second group isolates cities specialized in certain industries--northern mining towns and one-industry communities such as Sarnia and Pembroke. Small trade and industrial towns are grouped in the third category. Some of these (Lindsay, Orillia, Chatham) have been identified as obsolescent or declining, yet they are grouped with self-sustaining places on the basis of similar economic or functional structure, physical stock, and population composition.

The fourth and fifth groups are obvious. The fourth comprises two cities, Georgetown and Brampton, both outstanding in their recent growth as satellites of Metropolitan Toronto. The fifth isolates Toronto and Montreal, the two largest and only true metropolitan centres in the Ontario-Quebec system. In the sixth category, Fort William, Port Arthur, North Bay, and Kenora are combined. All are northern centres based more on transportation services than natural resources--they do not align with the mineral processing cities of group 2. Alma and Chicoutimi group together in the seventh category. Both are well-established commercial centres on the Saguenay River--a region unique in Ontario and Quebec.

Categories 8 to 13 comprise single centre groups, distinctive from any already grouped by the analysis. Three of these are

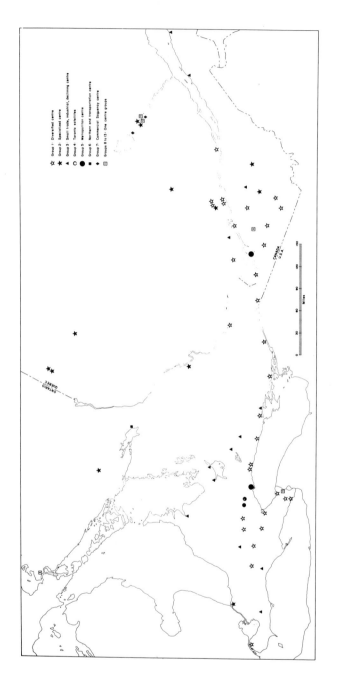

Figure 5.5 City groups, 1961 (Ontario and Quebec)

TABLE 5.4 CITY GROUPS, 1961: FOUR FACTORS

Group 1 (Diversified Centres)	Group 2 (Specialized Centres)	Group 4 (Toronto Satellites)
St. Catharines	Asbestos	Brampton
Whitby	Kenogami	Georgetown
St. Jérôme	La Tuque	
Cornwall	Sarnia	**Group 5** (Metropolitan Centres)
Granby	Noranda	
Brantford	Sudbury	Montreal
Drummondville	Timmins	Toronto
Kingston	Rouyn	
St. Jean	Val d'Or	**Group 6** (Northern and Transportation Centres)
Cobourg	Thetford Mines	
Sorel	Pembroke	
Valleyfield	Jonquière	
Brockville	Shawinigan-South	Fort William
Trois Rivières		Port Arthur
Guelph	**Group 3** (Small Trade, Industrial, Declining Centres)	North Bay
Magog		Kenora
Cap de la Madeleine		
Trenton	Joliette	**Group 7** (Commercial Saguenay Centres)
Shawinigan	Stratford	
Grand'Mère	Belleville	
Port Colborne	Lindsay	Alma
Welland	Orillia	Chicoutimi
Oshawa	Barrie	
Sherbrooke	Chatham	**Group 8** St. Hyacinthe
Woodstock	Peterborough	
London	Victoriaville	**Group 9** Sault Ste. Marie
Hamilton	Owen Sound	
Kitchener	St. Thomas	**Group 10** Sept-Îles
Ottawa	Rivière du Loup	
Windsor	Rimouski	**Group 11** Niagara Falls
Quebec		
		Group 12 Chicoutimi-North
		Group 13 Arvida

—undifferentiated

NOTES: After 60 iterations, between-group variance was 76 per cent. Order of cities within groups in approximate order of appearance in the grouping solution. The four factors from the 1961 analysis include:
1. Obsolescent Centre
2. Metropolitan Centre
3. Commercial Centre
4. Peripheral Centre

TABLE 5.5 CITY GROUPS, 1951: FOUR FACTORS

Group 1 (Diversified Centres)	Group 2 (Northern and Heavy Industrial Centres)	Group 5 (Metropolitan Centres)
Peterborough		Toronto
Stratford	Fort William	Montreal
St. Thomas	Port Arthur	
Cornwall	Sarnia	Group 6
Pembroke	Sault Ste. Marie	St. Hyacinthe
Belleville	Sudbury	
Brockville	Windsor	Group 7
Sherbrooke	North Bay	Arvida
Trois Rivières	Timmins	
Shawinigan		Group 8
Joliette	Group 3	Ottawa
Woodstock	(Small Trade and	
Brantford	Industrial Centres)	Group 9
Drummondville		Kingston
Kitchener	Barrie	
Guelph	Victoriaville	
Cap de la Madeleine	Owen Sound	
Grand'Mère	Orillia	
Trenton	Chatham	
Magog	Rouyn	
Hamilton	Jonquière	
St. Catharines	Thetford Mines	
Niagara Falls		
Welland	Group 4	
Valleyfield	(Administrative, Educational	
St. Jean	and Service Centres)	
Oshawa		
Granby	Chicoutimi	
St. Jérôme	Rimouski	
Sorel	London	
	Quebec	

NOTES: After 47 iterations, between-group variance was 77 per cent. Order of cities within groups in approximate order of appearance in the grouping solution.

The four factors from the 1951 analysis include:
1. Metropolitan Centre
2. Peripheral Centre
3. Educational-Occupational Structure
4. Declining Trade Centre

relatively new places in Quebec--Sept-Îles, Chicoutimi-North, a suburb of Chicoutimi, and Arvida, a company town specializing in aluminum processing. Of the three remaining places, two have an economic base and location unique in the Ontario-Quebec system--Niagara Falls (tourism and hydro-electric power), and Sault Ste. Marie (iron, steel, and transportation). St. Hyacinthe, sometimes called a typical "ville canadienne" appears not so typical of the present-day, but rather as a rare remaining example of the historical Quebec centre.

The 1951 grouping is summarized in Table 5.5. In this case, the four input factors are metropolitan, peripheral, declining trade, and educational centres. This is obviously not a direct counterpart of the 1961 input, though the first three factors are quite comparable. The most obvious difference between the two cluster analyses is that while 13 categories appear for 1961, only 9 appear for 1951. In part, this appears to index growth during the decade, and in part, structural change. Some stability is apparent. In both 1961 and 1951, the first and largest group comprises diversified places; the majority of places remained in group 1 over the decade. In 1961, however, a number of "new" (i.e., places that were under 10,000 in 1951) cities are added and a number of the 1951 group 1 places are found in group 3 in 1961 classified as small trade, industrial and declining centres. This confirms the earlier postulates that many small to medium-sized communities were in transition in 1951--Stratford, St. Thomas, and Belleville are good examples.

Both groupings yield categories descriptive of metropolitan, small trade, and specialized centres which are similar though not identical. In 1961, for example, the second grouping describes specialized manufacturing centres. In 1951, the group is limited to six northern centres and two heavy industrial centres in Ontario (Sarnia and Windsor). In 1961, several of these northern cities had moved to a separate category (no. 5, 1961) which describes isolated or peripheral cities lacking resource-oriented manufacturing bases but which are important as transportation and regional centres. Here the 1961 analysis is certainly much more definitive.

Category 3 is somewhat similar for both years except that in 1961 the group is larger as a result of the emergence of the obsolescence dimension. In 1951, a fourth group comprises administrative, educational and service centres. Since the dimension from which the group derives was not included in the 1961 grouping, there is no basis for comparison. Similarly, the satellite city (no. 4, 1961) does not appear in 1951. In both years, Toronto and Montreal are sufficiently distinctive to cause the two metropolitan areas to combine as an exclusive group. The 1951 grouping procedure leaves only four ungrouped places. Arvida and St. Hyacinthe for reasons given earlier are separate. So too, is the capital city of Ottawa, and the specialized institutional city of Kingston.

In general, the classification schemes produced here are considerably less rigorous than the factorial structures. First, only the most important dimensions were included in the analysis. More important is the fact that the results are combinatorial-- cities with different functions do, for example, group together when other attributes are similar. Certainly, the taxonomy provides an initial perspective on the state of the urban system in Central Canada. In accordance with King (1966), we would conclude that changes in urban dimensions or factors are more marked than changes in city typology over the ten year period. Since the data for the two time periods are not entirely compatable, we cannot comment further on King's thesis that this effect derives from strong regional contrasts.

Summary

The research presented here has provided a concise description of the Ontario-Quebec urban system in 1961 and 1951. In both cases eight components serve to summarize the overall structure of this system. In 1961, this comprises dimensions representative of obsolescent centres, cultural-linguistic contrasts, metropolitan centres, commercial and peripheral centres, educational-occupational structure, fast growing centres, and public administration and defense centres. In 1951 the dimensions include cultural-linguistic contrasts, metropolitan centres, centre-peripheral contrasts, educational-occupational structure, stagnant trade centres, institutional growth centres, public administration and defense centres, and transportation centres. Subsequent cluster analysis yielded 13 groups in 1961. The major ones are seven in number: diversified centres, specialized centres, commercial and declining centres, Toronto satellites, northern centres, transportation centres, metropolitan centres, and Saguenay commercial centres. Of the nine groups produced from the 1951 components, the five most important are one large group of diversified places, a group incorporating northern and heavy industrial centres, a contrasting group of small trade and industrial centres, a group termed administrative, educational and service centres, and a group isolating the two large metropolitan areas--Toronto and Montreal.

In general, our results are comparable to what has been achieved by previous analyses of this nature. Cultural or re-

gional, functional, locational, age–size, and growth dimensions
have been isolated. Excepting the educational-occupational component, there is no single index of socio-economic status. We
find that socio-economic variables do not provide a unique distinguishing dimension of the Ontario-Quebec urban system.
However, aside from these gross generalities, there is little
basis for comparison. Repeating our introductory argument, we
emphasize the distinctiveness of Canadian urban dimensions and
more specifically the dimensions of the heartland cities of Ontario and Quebec.

In addition to its specific regional focus, the present study
represents a preliminary step in the study of the dynamics of
Canadian urban systems. Indications of change between 1951 and
1961 are revealed by a significant variation in the factor structure
and complementary city grouping derived at each of the two time
periods. Elements of stability are certainly present in the
cultural-linguistic, educational-occupational, and public administration and defense components. This is not unanticipated
since each of the components represents considerable social and/
or structural investments which do not fluctuate rapidly over
time. There is, however, strong indication of changes in the
growth and nature of certain aspects of the urban system. The
results show an increase in metropolitanization and contempo-
raneously a decline for medium to small communities lacking
a strong economic base. The suggestion is that cities in this
size range are most susceptible to fluctuating growth rates.
The overall interpretation adhered to in this paper is that the
1951 urban structure evidences a transitional stage in the Ontario-
Quebec system. By 1961, the most important dimensions are
more tangible than those derived in 1951 when the structure is
characterized by a number of indications of growth and decline
but when no single dimension of this kind appears.

References

AHMAD, Q. 1965. Indian Cities: Characteristics and Correlates. Department of
    Geography Research Paper No. 102. Chicago: University of Chicago.

BERRY, B. J. L. 1964. Cities as systems within systems of cities. In J. Friedmann
    and W. Alonso, eds. Regional Development and Planning. Cambridge, Mass.:
    M.I.T. Press, pp. 116-37.

--------. 1968. A synthesis of formal and functional regions using a general field theory of spatial behavior. In B. J. L. Berry and D. Marble, eds. Spatial Analysis. Englewood Cliffs, N.J.: Prentice-Hall, Inc., pp. 419-431.

BERRY, B. J. L. and E. NEILS. 1969. Location, size and shape of cities as influenced by environmental factors. In H. S. Perloff, ed. The Quality of the Urban Environment. Baltimore: Johns Hopkins Press, pp. 257-304.

BLUMENFELD, H. 1965. The modern metropolis. Scientific American 213:3:64-74.

BRITTON, J. N. H. 1970. An occupational grouping of Ontario-Quebec cities. Research Paper No. 42, Centre for Urban and Community Studies, University of Toronto.

HADDEN, J. K. and E. F. BORGATTA. 1965. American Cities: Their Social Characteristics. Chicago: University of Chicago Press.

HODGE, G. 1971. Comparison of urban structure in Canada, the United States and Great Britain. Geographical Analysis 3(Jan., 1971):83-90.

KING, L. J. 1966. Cross sectional analysis of Canadian urban dimensions: 1951-1961. Canadian Geographer 10:4:205-24.

--------. 1967. Discriminatory analysis of urban growth patterns in Ontario and Quebec, 1951-1961. Annals of the Association of American Geographers 57:3: 566-78.

--------. 1969. Statistical Analysis in Geography. Englewood Cliffs, N.J.: Prentice-Hall, Inc.

MAXWELL, J. W. 1965. The functional structure of Canadian cities: a classification of cities. Geographical Bulletin 7:2:79-104.

MOSER, C. A. and W. SCOTT. 1961. British Towns. London: Oliver & Boyd.

RAY, D. M., et al. 1968. Socio-economic dimensions and spatial structure of Canadian cities. A Report on the First Phase of a C.M.H.C. Project. Waterloo: University of Waterloo. Mimeographed.

SIMMONS, J. W. 1967. Urban geography in Canada. The Canadian Geographer 11: 341-56.

SMITH, R. H. T. 1965. Method and purpose in functional town classification. Annals, Association of American Geographers 55:3:539-48.

THOMPSON, W. R. 1965. A Preface to Urban Economics. Baltimore: Johns Hopkins Press.

6

Economic structure of Ontario-Quebec cities: An occupational analysis

J. N. H. Britton

The objective of the investigation reported in this paper is to describe in a succinct fashion the economic structure of the cities in Ontario and Quebec. Groupings of these cities, based on similarities of economic functions are the means used here to achieve that description. The city groups and the account of their economic basis, complement patterns of interaction and their economic rationale; together these are the prime elements of the structure of the urban system.

Background Methodology

Classifications of cities may be arbitrarily divided according to whether or not the variables used for the classification are directly related only to economic functions (Smith 1965b). The study by Bunting (Paper 5), for example, may be regarded as a member of the group of studies concerned with function in an indirect fashion. Her terms of reference are first, to reduce the measurement of the characteristics of urban places to succinct dimensions; second, to examine city groupings based on these structural components; and third, to derive indices useful in the analysis of urban growth. In the final analysis her groupings are coloured strongly in functional terms; for example, the titles "metropolitan centre" and "commercial centre." Direct classifications which commonly use only employment variables (either by industries or by occupations) are probably best illustrated by the works of Maxwell (1965) and Smith (1965a). Maxwell developed a functional description of Canadian cities (1951 data on industrial employment) using the characteristics of "dominant function," "distinct function" and "degree of functional specialization." A current limitation of Maxwell's study is that the measures used are together relatively unwieldy, especially in the absence of an objective principle of classification.

Smith(1965a) carried the use of objective methods of direct classification considerably further. In a two-step procedure 422 Australian towns were first grouped into 91 classes by linkage analysis (correlations between towns calculated over 12 industry groups are used), and these were generalized to 17 groups by clustering a 91 x 91 matrix of Mahalanobis' D^2. To justify the groups, however, it is necessary to return to the original data and in that respect the method has a substantial subjective component (a point Smith acknowledges).

The results of these previous investigations are reflected in the choice here of:

1) a multi-variate statistical basis of analysis to ensure objectivity;
2) a "one-step" grouping method; and
3) one that not only identifies groups of cities but also identifies the main elements in the functional structure of each group.

Data

The use of occupational employment data to describe the economic profiles of the cities of Ontario and Quebec is based on the belief that they reflect more accurately, compared with industrial employment data, the job structure of a work-force. Problems in its use caused by the considerable difference in numbers of professional and non-professional workers are met by the standard occupational classification which subdivides non-professional occupations into industry-related classes.

The original data for this investigation have been obtained indirectly from the 1961 Census of Canada conducted by place of residence of each worker.[1] Modifications have been made to the standard occupational classes in order to derive a set of data for analysis (Table 6.1).[2] These are designed to bring to light groups (e.g., electronics) in the work-force that could

[1] Acknowledgement is made of the financial assistance given by the Department of Energy, Mines and Resources and Central Mortgage and Housing Corporation for the preparation of an initial data deck, and to Professors Robert Murdie and Michael Ray formerly of the University of Waterloo who kindly have permitted me to use these data.

[2] These modifications were:
a) 'occupation not stated,' 'farmers and farmworkers,' 'loggers and related workers' and 'fishermen, trappers, hunters' were deleted from further consideration owing to their minor importance in the cities under consideration.
b) At the same time, some of the occupational classes were subdivided to provide greater detail on occupations in the fields of (i) 'professional and technical occupations,' (ii)

TABLE 6.1 OCCUPATIONAL GROUPS USED IN ONTARIO-QUEBEC ANALYSIS

| Names | Percentage Employment by Cities | |
	Mean	Standard Deviation
1. Managers	10.03	1.97
2. Other professionals	4.25	1.33
3. Engineers	1.10	0.94
4. Scientists	0.26	0.38
5. Biological and agricultural scientists	0.11	0.13
6. Professors	0.26	0.41
7. Teachers	1.18	0.34
8. Health professionals	0.54	0.19
9. Physicians & Surgeons	0.48	0.22
10. Lawyers	0.28	0.12
11. Clerical	7.32	1.82
12. Sales	6.33	1.56
13. Services	8.71	4.70
14. Transport	1.53	0.94
15. Rail operators	0.96	1.59
16. Road operators	5.53	1.12
17. Miners	2.52	7.19
18. Other production workers	22.48	3.64
19. Spinners and weavers	1.59	3.71
20. Carpenters	3.19	1.57
21. Paper workers	1.86	2.94
22. Machinists	6.67	3.45
23. Electronics workers	0.30	0.66
24. Longshoremen	0.17	0.40
25. Labourers	6.89	2.36

n = 72

'transport and communication occupations,' and (iii) 'craftsmen, production process and related workers.' The more specialized occupational groups were defined on the basis of: (a) a priori expectations of distinguishing city characteristics and (b) the existence of possible sub-divisions of main occupational groups that are consistent with a systematic analysis of occupational distinctiveness of the cities. A more detailed list of modifications is found in Britton (1970).

85

distinguish the occupational structure of cities. Twenty-five
exclusive occupational groups are used, with data restricted to
the male labour force for ease of data handling. This restriction
is justified further on the grounds that female workers are not
broadly represented through the occupational classes but are
concentrated into clerical occupations which are not easily divis-
ible.

The geographical base for the study is the set of cities in
Ontario and Quebec with a population of 10,000 and over in 1961.
All of the cities included within the Census Metropolitan Area
(CMA) definition of the Dominion Bureau of Statistics were aggregated with their appropriate central cities to produce a total of
72 urban centres to be used in the analysis. In the case of
Montreal the cities on Montreal Island have been regarded as a
single metropolitan centre. The metropolitan area aggregation
procedure used here excludes from larger cities, basically non-
urban (in terms of the 10,000 population definition) administrative
areas. This is unlikely to produce different statistical results
from those that would be obtained using census metropolitan
definitions and furthermore it has meant considerable convenience in terms of assembling the necessary statistics.

The employment data were organized in a matrix of 25
occupational classes by 72 cities and the values were then transformed into percentages where each element in each city-column
is divided by the total male labour force in each city. This procedure is used to standardize for the size factor that would enter
into each set of correlations (between variables) calculated across
the same set of cities. While this new data-matrix could be used
for cross-sectional correlations of variables, that is traditional
R-mode analysis, the transpose of the matrix was used to obtain
structural correlations between cities, that is Q-mode analysis.

Relationship Between Occupational Variables
The form of the data is evaluated before proceeding with the main
objective of this paper. The hypothesis that the selected occupational variables when evaluated across the cities of Ontario
and Quebec are basically independent facets of urban structure is
considered first. To the extent that this assumption is substantiated, the data may then be used for an analysis of the functional
characteristics of the cities without depending on R-mode analysi

It can be anticipated, a priori, that the shapes of the frequency distributions for the occupational variables will vary con-

86

siderably; those occupational classes comprising the core of urban work-forces--sales, clerical etc., for example--can be expected to show a relatively uniform distribution of percentages over a narrow range of values. At the same time it can be anticipated that the occupational groups that have a relatively localized incidence in the set of cities will be characterized by distributions positively skewed to varying degrees. Examples of the various distributional shapes are shown in Figure 6.1 and the mean and standard deviations are given for each occupational group in Table 6.1.

A matrix of correlation coefficients between each of the occupational variables was found to contain only ten individual coefficients greater than 0.50.[3] The statistical dependence between the variables is of a fairly low order and is probably influenced by their construction: the variables are mutually exclusive for individuals.[4] Linkage and factor analysis shows only one substantial group of variables and in subsequent Q-mode analyses it has to be acknowledged that variables describing the "foundations" of the occupational structure of cities are not independent of each other.[5]

ANALYSIS OF OCCUPATIONAL STRUCTURE OF ONTARIO AND QUEBEC CITIES

Given some occupational variables have frequency distributions that are highly skewed in a positive direction while others, in

[3] Despite their non-normal distributions the variables have not been transformed. Reasons are as follows: (a) The data are already standardized (for size): normalizing does not seem a meaningful additional step given that no precise tests of statistical inference are to be made about the size of computed correlation coefficients. (b) No major hypotheses are being put forward about the associations between variables. It is expected that the occupations comprising the basic elements of the urban work force will follow a similar relative pattern of incidence throughout the set of cities, but localized occupations are expected to have low positive or even negative associations with one another. The former type of variable is least demanding of transformation and these variables (already with low variances) would probably behave poorly under a transformation which could only reduce their variance even further. The latter type of variable (localized occupations) is capable of being transformed (in terms of size of variance) but there seems little point as it is expected these are relatively independent of one another in locational incidence.

[4] The aggregation of such observations and the results of the analysis are paralleled by intra-urban investigations of land-use structure. See Bourne (1970).

[5] The loadings on this factor are managers (.58), professors (.55), health professionals (.74), physicians (.83), lawyers (.77), clerical (.56) and sales (.69).

87

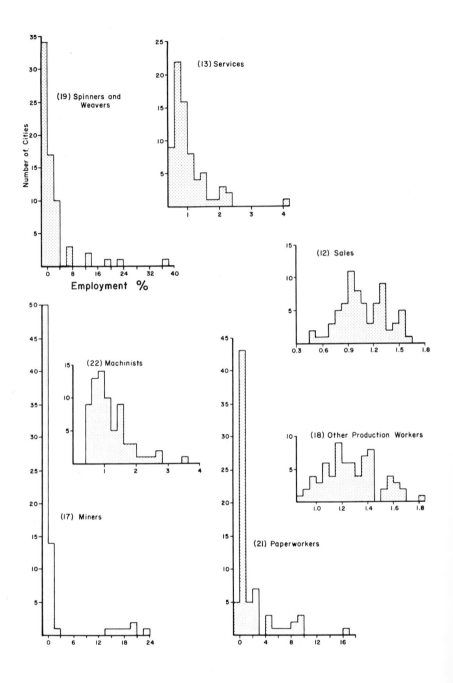

Figure 6.1   Selected proportional occupational measures: frequency distributions

particular the general urban occupational variables, have distributions that are reasonably symmetrical in shape, it can be anticipated that the occupational profile of each city will be a positively skewed distribution--the elements in the "tail" of the distribution will be the occupational groups distinguishing the particular functional structure of each city (Figure 6.2). Since it is intended to examine the association (correlation) between city occupational profiles, the question must be raised again whether the data should be transformed to more closely approximate to bi-variate normality: the decision has been taken against this step. [6]

Correlation coefficients between each of the 72 cities were calculated over the 25 occupational variables using the proportional (percentage) data and the similarity between occupational profiles has been explored using Q-mode factor analysis. At a later stage in the analysis a standardized set of occupational measures also is examined in comparative fashion using this technique.

Q-Mode Factor Analysis
A large number of high coefficients in the 72 x 72 correlation matrix attests to the expected basic similarities between cities

---

[6] The rationalization for this is as follows:
a) The data are already standardized into percentage form and additional normalizing would be a step that would cause difficulty in interpreting subsequent results in terms of city structure.
b) No precise tests of statistical inference are to be made about the size of computed correlation coefficients.
c) The expected results of an examination of the association between cities (similarity of occupational structure) is that: (i) city pairs highly associated with each other will be characterized by high proportions of the same "localized" occupational group, and low proportions of the general urban variables, (ii) city pairs registering lower levels of association will have similar low proportions of the general urban variables and high proportions of different "localized" occupational groups. These typical situations are illustrated in Figure 6.2. Transformation would result in no major change in calculated "r" values. It is to be noted that as general urban variables have a minor role in the recognition of city-groups (given the techniques used here) is not important that these observations (variables) are not strictly independent of one another.
d) If factor analysis is used to examine the correlations, the form of factor scores would be affected by the transformation of the percentage data so that they would better approximate symmetrical distributions. A consequence is that some ease of identifying distinguishing occupational classes by high factor scores (in a Q-mode analysis — see below) for each factor-group of cities would be lost. It can be argued, therefore, that the skew of the occupational profiles (city occupational distributions) can be used to advantage in the differentiation of the functional structure of cities.

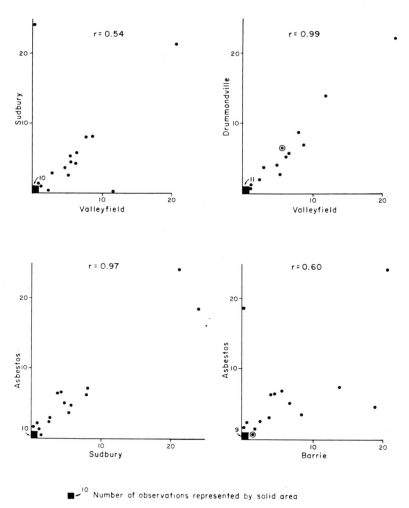

■-^{10} Number of observations represented by solid area

Figure 6.2   Selected city-pairs -- proportional occupational measures

throughout Ontario and Quebec.[7] A matrix of principal component loadings showed virtually all cities are associated in one group

---

[7]This similarity is strong enough to produce a principal eigenvalue of 59.8 equivalent to 83 per cent of the original total variance of the 72 cities; an additional 13 per cent of this variance is accounted for by 4 more dimensions with eigenvalues $\geq$ 1.0. The compound ratio:

$$E_c^O \ / \ E_c \ / \ E_t^O \ / \ E_t \ = \ LQ_c^O$$

provides a location quotient, where E = employment; ^{O} = occupational group, group 1, ...25, $_c$ = city, 1,...72; $_t$ = provincial total for Ontario-Quebec, when superscript absent symbol indicates aggregate of all occupational groups.

on Component I. The major exceptions are 5 centres dominated by mining activities which have the highest loadings on Component II. A rotation of the components to form a factor analytic solution (according to the principles of simple structure) will emphasize similarities within subsets of cities in terms of occupational structure.

All components with eigenvalues ≥ 1.0 were rotated and a summary of the pattern of loadings for five factors is presented in Table 6.2. Of the total number of cities, 47 have <u>one</u> significant loading, the remainder (classified more than once) indicate complex differences in occupational structure. Of the remaining 25 cities, however, 12 have dual loadings on 'service' and 'paper workers' and even the remaining 13 cities are relatively concentrated into a few of the potential loadings-patterns (see legend Figure 6.3).

Q-mode varimax factor analysis is an effective grouping algorithm in the case of Ontario-Quebec cities. More specifically, in Figure 6.3, the following groupings are shown:

1) centres specializing in mining activity are clearly delineated;

2) some centres have the 'service' occupational group represented in greater than average fashion and this is paralleled by strong representation of 'managers' and 'clerical' workers;

3) three factor groups are distinguished by special manufacturing functions which accompany generally strongly represented proportions of 'other production workers.' The three groups of centres are concerned with (i) metal manufacturing, engineering, and machinery industries ('machinists'); (ii) paper production and chemicals, ('paper workers') and (iii) textiles ('spinning and weaving').

The overwhelming similarities between cities must be accepted as a 'given' fact, and filtered from the data. In addition to using absolute occupational profiles another city grouping can be made, using relative profiles, that would have a somewhat different meaning. To test this methodology, the data describing the occupational structure of each city have been standardized by converting all percentages to location quotients (L.Q.)[8].

The location quotient form of the data takes into account the basic similarities between cities and places in relief, the occu-

---

[8]See Florence (1943), and Hoover and Vernon (1959).

TABLE 6.2 OCCUPATIONAL CHARACTERISTICS OF FACTOR-GROUPS OF CITIES:
Q - MODE FACTOR ANALYSIS — 25 PROPORTIONAL MEASURES, 72 CITIES

Factor Number	Per Cent Variance	Distinguishing Occupational Variables		High Factor* Score
I	16.0	22	Machinists	3.7
		18	Other production workers	2.0
		21	Paper workers	- 1.6
II	13.6	17	Miners	4.3
		18	Other production workers	1.4
III	33.0	13	Service	3.5
		1	Managers	1.7
		11	Clerical	1.1
		17	Miners	- 1.1
		21	Paper workers	- 1.0
IV	8.5	19	Spinners & weavers	4.2
		18	Other production workers	1.4
V	25.0	18	Other production workers	2.8
		21	Paper workers	2.7
		25	Labourers	1.7
		13	Service	- 1.1

*Factor Score $\geq$ 1.0

pations in each that are of greater or lesser than usual importance (Figure 6.4)--much of the common variance in the occupational profiles of the cities is removed and the analysis of the
transformed data reveals less similarity in the city structures.
The changes in proportions of total variance associated with each
principal component are correspondingly less steep, starting at
21 per cent rather than 83 per cent found with the percentage
data. The groups of cities which are formed from transformed
data have occupational profiles with similar relative structure.
    The general output from the varimax rotation of the compo-
nents is as follows: 58 of the 72 cities have loadings $\geq$ 0.5 on
only one factor; the other 14 cities have 2 (3 in one case)'significant' loadings on 12 different combinations of factors; only factors VI, VII and VIII are poorly represented among the cities of
mixed classification. The meaning attached to the factor groups
has been developed from the factor scores (See Table 6.3).

92

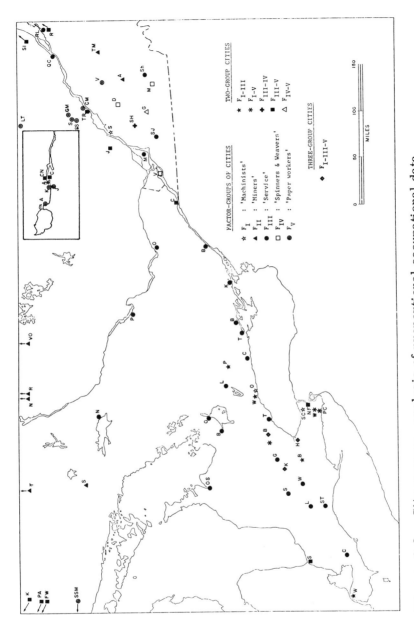

Figure 6.3   City groups: analysis of proportional occupational data

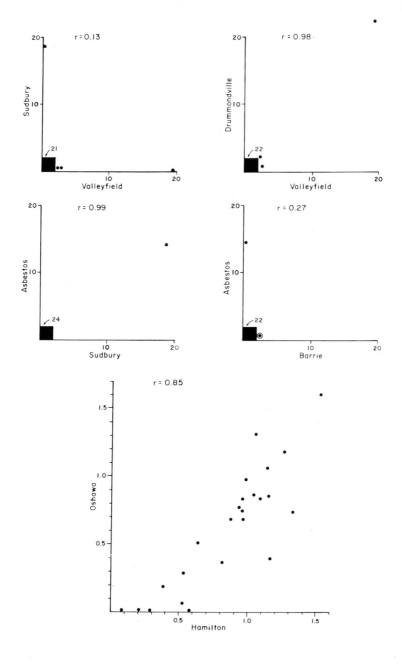

Figure 6.4   Selected city-pairs -- location quotient occupational measures

There appear to be similarities to some of the loadings from
the percentage data; there is a tendency, for example, for basic--
secondary and primary--urban functions to characterize absolute
and relative urban occupational profiles. Possibly this is due to
economies of scale of individual enterprises (for example, mining)
and/or agglomeration (localization) economies leading to the
important position of certain manufacturing activities (for example,
spinning and weaving) in some cities. Generally tertiary and
quaternary activities are present in smaller quantities and these
lead to relative specializations in a smaller number of centres.
In absolute terms, these functions are marked by 'service' occupational employment which characterizes a large number of centres
fulfilling the role of central places. For 14 centres a complex
classification into several structural groups is required owing
to their loading patterns.[9] In addition, it can be argued that the
two major metropolitan centres, Montreal and Toronto, have
shown themselves to be significantly different from all other
urban centres in Ontario and Quebec by virtue of their low loadings on group-dimensions which have been built primarily upon
the basis of the characteristics of the other 70 cities. Montreal
and Toronto must be regarded as metropolitan centres possess-
ing broadly based employment structures which distinguish them
from smaller urban nodes.

SPATIAL PATTERNS OF OCCUPATIONAL GROUPS

Among the groups formed on a proportional basis, 'service'
centres have the most extensive distribution, from Kenora, at one
extreme, to Rimouski and Sept-Îles, at the other (Figure 6.3).
They are, however, concentrated relatively and absolutely within
Ontario. The settlement distribution in the St. Lawrence Lowlands in Quebec is more contained and as a consequence of the

---

[9]Alternative simple-structure principles of rotation also were used, in addition to that
of the varimax routine, to attempt grouping of the cities. The quartimax rotational
scheme (also orthogonal), concerned with simplifying the row-wise distribution of factor
loadings, did not produce results of great difference or easier interpretation. Likewise
hypotheses of non-orthogonal groupings of cities were not substantiated as a preferable
basis for describing these cities when an oblique rotation scheme (oblimin) was used.
The majority of analyses were run using programme BMD 03M (see Dixon 1968) but for
the additional investigations mentioned in this footnote programme BMD X72 was used
(see Dixon 1969).

TABLE 6.3 OCCUPATIONAL CHARACTERISTICS OF FACTOR-GROUPS OF CITIES: Q-MODE FACTOR ANALYSIS — 25 LOCATION QUOTIENT MEASURES, 72 CITIES

Factor Number	Per Cent Variance	No. of Cities Single Loading ≥ 0.5 **	Distinguishing Occupational Variables		Highest Factor Scores*
I	9.7	3	22	Machinists	3.3
			3	Engineers	1.2
			18	Other production workers	1.2
			5	Biological-agricultural workers	-1.3
II	15.8	11	19	Spinners and weavers	-4.6
III	14.4	10	21	Paper workers	-4.6
IV	13.6	9	15	Rail operatives	4.5
V	10.3	7	6	Professors	-4.2
			23	Electronics workers	1.4
VI	10.4	7	17	Miners	-4.6
			23	Electronics workers	1.0
			24	Longshoremen	1.1
VII	4.0	2	4	Scientists	-4.3
			3	Engineers	-1.3
			24	Longshoremen	1.0
VIII	4.1	2	5	Biological-agricultural workers	-4.3
			13	Service	1.1
			24	Longshoremen	1.1
IX	5.0	3	14	Transport	4.4
			24	Longshoremen	1.1
X	6.8	4	13	Service	2.6
			20	Carpenters	1.3
			3	Engineers	-1.5
			6	Professors	-1.6
			22	Machinists	-1.1
			23	Electronics workers	-1.5
			24	Longshoremen	-1.3

*   Factor scores   ≥ 1.0
**   Other cities have combinations of loadings on more than one factor, viz.:
     I-III (2), I-V (1), I-X (2), II-III (1), II-V (1), II-IX (1), III-VII (1),
     IV-V (1), IV-IX (1), IV-X (1), VIII-X (1), III-IV-IX (1).

higher density of towns and cities there is less need for numerous centres catering primarily to an areal service base. Many service cities however, have additional functions in their economic base--mainly types of manufacturing specialization. Three such categories emerge in the analysis as a joint product of the occupational classes used here and the actual nature of industrial production. 'Machinists' for example, characterize a small group of cities--Windsor, Kitchener, Brantford, Hamilton, St. Catharines, Whitby, Oshawa, Welland, Port Colborne, Peterborough and Arvida. The location of these cities (primarily in Ontario) reflects the difference in the technological-industrial base of the economies of the two provinces: the number of 'machinists' in Ontario is 1.86 times the number in Quebec, the comparable figure for 'other production workers' is 1.40 and for occupations 1.32. Quebec's domination of the textile industry (ratio of 1:2.29) is reflected, however, in the spatial distribution of centres characterized by larger numbers of 'spinners and weavers.' 'Paper (and chemicals) workers' are distributed about evenly between the two provinces; more Quebec cities, however, have this occupational group as a primary functional description--there are five such cities on the Saguenay and nine others in the St. Lawrence area.

Mining centres are distinguished by the analysis and as expected these are located mainly on the Shield: the exceptions are Asbestos and Thetford Mines. Mining centres were classified in identical fashion in both percentage and location quotient analyses: this degree of spatial conformity between the two analyses is not repeated to the same extent for all other groups of cities. The centres specializing in 'spinning and weaving' (Figure 6.5) however, are essentially the same but there is a spread into Ontario of cities with relatively important elements of their structure devoted to this occupational class--Kitchener, Woodstock, Brantford and Welland of the former 'machinist' group, show textile activity as a relatively important industrial component.

Most of the cities formerly classified as service centres have other relatively important functions which have assisted in their re-classification: this applies to all but Toronto (weak loading), Pembroke, Cobourg and Chicoutimi North--perhaps the factor of local armed forces bases is significant in adding to the underlying central place type of economic support for these latter three centres. Orillia and Barrie have mixed functions, including service, and Chatham's relative structure is a combination of 'service occupation' employment and a high proportion of 'agricultural-biological workers.' The latter occupation class

97

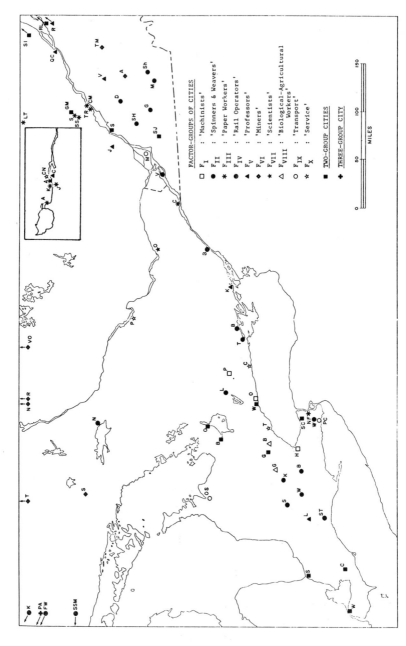

Figure 6.5   City groups' analysis of location quotient data

is also the basis for Guelph (agricultural college) and Brampton (nurseries) being grouped together in this analysis.

The relative importance of university employment (professors) in a number of small and medium sized centres is revealed in Figure 6.5 and it is an element of urban structure that is widespread in its incidence. However, a number of cities with sizeable university employment, have this function masked by other dominant occupational classes--Hamilton, for example, is in this category. 'Machinists' are the distinctive occupational class for Hamilton which groups with Oshawa, Peterborough, Windsor, Georgetown, St. Catharines, Orillia, Whitby--many of which were similarly classified in the percentage analysis. No Quebec cities enter this group thus revealing even more clearly than previously an urban translation of this·element of economic difference between the provinces.

Quebec's textile industry specialization is supplemented by the importance of 'paper workers' in cities on the Saguenay and in the central portion of the lowlands. This specialization carries over to some Ontario centres, identifying the importance of the chemical industry in Sarnia, and paper manufacturing in St. Catharines, Niagara Falls and Georgetown.

The last three occupational groups of cities requiring mention are:

1) the centres with relatively large proportions of 'rail operatives' which are major regional transportation junctions or terminals in the two provinces, though some members of the group are rail-depot towns along the Windsor-Montreal axis, such as Belleville;

2) a small number of centres have relatively high proportions of their work forces in 'transport' (and communications); Montreal is poorly described by this factor; and

3) centres with relatively large proportions of 'scientists' are a product of industrial activities in the cases of Sarnia and Arvida, and Federal Government employment in the obvious case of Ottawa-Hull.

COMPARISON OF RESULTS WITH THOSE OF THE STUDY OF URBAN DIMENSIONS

To the extent that some of the "dimensions" produced by the work of Bunting (Paper 5) also have a functional basis, a brief comparison of these dimensions with the Q-mode results obtained here may be valuable. It is to be stressed, however, the <u>functional</u> factors in the previous study are only <u>part</u> of a larger output not aimed principally at producing a functional grouping of cities.

Meaningful comparison is very difficult. Some of the factors from her 1961 analysis, however, refer to urban functions-- commercial metropolitan, peripheral, educational-occupational structure and public administration and defense types of centres. "Metropolitan centres," however, were defined with their highest loading on "population 1961," whereas the comparable group in this study has been identified only on the basis of occupational structure. The "commercial centre" appears in the percentage Q-mode analysis in the form of factor groups III, V and jointly classified cities: there are too few classified as "commercial centres" for there to be value in the apparent similarity. The "peripheral centre" of Bunting has a relatively high loading on "per cent in transportation industry" (in its total structure), and thus similarity with cities loading on L.Q. factor groups IV (rail operatives) or IX (transport and longshoremen) may be expected. The six cities with factor scores ≥ 1.50 have been examined and the pattern is as expected, thus yielding another point of contact for the two classifications. It is to be noted, however, that the other member of L.Q. factor groups IV and IX are classified differently in Bunting's analysis. The reason is the loading pattern attributable to the "accessibility," "situation" and "urban population in commuting radius" variables in that analysis. The present study shows a number of cities have rail transport occupations as a distinguishing functional characteristic. The inclusion of the spatial variables in Bunting's analysis, however, precludes the development of a functional grouping based on rail service. As the spatial variables are related to one another, "peripheralness" is associated with a large transport work force and cities accessible to the market foci have a sizeable manufacturing work force. The "educational-occupational structure" factor in that study has its counterpart in this analysis in the form of L.Q. factor groups V (professors) and VII (scientists). The "public administration and defense centre" factor similarly has some relation to functional group-ings developed here. Three of the high scoring cities are mem-bers of the small service specialization group derived in this analysis and armed forces' bases may well explain the functional group identified here--however, the possibility of an area-based function for these three centres also merits further consideration.

As the groupings of cities (based on factor scores) in the work by Bunting is based on only four factors it was not expected to offer a grouping exactly comparable with that developed here. This is borne out in fact--only the two metropolitan centres have identical postions in the two classifications.

EVALUATION OF Q-MODE ANALYSIS

The differences in results between the work of Bunting and that reported here are largely a function of the data. It has been considered important, however, to check the importance of the difference in methods of analysis used in the two studies. Therefore, an alternative indirect type of analysis has been used.

Scores for 8-factor, 12-factor, and 12-component, R-mode analyses of the Ontario-Quebec occupational data have been used to group the cities. The scores for 12-factors produce results most like the Q-mode analyses when used in grouping the cities in hierarchical fashion.[10] The multiple classification of some cities using factor analysis, however, recognizes the complexity of comparisons of city structure and is preferable to the intuitively less defensible simple grouping of cities obtained using the alternative.[11]

The value of Q-mode analysis is that the allocation of cities to groups can be achieved using factor loadings while the occupational characteristics (which may be complex) associated with each group are revealed in factor scores. In R-mode analysis cities score on the factor groups of variables and there is no guarantee that the allocation of cities to groups can be achieved easily using this output directly: the multiple "classification" of observations according to factor scores is usually so great that recourse is taken to grouping algorithms using factor-score input (see above). The ease with which Q-mode output can be interpreted is a strong point in its favour. For investigations such as this, where there is no redundancy in the set of variables used for analysis it can be argued that the Q-mode technique is intuitively and statistically (in variance terms) more defensible than the grouping procedure that depends on R-mode analysis.

[10] The program H-GROUP was used (see Veldman 1967).

[11] For an authoritative review of work in this field up to 1965 see Smith (1965b).

101

References

BOURNE, L. S. 1970. Dimensions of metropolitan land use: cross-sectional structure and stability. Research Paper No. 31, Centre for Urban and Community Studies, University of Toronto.

BRITTON, J. N. H. 1970. An occupational grouping of Ontario-Quebec cities. Research Paper No. 42, Centre for Urban and Community Studies, University of Toronto.

DIXON, W. J., ed. 1968. BMD Biomedical Computer Programs. University of California Publications in Automatic Computation No. 2. Berkeley and Los Angeles: University of California Press.

--------, ed. 1969. BMD Biomedical Computer Programs, X-Series supplement. University of California Publications in Automatic Computation No. 3. Berkeley and Los Angeles: University of California Press.

FLORENCE, F. 1943. The technique of industrial location. The Architectural Review 93:59-64.

HOOVER, E. M. and R. VERNON. 1959. Anatomy of a Metropolis. Cambridge, Mass.: Harvard University Press, pp. 283-87.

MAXWELL, J. W. 1965. The functional structure of Canadian cities: A classification of cities. Geographical Bulletin 7:2:79-104.

SMITH, R. H. T. 1965a. The functions of Australian towns. Tijdschrift voor Economische en Sociale Geografie 56:3:81-92.

--------. 1965b. Method and purpose in functional town classification. Annals, Association of American Geographers 55:539-48.

VELDMAN, D. J. 1967. Fortran Programming for the Behavioral Sciences. New York: Holt, Rinehart and Winston, pp. 311-17.

III

Growth Characteristics of the Urban System

7

Editors' comments

Growth is inevitably the most difficult aspect of system behaviour to analyze. An appropriate research strategy is to marshall as much information as possible on historical occurrences, cross-sectional characteristics, and activity interrelationships, before initiating an intensive study of growth, its distributions and mechanisms and raison-d'être. The papers in this section represent an introductory foray into some of the interrelationships between the structure of the cities in Ontario and Quebec and their recent growth characteristics. Initially, this section provides a comparative context of the relationships between economic and population structure and rates of urban growth, among Canadian and U.S. cities.

The distinction between two kinds of growth drawn by Boulding (1953) offers one context to facilitate understanding the growth of urban areas.[1] In his terms, simple or proportional growth refers to the direct expansion or contraction of an object or system by the addition or deletion of members of elements. Proportional growth implies that a system is inhomogeneous, but more important that it exists as a population with a definite age distribution. The second type of growth form, structural growth, on the other hand, involves a process of adjustment in the interrelationships between parts of an aggregate system. It is this process which is of particular interest here.

[1]See also Thompson (1919).

104

Boulding also differentiates between several principles of
structural growth, three of which are relevant to the analysis
of an urban system. The first states that "at any moment the
form of an object, organism, or organization is a result of its
laws of growth up to that moment," and further that "growth
creates form, but form limits growth." The relevance of this
principle to the spatial structure of an urban system is self-
evident. [2] Growth requires an adjustment in structure whether
an increase in size occurs or not. The second principle is an
argument as to why an orderly structure should exist at all.
This is the principle of equal advantage, which provides instruments for and governs the distribution of increments of growth
among the competing parts of the structure involved. In economic
systems such as ours the advantage principle is most frequently
defined as monetary reward or profit. In other more regulated
economic systems the instruments of adjustment may be defined
as a blueprint guiding the process of growth. It will also be
recognized that the principle of advantage is the fundamental
premise of location theory. The third principle is that of non-
proportional change. As any structure grows, such as an urban
system, the proportional relationships of its parts and characteristics cannot remain constant simply because of differential
change among the components of that structure. Growth always
involves a compensatory change in the relative sizes of parts of
a system and in the linkages between these parts. These principles provide a logical framework for the analyses of urban
structure and growth in this section.

In the first paper, Gerald Hodge examines the relative
distribution and components of growth for ten metropolitan areas
in Canada employing a technique defined as "regional-structural"
analysis. [3] Briefly, this technique partitions the growth of an
urban centre, for example the rate of population growth, into
two parts, one it is argued derives from the local structure (of
the population of that city) and the other is a competitive effect
deriving from comparative advantages in the city's relative
location. This particular approach has met with considerable
success in studies of changing employment structures in U.S.
cities and counties. [4] Having achieved this partition for both

[2] See Guttenburg (1960).

[3] This technique is similar in origin and purpose to "shift-share" analysis. A recent
review of shift-share analysis is given in Krumme (1969).

[4] Some of these applications are reviewed in Berry (1967).

employment and population for Canadian cities, Hodge elaborates
on the insights provided by this model through a comparative
analysis with selected U.S. metropolitan areas.

The second paper introduces the Ontario-Quebec situation
specifically. Golant begins with a two-fold hypothesis regarding
the interrelationships between the structure of the set of cities
and variations in recent rates of growth. The hypothesis states,
first, that variations in past growth performance are reflected
directly in differences in urban structure, and second, that it is
possible to isolate growth potential from existing structural
conditions. Do growing cities have different structures? Regression equations are described for population, employment, and
building permit change as surrogates for demographic, economic,
and physical growth. The data and cities used in the analysis
are the same as those on which Paper 5 is based. Of course the
differentiation of structure and process is extremely difficult and
in fact open to interpretative questions. Yet, as an introductory
phase in the treatment of growth such cross-sectional comparisons are a useful building block for subsequent research.

Thus far, the papers have been concerned primarily with
the growth of the larger cities in Ontario and Quebec. What has
been the recent growth experience of smaller communities? Do
they behave in the same way as the metropolitan centres? Or,
as many observers feel, have these cities been overlooked in
the rapid urbanization of recent decades? Suggestions of the
death of small towns abound. In the third paper John Hodgson
undertakes two specific analyses to counter these arguments.
First, he extends previous analyses of growth characteristics,
by Davies in Paper 3 and Golant in this section, to include small
cities in the province of Ontario. Second, he adds a new component to the approaches outlined thus far by attempting to evaluate a regional effect in urban growth. If variations in the rate
at which cities are growing contain a significant spatial component, that is if cities in one region are growing consistently
faster than those in other regions, or if a city has a higher
probability of growth the nearer it is located to a rapidly growing
city, then it should be evident in the clustering of cities with
similar growth rates. Using techniques of nearest neighbour
analysis, the author demonstrates that urban growth clearly does
have a significant regional component. One of the factors in such
regional variations in urban growth are the networks of transportation, flows and interaction, the subjects of the following section.

There are of course other approaches to the analysis of differential growth rates for cities. In the final paper Barber begins by grouping Ontario-Quebec cities into three categories -- growing, unstable and declining--according to their position relative to the overall mean population growth rate, and then utilizes discriminant analysis techniques to identify those variables which differentiate between the groups. The key discriminants of urban growth emerge as accessibility and employment in manufacturing, community service and construction industries; results which both complement and question those obtained previously.

References

BERRY, B. J. L. 1967. Strategies, Models and Economic Theories of Development in Rural Regions. Washington, D.C.: U.S. Department of Agriculture.

BOULDING, K. E. 1953. Toward a general theory of growth. Canadian Journal of Economics and Political Science 19:326-40. Reprinted in J. J. Spengler and O. D. Duncan, eds Population Theory and Policy. Glencoe, Ill.: The Free Press, 1956, pp. 109-24.

GUTTENBURG, A. Z. 1960. Urban structure and urban growth. Journal of the American Institute of Planners 26:104-10.

KRUMME, G. 1969. Identifying regional economic change: A variation of the theme shift and share. Canadian Geographer 13:76-80.

THOMPSON, D. W. 1919. On Growth and Form. Cambridge, England: The University Press.

8

Regional and structural components of urban growth

G. Hodge

In this paper growth rates in two aspects of urban structure--population and employment--are examined for a number of Canadian and U.S. metropolitan areas and the reasons for differences in growth rates are probed. These probes are made through a type of shift/share analysis called Regional/Structural Analysis.[1] The basis of the technique is a comparison of the growth rate of some element (in our case, metropolitan areas) with the growth rate of some relevant and larger aggregate (in our case, the nation) of which the element is a part, through an examination of differences in the structure of each. Differences in growth rates are explained in terms of two components: the structural component, which describes the tendency for a metropolitan area to grow slowly or fast because of its own population composition, and the regional component, which describes the tendency for the same area's growth rate to be influenced by factors not accounted for in its population composition.[2]

Four separate regional/structural analyses are reported on here, and shown in Figures 8.1 through 8.4. They involve metropolitan areas in Canada and the U.S., analyzed separately in terms of their population and employment growth during the 1950's. Population growth is viewed through age composition, by 5-year age groups. Employment growth is viewed through standard industry group composition.

Derivation of Technique
In order to gain maximum benefit from the graphical representations, some further explanation of the derivation of the two components is necessary. The structural and regional compo-

---

[1] An excellent presentation of this technique and a review of pertinent literature is found in Paris (1969).

[2] General reviews of similar techniques of regional economic analysis are reviewed in Dunn (1960), Perloff et.al. (1960), and Stilwell (1969).

nents of population or employment growth derive from the calculation of a "hypothetical growth rate" for each metropolitan area:
i. e., the growth rate which would have occurred if each of its
sectors (age groups, industry groups) had grown at the same
rate as the corresponding sectors in the nation as a whole.

Thus, using population growth as an example, if a metropolitan area has the same age distribution as the nation, the
hypothetical growth rate for the area would equal the actual growth
rate for the nation. In that situation the structural component
would show a score of zero--or be at the origin on our graph
with respect to the NW - SE sloping axis. A positive structural
component (a shift to the SE) results when the metropolitan
area's age distribution is more concentrated in those age classes
which have been experiencing high positive rates of change.
That is, the area possesses an advantage for growth by virtue
of its population structure. A negative structural component
(a shift to the NW) results when an area's age distribution is
more concentrated in declining age or slowly growing classes.
An area is, therefore, disadvantaged by its structure.

The regional component is simply the difference between
the observed population growth rate of the region for the particular period and the hypothetical growth rate, as already defined.
Thus, a positive score on the regional component indicates a
fast rate of population growth which cannot be attributed to the
area's age structure, and will be found on the NE - SW sloping
asix toward the NE. It might, for example, be due to differences in net in-migration rates, mortality or birth rates, economic structure, and so forth. This would constitute a special
advantage for growth in a region not generally available to all
other regions. A negative score on the regional component (a
shift to the SW) is the result of factors in the region, other than
age structure, which have tended to restrain population growth
such as a low or negative rate of migration or economic growth,
or of constraining cultural factors.

Actual growth in any region is most often subject to a
combination of structural and regional advantages or disadvantages.
Thus, the metropolitan areas on our graphs tend to fall in the
quadrants between the two sloping axes. Those falling in the
right hand quadrant, possess the best combination of structural
and extra-structural advantages for growth. Those in the left
hand quadrant have no absolute advantages, regional or structural, for growth. The upper quadrant reflects the presence of

109

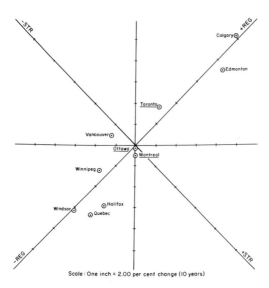

Scale: One inch = 2.00 per cent change (10 years)

Figure 8.1   Population shifts in
Canadian metropolitan areas, 1951-
1961. Note: Base for comparison:
total metropolitan population

regional advantages but no structural advantages for a metropolitan area's growth; the lower quadrant reflects the opposite.

Canadian Metropolitan Population Growth, 1951-1961

Ten Canadian census metropolitan areas (CMA's) were subjected
to regional/structural analyses of their population growth rates
in light of their age distributions measured in 5-year age groups
(Figure 8.1). Two different aggregates were used as a base for
comparison: total Canadian population and the population of the
ten CMA's in the sample. The latter is reproduced here in view
of the finding that there was virtually no difference in the results--
a fact which testifies to the high degree to which Canadian population growth has recently been dominated by the growth tendencies of its major metropolitan areas.

Three distinct groupings of Canadian metropolitan areas
appear on the graph. First, there are those that have strong
regional components affecting their growth rates--Edmonton,
Calgary, and Toronto. The two western centres are particularly strong. Edmonton enjoys substantial structural advan-

110

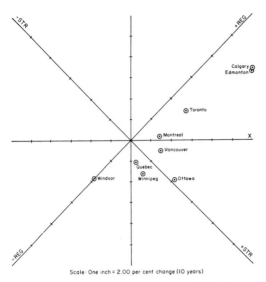

Scale·One inch = 2.00 per cent change (10 years)

Figure 8.2   Employment shifts in
Canadian metropolitan areas, 1951-
1961. Note: Base for comparison:
total Canada

tages as well, while the other two have small structural disadvantages but these are not sufficient to offset their regional
advantages.   A second group falls close to the origin of the axes--
Montreal, Ottawa, and Vancouver--indicating that they are
neither substantially favoured nor disfavoured by their population
structure or regional situation.   A third group shows large
disadvantages attributable to their age structure composition--
Windsor, Quebec, Halifax, and Winnipeg.   That is, they are
either weak in those age groups which are enjoying fast growth
in the aggregate, or strong in the slow-growing groups, or
usually both.

Canadian Metropolitan Employment Growth, 1951-1961
In a similar type of analysis, the employment growth rates of
nine of the same Canadian metropolitan areas were analyzed and
plotted (Figure 8.2).   The structural elements were employment
by nine industry groups: manufacturing, construction, transportation, wholesale, retail, finance, service, government, and
all others.   The aggregate used as a base of comparison was
total employment in Canada, its structure and changes from
1951 to 1961.

111

From the graph we see that all but one of the metropolitan areas, Windsor, possesses substantial advantages for growth through their industry-employment group structure. Ottawa, in particular, enjoys the greatest structural advantage. Four other centres besides Ottawa also enjoy large regional advantages for employment growth with Calgary and Edmonton again leading, as they did in the analysis of structural growth. Toronto also shows up with a large regional advantage, significantly better for example than Montreal. Quebec City and Winnipeg, while enjoying some structural advantages, show no special strength through their regional situation. Windsor is clearly weak in both directions.

Probing the relationship between rates of employment growth of individual centres and their employment in the nine industrial sectors shows the following: (1) diversity in employment structure is more consonant with growth than is dominant strength in one sector;[3] (2) strength in manufacturing employment is inversely related to rate of growth; but (3) strength in construction, transportation, and finance sectors goes with high growth rates; while (4) proportions in retail, service, and government are generally not associated with either growth or decline rates.

U.S. Metropolitan Population Growth, 1950-1960

Twelve United States metropolitan areas (SMSA's), selected to include a range of city sizes and locations as well as several representative Great Lakes' cities, were subjected to similar regional/structural analyses of their 1950-1960 population growth rates. Five-year age groups were used, as in the Canadian test, and the aggregate base for comparison was the total population of the twelve SMSA's in the sample. The results are illustrated in Figure 8.3.

As in the Canadian example, the newer "western" centres such as San Diego, Los Angeles, and Houston, show up with exceeding strong regional components contributing to their substantially better-than-average growth rates in the period. Houston, as well, enjoys the highest structural advantages among all the centres. Washington is the only other centre to have some regional advantages; these are combined with a high structural advantage. Interestingly, Washington occupies a similar position in the array of U.S. metropolitan centres as does Ottawa in the Canadian array. This is likely some reflection

---

[3] This is confirmation of a similar proposition in Thompson (1968).

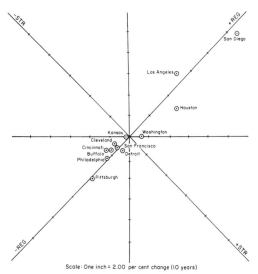

Scale: One inch = 2.00 per cent change (10 years)

Figure 8.3   Population shifts in
U.S. metropolitan areas, 1950-1960
Note: Base for comparison: SMSA
total

of the importance of national capital functions as a force for
generating growth.

The four U.S. Great Lakes' metropolitan centres--Buffalo,
Cincinnati, Cleveland, and Detroit--all show substantial regional
disadvantages and, except for Detroit, none have structural
advantages. San Francisco-Oakland, unlike its sister western
cities, falls in the latter range along with Philadelphia, and
Pittsburgh. Kansas City falls near the origin which indicates
no great advantages or disadvantages due to either structural
or regional effects; that is structure and growth rate are much
the same as in the aggregate.

U.S. Metropolitan Employment Growth, 1950-1960
For the twelve U.S. metropolitan areas analyzed for population
growth, employment growth in terms of ten industry groups was
also examined. The ten industry groups differ slightly from
those used in the Canadian analysis, but the parallels should be
obvious. The U.S. industry groups are: construction,
manufacturing-durables, manufacturing-non-durables, transpor-
tation-utilities, wholesale-retail, finance, business services,
professional services, public administration, and all others.

113

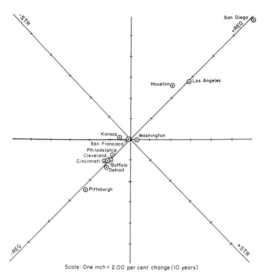

Scale: One inch = 2.00 per cent change (10 years)

Figure 8.4   Employment shifts in
U.S. metropolitan areas, 1950-1960
Note: Base for comparison: SMSA
total

The aggregate base for comparison is the total employment for
the 12 SMSA's in the sample.

The metropolitan areas array themselves in employment
growth in a very similar way to their array in population growth
(Figure 8.4). That is, a western group of cities with very
strong regional components emerges--San Diego, Los Angeles,
Houston, Kansas City, and San Francisco, as well as Washington, cluster near the origin, neither strongly advantaged nor
disadvantaged by their structure or region; and the eastern
cities, including Buffalo, Detroit, Cleveland, and Cincinnati,
with industry structures and regional conditions that are of no
advantage to them in employment growth. It should also be
noted that, because structural components are universally small
for these centres, the array as illustrated by Figure 8.4 is
mainly on regional components and is also indicative of decreasing employment growth rates from right to left.

Several characteristics of industry group structure emerge,
as they did in the Canadian metropolitan areas, as being closely
associated with employment growth rates. These are: (1)
strength in manufacturing employment, durable and non-durable
combined, is inversely related to employment growth rates; but

114

(2) strength in construction, finance, business services, and professional services goes with high growth rates; while (3) strength in public administration employment is not regularly associated with either growth or decline; and (4) general diversity may be the best employment structure to achieve consistently high growth rates.

Population and Employment Growth: Canada and the U.S.

In each of the sets of metropolitan areas studied, Canadian and U.S., there is a high degree of coincidence of the position of centres on the regional/structural axes for both population growth and employment growth. That is, the metropolitan areas in both countries show high, or low regional and structural components of growth in very much the same manner whether measured in terms of population or employment. Cities like San Diego, Calgary, Houston, or Toronto, for example, have gained advantages in population and employment growth from strong regional conditions. Cities that have been weak regionally in population growth are also weak regionally in employment growth achievement. At least in the 1950-1960 period, the population structural feature would have been a good predictor of employment growth rates, and vice versa.

One could study intensively the possible constraining influences of certain population age structures or industry group structures on one another. While these have not been considered here, two generalizations do emerge: first, where the age and industry group structures have not been dominated by one or a few groups, that is where structure is diversified, overall growth has been achieved. Second, structural strength in sectors consistent with the current conditions for growth, such as young age groups or service industry groups, can add weight to growth prospects. While there seem to be some regional conditions giving strong advantages to western cities in both countries, it is not uniform. Moreover, such eastern cities as Toronto, Ottawa, and Washington also show up strongly in this regard.

A short addendum to the foregoing analyses explored the position that might be assumed by Toronto, Montreal, Ottawa, Edmonton and Calgary in the U.S. population arrays if, with their own age structures, they had to relate to the U.S. aggregate for the same age groups. This analysis had many "rough" statistical edges (such as the difference in the census period),

115

and is not, therefore, reproduced here, but it is useful to convey some of the general impressions. First, Toronto, Montreal, and Ottawa showed up in a U.S. context as having extremely strong structural components, far and above anything achieved by the U.S. centres. Secondly, Edmonton and Calgary maintained their strong regional advantages along with the strong western U.S. cities. Referring to our first point, it is clear that Toronto, Montreal and Ottawa all possess substantial potential for growth, probably much in excess of their U.S. counterparts in the Great Lakes Megalopolis--Detroit, Cleveland, Cincinnati, and Buffalo. Toronto shows up in the strongest position.

In summary, these analyses, comparing growth behaviour within sets of Canadian and U.S. metropolitan areas regarding population and employment, showed distinctive types of centres according to their age group and industry group structure. There were the fast-growing "western-type" centres exemplified by Los Angeles, Houston, Calgary and Edmonton. Toronto, also enjoyed many of the same structural and regional advantages as the latter cities in both population and employment growth. More important, the three major eastern Canadian cities appear to enjoy substantially superior conditions for growth than most large cities in the U.S. midwest and Great Lakes regions.

References

DUNN, E. S., JR. 1960. A statistical and analytical technique for regional analysis. Papers and Proceedings of the Regional Science Association 6:97-112.

PARIS, D. 1969. Regional structural analysis of population change. Unpublished paper. Department of Urban and Regional Planning, University of Toronto.

PERLOFF, H. S., et al. 1960. Regions, Resources and Economic Growth. Baltimore: Johns Hopkins Press, for Resources for the Future, Inc.

STILWELL, F. J. B. 1969. Regional growth and structural adaptation. Urban Studies 6:2:162-78.

THOMPSON, W. 1968. Internal and external factors in the development of urban economics. In H. Perloff and L. Wingo, Jr., eds Issues in Urban Economics. Baltimore: Johns Hopkins Press, for Resources for the Future Inc., pp. 43-65.

9

Regression models of urban growth in Ontario and Quebec

S. M. Golant

In this paper the urban centres of Quebec and Ontario are treated as a system described by a wide range of interacting social, economic and physical variables over a twenty-five year period. In particular, this study focuses on the obvious but complex relationships between urban growth and spatial structure. At any point in time the structure of a system of cities both reflects past growth behaviour and provides the basic infrastructure for future growth. As Blaut (1961) expresses it, "...structures of the real world are simply slow processes of long duration, the more slowly changing elements in any spatial-temporal segment."

This study attempts to reveal some of the more important cross-sectional structural variables related to variations in population and economic growth among cities in the Ontario-Quebec system. Is it possible to account for differential urban growth rates with a set of attributes describing the structure of these cities? In this context, growth rates become the dependent variables, to be explained by a set of hypothesized structural variables.

Such an approach implicitly involves two assumptions: first, that the aggregation of urban centres in Quebec and Ontario pos-sesses the properties of, or operates as, a system; and second, that the interval of time over which the system is being studied will provide a clear representation of the spatiotemporal relation-ships. In partially dealing with the first assumption, Quebec and Ontario centres are analyzed separately as distinctive urban aggregates or subsystems. Then the centres of both provinces are examined with regard to such parameters as size and func-tion in determining the appropriateness of including both sets in the same system. In reference to the second assumption, sev-eral time-intervals are considered in the analysis of the system growth, and the structure of the urban centres is examined at two points in time (see Paper 2).

This study closely parallels the analysis of urban growth dimensions for Canadian central cities by King (1966, 1967), the econometric models of Matilla and Thompson (1968) for metropolitan growth in the United States, and the study of urban growth poles in eastern Ontario by Hodge (1966). King (1967) is of particular relevance here in that this study deals with much the same region over a similar time period. This study differs from several urban growth analyses in that its variables are not limited to depicting economic components and it primarily emphasizes cross-sectional structural, concomitant variables as an expression of growth. [1]

The Data and Analytical Procedures

All urban centres in Ontario and Quebec with populations over 10,000 at the 1961 census are included. [2] Those centres contained within census metropolitan areas (CMA's) are treated as part of the CMA's and not as separate entities. [3] By these criteria, a total of 40 Ontario and 33 Quebec urban centres are included. The variables describing this system are grouped into five categories: (A) population and economic growth; (B) demographic and social structure; (C) employment and occupational structure; (D) physical structure and development; and, (E) relative location and hinterland characteristics (see Bunting, Paper 5).

Growth of the urban system is measured in three ways: i) population growth--percentage change in population; ii) economic growth--percentage change in employment; and iii) physical growth--percentage change in total value of building permits issued. Four time intervals are considered: 1941-1961; 1951-1961; 1956-1961; and 1961-1966. Both 1951 and the 1961 structural variables are included where possible. These and the growth variables have been obtained primarily from 1951 and 1961 census publications. Category E data, measuring the location accessibility of the urban centres, have been obtained from provincial data sources and by direct extrapolation from official maps.

The inevitable limitations imposed by inconsistent time

[1] For a summary of these variables, see Czamanski (1964).

[2] The threshold population level of 10,000 is a limitation imposed upon the study by the availability of census data.

[3] The assumption is made here that considerable distortion would arise if metropolitan area figures had not been used. Similar grouping should have been carried out for census major urban areas, but this was prohibited by limited data availability.

series data have necessitated modifications in the number of observations and variables employed. The most complete data inventory has been prepared for 1961 for all 73 urban centres; however, to achieve compatability among critical variables for both 1951 and 1961, 70 cities are used in the 1961 analysis. Only 56 cities are employed in the limited 1951 analysis as many fell below the 10,000 population threshold.

The relationships between growth and structure are calculated using least squares stepwise multiple regression. Initially the structural variables are transformed into percentages to eliminate the obvious and dominant effects of relationships statistically collinear with city size. Through a progressive sequence of testing and deletion, a final set of predictor variables is derived for each growth index.

Two approaches are employed: first, an attempt to predict urban growth differentials by utilizing differences in cross-sectional structure prior to the period of growth; and second, an examination of the relationships between growth rates and the structure of cities at the end of the growth period.

Derivation and Assumptions of Regression Equations

The general linear multiple regression analysis may be expressed as

$$\Delta Y = b_0 + b_1 X_1 + b_2 X_2 + \ldots + b_K X_K + e$$

where Y is a dependent growth variable, X_1, X_2, .., X_K represent the values taken by the independent structural variables, b_0 is a fixed constant, b_1, b_2, .., b_K are linear coefficients and e is an error term.

Stepwise multiple regression procedures are used to identify the most relevant predictor variables among the structural data (Table 9.1). The systematic procedure by which the final sets of independent variables are selected is of critical importance in evaluating the final results. The task of isolating the most meaningful independent variables from an original matrix of over 100 is difficult and time consuming. Six dependent growth variables (category A) are estimated. For each one the procedure consists of four stepwise regression analyses on members of the four initial variable groupings (categories B to E) to obtain the "best" predictors. This reduces the original independent variables to a final set of 24 which are common to all six of the dependent variables (Table 9.1). The stepwise regression anal-

119

TABLE 9.1 VARIABLES USED TO DESCRIBE CITIES IN ANALYSES OF URBAN GROWTH

Population and Economic Growth (dependent) - Category A

		Code
1.	Per cent change in population, 1941–61	PC4161
2.	Per cent change in population, 1951–61	PC5161
3.	Per cent change in population, 1956–61	PC5661
4.	Per cent change in population, 1961–66	PC6166
5.	Per cent change in total urban employment, 1951–61	EC5161
6.	Per cent change in total value of building permits issued, 1951–61	BP5161

Demographic and Social Structure - Category B

7.	Per cent of population 14 years or under, 1961	POPU14
8.	Per cent of population with single status, 1961	POPU14
9.	Per cent of population widowed or divorced (other) status, 1961	POPSIN
10.	Per cent of population immigrated into urban place since 1946 (foreign immigration) , 1961	PIMM46
11.	Per cent of families earning less than $3,000, 1961	FA3000
12.	Per cent population with university education, 1961	POPUNI
13.	Sex ratio: number of males per 100 females, 1961	SEXRAT
14.	Average income per family, 1961	FAMINC

Employment and Occupational Structure - Category C

15.	Per cent unemployed, 1961	UNEMPL
16.	Female, per cent in labour force, 1961	FEMLAB
17.	Per cent in managerial occupations, 1961	MANOCC
18.	Per cent in professional occupations, 1961	PROOCC
19.	Per cent employed in manufacturing industry, 1961	MANIND
20.	Per cent employed in community, business and personal service industries, 1961	PERIND

Physical Structure and Development - Category D

21.	Percentage of dwelling units (still standing) constructed before 1920	DU1920
22.	Percentage of owned dwelling units, 1961	DWUOWN
23.	Percentage of rented dwelling units, 1961	DURENT
24.	Percentage of dwelling units in need of major repair	DWUFIX
25.	Percentage of dwelling units occupied by head of household for more than 10 years	DU10YR
26.	Per cent change in value of industrial permits issued, 1951–1961	IP5161
27.	Per cent change in value of residential permits issued, 1951–1961	RP5161

Location and Hinterland Characteristics - Category E

28.	Nodality index (the number of major provincial highways that enter the urban boundary), 1966	NODIND
29.	Situation (the number of cities of over 5,000 population within 50 miles of urban place), 1966	SITNUM
30.	Urban population in surrounding area (commuting radius --total population of towns over 5,000 within 50 miles of urban place), 1964	SITPOP

ysis is repeated again for each dependent variable, further
reducing the number to 3 or 4 in each case. Finally, the analysis
is repeated separately for Ontario and Quebec cities, both with
a common set of independent variables to test their stability and
also allowing other variables to enter the equations.

The basic assumptions of the regression model may be
summarized as follows:

    i) that true linear relationships exist between the dependent
       and the independent variables.

    ii) the errors-of-estimate (e) are distributed independently
       of the X's and are normally distributed with zero mean
       and unit variance.

    iii) the independent variables are not interrelated with one
       another in reality

In this analysis it is admitted that not all the independent variables
used satisfy the first assumption. Nevertheless, it is argued
that the often stated alternative of transformation of one or more
but not all of the independent variables, creates statistical and
interpretative problems of even greater magnitude. With respect
to the second point, as this study makes no assumptions about
the underlying distributions, it cannot evaluate the "goodness"
of the equation. In addition, as this study is in fact dealing with
a "population" rather than with a "sampling distribution," the
theoretical necessity of such tests is not apparent. The third
assumption is considered the most crucial. As the effects of the
independent variables are additive, the insertion of substantially
intercorrelated variables produces unrealistically large coefficients of determinations, and creates ambiguity in separating
the influences of each independent variable. In this study,
unreasonably high intercorrelations between independent variables
were rigorously avoided often at the sacrifice of considerable
"explained" variance. The simple correlations between all
variables are summarized in Table 9.2.

Effectiveness of the Regression Models
The effectiveness of the regression equations (Tables 9.3 to 9.5),
reflected in the proportion of variance explained (R^2), varies
according to the length of the growth period under analysis and
to whether the provinces of Ontario and Quebec are treated separately or combined.

    The highest proportion of variance explained is for differ-

TABLE 9.2 SIMPLE CORRELATION MATRIX OF ONTARIO-QUEBEC GROWTH AND STRUCTURAL VARIABLES
(decimals omitted)

VARIABLES*	1	2	3	4	5	6	7	8	9	10	11	12	13	14	15	16	17	18	19	20	21	22	23	24	25	26	27	28	29
1. PC4161																													
2. PC5161	72																												
3. PC5661	47	80																											
4. PC6166	-03	06	01																										
5. EC5161	60	83	63	05																									
6. BP5161	01	08	13	-03	06																								
7. POPU14	51	14	04	-35	08	18																							
8. POPSIN	19	-16	04	08	-18	04	74																						
9. POWIDI	-47	-13	-03	-31	-10	-16	-90	-84																					
10. PIMM46	09	36	-03	29	40	-02	-41	-77	48																				
11. FA3000	-28	-31	26	52	-38	-16	04	46	-12	-62																			
12. POPUNI	10	13	-21	-09	16	-20	-26	-20	16	34	37																		
13. SEXRAT	28	13	11	11	14	24	46	10	47	18	-36	-17																	
14. FAMINC	28	30	06	-04	38	02	-11	-42	13	64	-86	63	27																
15. UNEMPL	-11	-10	21	20	-15	-19	-24	-08	27	-08	40	-28	-33	-42															
16. FEMLAB	-36	-06	-08	06	00	-26	-70	-37	50	18	40	23	-72	-16	28														
17. MANOCC	-06	09	-05	20	12	-12	-48	-48	-22	30	-11	29	-28	13	48	44													
18. PROOCC	18	-02	13	08	-02	-16	16	31	01	-22	-14	68	-15	33	-28	-01	08												
19. MANIND	28	28	01	-25	14	-03	-40	-10	36	05	04	-12	-09	06	-04	-06	-28	-17											
20. PERIND	-35	-28	17	12	-21	-24	-73	03	83	-08	21	30	-52	-13	13	57	30	47	-43										
21. DU1920	-54	-24	-13	03	-22	-20	-28	-59	47	16	07	09	-60	-05	34	59	42	-10	03	35									
22. DWUOWN	15	27	-13	13	28	04	29	-68	52	65	61	09	13	55	-02	01	32	-09	11	-06	32								
23. DURENT	-16	-27	20	-24	-29	-03	-41	67	52	-66	01	-10	-12	-56	03	-03	-32	08	-11	05	-32	-99							
24. DWUFIX	-49	-27	-17	-09	-15	01	-38	-39	-12	10	16	-22	-06	-10	18	23	14	-31	-22	18	42	16	-16						
25. DU10YR	-50	-40	-23	12	-42	01	06	-29	52	-06	01	-31	-22	-21	26	18	17	-23	-05	19	64	38	-37	39					
26. IP5161	40	21	12	04	20	03	09	10	-12	01	16	07	17	06	02	-18	00	16	16	-05	-14	04	-04	-17	-18				
27. RP5161	-02	19	32	-07	22	37	-52	08	-47	-10	16	-08	06	-13	11	-02	02	-06	-11	17	23	-18	16	23	-07	-08			
28. NODIND	-13	07	06	16	09	-15	-20	-47	-28	51	-18	44	-21	33	-09	46	47	-02	-06	17	04	14	-16	11	-09	-09	-04		
29. SITNUM	27	46	27	29	40	02	-24	-28	-24	40	11	11	-13	18	08	20	04	-18	57	-26	04	12	-21	-29	-17	22	-05	31	
30. SITPOP	20	43	43	36	31	03	-24	-24	-24	32	00	-06	-11	-04	-11	17	04	-29	44	-15	07	12	-10	-20	-13	24	00	15	61

* See Table 9.1

ences in population growth among cities in the twenty year period from 1941 to 1961. This amounts to 66 per cent in the Ontario-Quebec system and 76 and 69 per cent respectively, for Ontario and Quebec cities separately. Over long periods, in this case 20 years, short-term fluctuations in growth are apparently smoothed out; the cross-sectional structure thus more clearly reflects the consequences of growth trends. It is difficult to predict successfully anything but a small proportion of the variance for the 1956-1961 and 1961-1966 five year periods. For the Ontario subsystem the coefficient of determination for population change 1956-1961 (PC5661) is .44, and for population change 1961-1966 (PC6166) is .42. For Quebec, these two values are .45 and .43 respectively. For Ontario-Quebec cities, no satisfactory equations could explain more than 22 per cent of the variance of 1956-1961 population growth and this period is therefore excluded from subsequent analysis. Finally, for population growth from 1961 to 1966 less than 30 per cent of the variance is explained in the Ontario-Quebec analysis, and 39 per cent in the Quebec analysis, and the former equation is also subsequently excluded.

In most cases, the level of explanation is considerably higher or lower for Ontario and Quebec analyzed separately than for Ontario-Quebec centres combined. Ontario's growth equations reveal, for example, generally much higher variances explained than those found in the larger system. Clearly, Ontario centres act more consistently as a system, at least in terms of the allocation of growth. This is particularly true in the prediction of the PC5161 and EC5161 growth variables. In Quebec the amount of explanation of PC5161 and EC5161 is much lower than in Ontario-Quebec system and these equations, in fact, are not deemed satisfactory as regression models. In the prediction of PC5661, on the other hand, both the Quebec and Ontario equations explain relatively more variance than for Ontario and Quebec combined. The latter equations perform so poorly that they have been dropped from further analysis.

These results suggest that the urban growth-structural relationship is not spatially homogeneous, and that the urban systems in Quebec and Ontario are sufficiently distinctive to warrant separate attention. While this conclusion suggests that for greater precision, a spatial allocation model should deal with individual urban subsystems, it does not clearly show whether a general allocation model would be applicable to several urban subsystems. For further evidence regarding this question, the independent variables in each of the Ontario-Quebec growth equations have been related to the respective dependent variables in both subsystems. The results show that for the 1941-1961 growth period, the generalized Ontario-Quebec equation is capable of being extended to the individual urban subsystems; but, for other urban growth periods, the Ontario-Quebec model proves to be entirely unsatisfactory. These results are entirely compatible with two previous studies that employed quite different statistical techniques--Ray's and Berry's (1965) study of socioeconomic regionalization in Central Canada using factor analysis, and King's discriminant function analysis of growth patterns in Ontario and Quebec. King (1967) concludes that

"as a guide to the structuring of a model of the growth and development of a systems of cities, ... such (Ontario-Quebec) regional contrasts will have to be recognized, either by a corresponding weighting of selected variables, or by an emphasis on less generalized models for regional sybsystems of cities."

Attempts to explain the rate of change in value of building permits issued between 1951 and 1961 as a measure of growth in the urban physical plant, have proved largely unsuccessful. No more than 30 per cent of the variance could be accounted for in any of the regression models. This suggests that other additional predictor variables are required to explain the physical growth process, or that given the fluctuations common to the building industry (despite the use here of three-year moving averages), some other proxy variable for physical growth should be examined.

The Critical Independent Variables
An examination of the growth equations (Tables 9.3 to 9.5) reveals the dominance of certain categories of variables and a consistent repetition of a small group of individual variables. There is also a significant distinction between those equations which attempt to explain growth in relation to a base of initial cross-sectional structure and those which relate growth to the terminal structure at the end of the growth period. Only the equations for PC6166, and the one equation for 1951-1961 employment change based on 1951 structural data (Table 9.6) are in this first group. In the following sections, rather than discuss each equation individually, emphasis is given to those variables which are common to several of the equations.

TABLE 9.3 REGRESSION EQUATIONS FOR ONTARIO URBAN GROWTH

$$PC\ 4161\ =\ \underset{(31)}{65.49} +\ \underset{(25)}{7.87\ POPU14} -\ \underset{(20)}{3.90\ DU10YR} +\ .00003\ SITPOP$$

$$(R\ =\ .87\quad R^2 =\ .76)$$

$$PC5161\ =\ 132.84 -\ \underset{(40)}{3.17\ DU10YR} +\ \underset{(22)}{.00002\ SITPOP}$$

$$(R\ =\ .79\quad R^2 =\ .62)$$

$$PC5661\ =\ 267.38 +\ \underset{(5)}{5.64\ POPSIN} +\ \underset{(21)}{.39\ MANIND} +\ \underset{(18)}{.00002\ SITPOP}$$

$$(R\ =\ .66\quad R^2 =\ .44)$$

$$EC5161\ =\ 168.08 -\ \underset{(37)}{10.32\ POWIDI} -\ \underset{(16)}{2.56\ DU10YR} +\ \underset{(10)}{.00001\ SITPOP}$$

$$(R\ =\ .79\quad R^2 =\ .63)$$

$$PC6166\ =\ 95.47 -\ \underset{(8)}{2.59\ POPU14} +\ \underset{(30)}{3.10\ PIMM46} -\ \underset{(4)}{2.59\ PROOCC}$$

$$(R\ =\ .65\quad R^2 =\ .42)$$

NOTES: The per cent variance explained by each independent variable is given above the regression coefficient. Only those coefficients significant at the .05 level are included. Tables 9.3 to 9.6 employ 1961 cross-sectional independent variables.

TABLE 9.4 REGRESSION EQUATIONS FOR QUEBEC URBAN GROWTH

$$PC4161\ =\ 277.22 -\ \underset{(35)}{2.97\ DU1920} -\ \underset{(16)}{2.24\ DURENT} +\ \underset{(18)}{.07\ IP5161}$$

$$(R\ =\ .83\quad R^2 =\ .69)$$

$$PC5661\ =\ 15.09 -\ \underset{(20)}{1.63\ DU1920} +\ \underset{(16)}{1.84\ NONIND} -\ \underset{(9)}{.69\ SITNUM}$$

$$(R\ =\ .67\quad R^2 =\ .45)$$

$$PC6166\ =\ 10.34 +\ \underset{(20)}{.37\ FA3000} +\ \underset{(11)}{.34\ PERIND} +\ \underset{(8)}{1.06\ NONIND}$$

$$(R\ =\ .62\quad R^2 =\ .39)$$

125

TABLE 9.5 REGRESSION EQUATIONS FOR ONTARIO-QUEBEC URBAN GROWTH

$$\overset{(26)}{PC4161} = 72.14 + \overset{(26)}{7.46} POPU14 - \overset{(10)}{2.16} DURENT - \overset{(10)}{5.61} DWUFIX - \overset{(14)}{4.16} DU10YR$$

$$\qquad\qquad + \overset{(6)}{.045} IP6151$$

$$(R = .81 \qquad R^2 = .66)$$

$$\overset{(7)}{PC5161} = 49.83 + \overset{(7)}{1.01} DWOUWN - \overset{(29)}{2.69} DU10YR + \overset{(8)}{2.87} SITNUM$$

$$(R = .66 \qquad R^2 = .44)$$

$$\overset{(8)}{EC5161} = 156.51 - \overset{(8)}{1.10} DURENT - \overset{(32)}{2.91} DU10YR + \overset{(4)}{2.04} SITNUM$$

$$(R = .66 \qquad R^2 = .44)$$

TABLE 9.6 REGRESSION EQUATION FOR RATE OF EMPLOYMENT CHANGE,
1951-1961, USING 1951 CROSS-SECTIONAL VARIABLES

$$\overset{(3)}{EC5161} = 74.03 + \overset{(3)}{3.70} POPU14 + \overset{(37)}{15.45} PIMM46 - \overset{(9)}{1.94} DURENT$$

$$(R = .70 \qquad R^2 = .49)$$

<u>Relative Importance of Variable Categories</u>   On the basis of the
amount of variance contributed by each independent variable in
the growth equations, the physical structure and development variables dominate the analysis. These variables appear more sensitive in their response to and reflection of urban growth than the
socio-economic variables. Second in importance as a group are
the demographic variables, followed by the location relationships.
The demographic group unlike the structural variables, plays
a more direct and fundamental role in explaining different rates
of urban population growth. Of a different nature are the external
structural relationships of an urban centre with neighbouring
cities and the tributary hinterland. The importance of location
and proximity to cities of a similar size in the viability of an
urban centre has been well documented and is fundamental in
understanding the growth process. Very weak results are obtained with the employment variables, which on the whole con-

126

tribute little to the equations. King (1967) obtains similar results in his study, but provides no satisfactory explanation in the context of urban growth in Ontario and Quebec.

Physical Structure and Development Variables--The variable DURENT, and conversely DWUOWN, reflect the close association between rate of growth, housing demand, and type of residential construction. The negative sign for DURENT indicates the emphasis on single-family housing construction in urban areas during the 1941-1961 period, and the dominance of the home ownership market. The appearance of variables DWUFIX and DU1920, the age and condition of the dwelling stock, both with negative signs, expresses a basic relationship between urban growth and change in the structural inventory. Population growth stimulates expansion and rearrangement of land uses within a city which in turn affects the pace of urban development. Old and deteriorated structures in a rapidly growing centre make up a small and decreasing percentage of the housing stock, not only through simple expansion of the housing inventory, but also through the replacement of existing units.

The most prominent structural variable DU10YR, in this case a negative relationship, reflects the process of ecological succession and neighbourhood transition. Simply, the stages in the life cycle of a residential unit include the sequential occupancy of different social groups, often of decreasing income levels with deterioration continuing until replacement is feasible. This cycle is stimulated by rapid growth and accompanying high levels of new residential construction.[4] The variables DU10YR and DWUFIX, it might be noted, are not highly intercorrelated, indicating that residential succession is not merely a function of building deterioration, and the reverse, but of a whole host of factors relating to growth and the provision of new residential accommodation. Variable IP5161 with a positive sign, appearing only in the 1941-1961 equations, is the only indication of the anticipated strong relationship between urban growth and the scale of investment in industrial plant construction. Variability in the construction industry again reduces the effects of building permit variables.

Demographic Structure--Rapidly growing areas almost inevitably have relatively young populations, whether the growth comes

[4] On urban growth and structure, see Hoover (1968). For a review of concepts relating to structural change, see Bourne (1967).

from natural increase or from in-migration.[5] This is clearly reflected in the positive signs for variables POPU14 and POPSIN, which differentiate cities on the basis of age structure, and the negative sign for POWIDI. The latter variable acts as a proxy measure of aging populations, while the former reflects the youthful age-specific nature of migration streams into the city.

Accessibility Relationships--The variables SITPOP and SITNUM, both of which measure proximity to urban populations, appear frequently in the growth equations. Their positive signs reinforce the importance in urban economics of external linkages in generating agglomerations of urban and industrial activity.[6] Further, they emphasize that growth is cumulative and does not occur in physical or spatial isolation.

Employment Structure--The fact that employment and occupational structure play no significant role conflicts with the results of many previous studies. It may be argued that the cities of Ontario and Quebec represent a sufficient diversity in the scale and mix of economies and growth patterns to eliminate employment structure and occupational status as indicators of growth centres. There are, for example, rapidly growing industrial centres, many of them small single-enterprise communities, as well as declining industrial centres. This is not to say that growth and economy are not related, but that it cannot be proven at this scale and with these data.

Clearly, the inclusion of smaller centres in this study allows for wider variations in local economic mix, effectively reducing the expected associations with growth. What holds for large metropolitan areas, as in previous American studies, does not seem to hold for a larger cross-section of the urban size hierarchy in Canada. It is also likely that the standard employment and occupational classifications in the census tend to obscure underlying relationships between growth and economic structure.

Population Growth 1961-1966--Two equations for Ontario and Quebec cities (Tables 9.3 and 9.4), relate the cross-sectional structure at the beginning of the period to the rate of growth in that period. In these equations the demographic variables clearly were dominant. Variable PIMM46 was the strongest contribution

[5]For a discussion of migration and age distribtution, see Stone (1967).

[6]See Thompson (1965) and Lampard (1968).

128

indicating the importance of the immigration component in the recent growth of larger Canadian cities, particularly in Ontario. The negative sign of POPU14 in the Ontario equations reflects age structure and by inference, the low fertility ratios of the urban population. The positive sign of the income variable FA3000 with population growth is related to the fact that low income populations tend to have higher birth rates and usually, although not necessarily, higher rates of natural increase. The appearance of variables PERIND and PROOCC in the Quebec subsystem, the only contribution made by employment variables, is indicative of the importance of community and personal service employment in the growth of the Quebec economy. The variables NODIND in the same equation, while suggesting the obvious importance of transportation linkages in the urban growth process, since it did not appear in other equations, can best be interpreted as a reflection of the limited accessibility of many cities and towns in Quebec.

Employment Change 1951-1961--The regression of rate of employ-ment change 1951 to 1961 on the 1951 cross-sectional variables produces quite reasonable results (Table 9.6). Employment change potential seems to derive largely from a youthful age structure (POPU14) and high rates of immigration (PIMM46), which are the explicit internal and external components of an expanding labour force, rather than from any particular attributes of the local urban economic structure. It should be noted that this is not a measure of employment shifts but simply of employ-ment growth.

Summary and Conclusions
Urban structure clearly reflects growth performance. In most instances it is possible to predict over 50 per cent of the varia-bility of growth in population and employment among Ontario and Quebec cities, with only three or four independent structural variables. The highest proportion of variance explained, 76 per cent, is achieved for the longest time period considered, 1941 to 1961, perhaps an indication of the lag between changes in the rate of growth and substantial adjustment in urban structural character. Analyses based on 5 year periods are inconclusive, largely because of this lag effect and the tendency for short-run growth rates, particularly for smaller centres, to be highly unstable. Unfortunately, this meant that equations for the most recent census period 1961-1966, for which substantial data are

available, were only of marginal significance. The appearance
of 1971 census data will greatly facilitate such analyses in the
future.

The critical independent variables, as theory suggests
relate to demographic structure and physical development. The
dominance of developmental variables indicates a strong relationship between rate of urban growth and the internal pattern and
structural inventory of the city. The character, quality, and
stability of the housing inventory in particular, appears prominently in several analyses. This occurs although attempts to
predict growth in the urban building inventory, employing
building permits as variables, has been unsuccessful even with
permit values considered as three-year moving averages to
reduce fluctuations. Demographic variables, particularly age
structure and marital status, appear as obvious direct components of population and employment growth. As independent
variables, employment and occupational structure, on the other
hand, are weak, suggesting that local economic mix is not a
uniform indicator of growth. Also, standard industrial classifications and the range of urban centre sizes may have obscured
important variations in the sensitivity of such variables to
differences in urban growth.

Accessibility and location differentials also appear as positive factors related to growth. Nodality with respect to transportation facilities, and proximity to extensive populations in nearby
centres and rural hinterlands, are logical concomitants of higher
urban growth rates. That these appear prominently in almost
all equations is evidence of the importance of market access
and the availability of an existing urban infrastructure in influencing growth.

The parameters of growth are not, however, strictly consistent. Although no large differences appeared in the major
categories of significant predictor variables between Ontario
and Quebec cities, specific variables may change and the power
of the models varies considerably. The Ontario-Quebec growth
equations are seldom as successful as those treating the provinces separately, with the Ontario equations showing the highest
variance explained. One possible explanation for this is that
differences between the two provinces tend to counter-balance
and lower the power of the joint equations. Also, the urban
centres of Ontario generally display a greater complexity and
more continuous variance in structural character.

References

BLAUT, J. M. 1961. Space and process. The Professional Geographer 13:4.

BOURNE, L. S. 1967. Private Redevelopment of the Central City. Department of Geography Research Paper No. 112. Chicago: University of Chicago, pp. 17-49.

CZAMANSKI, S. 1964. A model of urban growth. Papers and Proceedings of the Regional Science Association 13:177-200.

HODGE, G. 1966. The Identification of Growth Poles in Eastern Ontario. A Report to the Ontario Department of Economics and Development. Toronto, Ontario.

HOOVER, E. M. 1968. The evolving form and organization of the metropolitis. In H. S. Perloff and L. Wingo, Jr., eds Issues in Urban Economics. Baltimore: The Johns Hopkins Press, for Resources for the Future Inc., pp. 237-84.

KING, L. J. 1966. Cross sectional analysis of Canadian urban dimensions, 1951 and 1961. Canadian Geographer 10:205-24.

--------. 1967. Discriminatory analysis of urban growth patterns in Ontario and Quebec, 1951-1961. Annals Association of American Geographers 57:3:566-78.

LAMPARD, E. R. 1968. The evolving system of cities in the United States: urbanization and economic development. In H. S. Perloff and L. Wingo, Jr., eds Issues in Urban Economics. Baltimore: The Johns Hopkins Press, for Resources for the Future Inc., pp. 81-139.

MATILLA, J. M. and W. R. THOMPSON. 1968. Toward an econometric model of urban economic development. In J. S. Perloff and L. Wingo, Jr., eds Issues in Urban Economics. Baltimore: The Johns Hopkins Press, for Resources for the Future Inc., pp.63-80.

RAY, D. M. and B. J. L. BERRY. 1965. Multivariate socio-economic regionalization: A pilot study in Central Canada. In S. Ostry and T. K. Rymes, eds Papers on Regional Statistical Studies. Toronto: University of Toronto Press, pp.75-122.

STONE, L. O. 1967. Urban Development in Canada. Census Monograph No. 1. Ottawa: Queen's Printer, pp. 113-18.

THOMAS, E. N. 1968. Maps of residuals from regression. In B. J. L. Berry and D. F. Marble, eds Spatial Analysis, A Reader in Statistical Geography. Englewood Cliffs, N. J.: Prentice Hall, Inc.,pp.326-52.

THOMPSON, W. R. 1965. A Preface to Urban Economics. Baltimore: The Johns Hopkins Press, for Resources for the Future Inc., esp. pp. 11-60.

131

10

Variability in the growth of small urban areas

M. J. Hodgson

The tendency for Canada to become increasingly urbanized has
been widely documented. In the provinces of Ontario and Quebec
nearly two-thirds of the population live in large metropolitan
centres or major urban areas. Yet what of the growth of smaller
cities in this system? Serious difficulties face those communities which have not been caught up in this rapid growth process.
As there is a relative increase in the metropolitan sector, there
must of course be a relative decline in the non-metropolitan
sector. The latter we may think of as comprising two groups:
rural population, and the population living in small urban centres.
     Increased agricultural efficiency encourages and supports
urban growth. Current agricultural policy is directed toward
even greater agricultural efficiency and to the encouragement,
at least indirectly, of the movement of redundant rural populations into urban areas. While farm incomes remain low and the
cities continue to be fed, rural depopulation per se cannot be
considered to be a problem.
     Harris and Ullman (1959) have listed the basic functions of
urban areas as: 1) the provision of goods and services for a
surrounding area; 2) the provision of transportation facilities;
and 3) the provision of specialized goods and services for a
large area, perhaps for the country as a whole. As the number
of rural dwellers declines, the number of providers of low-
order goods and services in rural service centres must also
decline. As those who remain in the rural areas experience a
growth in real income, a larger proportion of rural demand will
be redirected to higher order goods and services. As travel
times and costs decline, rural residents are able to visit with
the same transportation expenditures larger centres with a
greater variety of goods and services. It would seem, therefore, that the urban function of providing comprehensive services

to a hinterland will increasingly accrue to the larger urban centres at the expense of the smaller ones.

As the number of persons in the rural hinterland decreases, while at the same time transportation efficiency increases, the importance of the small urban centre as a provider of transportation services will also decline. [1] The role of the small centre in the production of specialized goods and services has never been particularly large, and the increasing orientation of specialized industry toward larger metropolitan markets is a well documented phenomenon. Hoover (1963) indicates that as industrial and transportation technologies improve, the importance of the "economies of urban concentration" will continue to rise.

Thus we see a general tendency for smaller centres to decline in importance as technology advances. A parallel decrease in population is to be expected. It might be argued that this is inevitable and that our attention should be directed toward the orderly relocation of individuals from smaller to larger urban areas. In some countries such policies are currently in effect.

Apart from the problems that this would involve at the level of the small centre, however, such a policy would add dramatically to the problems being faced by the metropolitan areas. Hodge (1966) suggests that some of the smaller centres can survive the metropolitanization trend.

This paper has two objectives in response to these general themes: first, to examine the growth of small urban centres in southern Ontario, and thus to make some contribution to an understanding of their spatial pattern; second, to determine whether urban growth displays a regional component, through the use of nearest neighbour spatial statistics.

The Area of Study
A small urban centre is defined as any incorporated village, town, or city with a population larger than 1,000 in the 1961 census and which did not constitute part of a metropolitan or major urban area in the 1961 census. Smaller municipalities incorporated within these large urban areas are excluded, for they are considered to be closely linked economically and soci-

[1] An example of this type of phenomenon is the decline in small centres as stops for long -distance trucking operations since the innovation of "Piggyback" trucking operations. This in itself may be relatively unimportant, but is an example of the trend for the importance of the small urban centre as a transportation centre to decline with improving technology.

ologically with their central cities, and do not represent independent urban places.[2] This study deals with such centres in southern Ontario. "Southern Ontario" is defined quite arbitrarily as including the counties of Muskoka, Haliburton, Hastings, Renfrew, and all those to the south and west.

The time period under consideration is the 1951-61 intercensal period. Growth is simply defined as the actual percentage change in population during this period.[3] Growth is a continuous process and there is some danger in the use of only one time period as a basis for defining relationships. In this exploratory study, however, some spatial aspects of a single growth period are analyzed rather than time-series characteristics of the same problem.

Urbanization in the Study Area--1951 and 1961

Variations in the rate of urban growth by city size are considerable. Table 10.1 presents basic population and growth figures for Ontario, southern Ontario, and the three types of population classification mentioned in the above discussion. It is clear from these data that the metropolitan and major urban areas are enjoying much higher growth rates than either of the other two sectors of the urban system. Note, however, that the rate of relative population decline of the smaller urban centres is actually quite slight, especially in comparison with the rate of rural population decline. This suggests that the problem of the small centre decline may be exaggerated, and is not presently one of major proportions, although if the study period can be taken as indicative of general trends, the process is indeed underway.

The paper now turns to three approaches to examining the growth rates of the smaller urban centres. These three are: a comparison of the rank-size regularities for large and small centres; the degree of regional clustering of growth rates; and the evaluation of a set of spatial variables in accounting for differences in growth rates between cities.

Rank-Size Relationships Among Large and Small Urban Centres

The "rank-size rule" states that within a system of cities, the

[2] One problem in dealing with cities of this size range, for which no compensation could be made here, is that of annexation. The smaller the centre the more significant the effects of annexation on time-series analyses tend to be.

[3] The actual method of calculation is: GROWTH = $\frac{1961 \text{ Population} - 1951 \text{ Population}}{1951 \text{ Population}} \times 100\%$

134

TABLE 10.1 POPULATION GROWTH IN ONTARIO , 1951-1961

	1951	1961	Per Cent Change 1951 - 1961
Ontario population	4,597,542	6,236,092	+ 35.64
Counties of southern Ontario, population [a]	4,033,777	5,484,286	+ 35.96
Population of southern Ontario as per cent of province	84.74	87.94	+ 3.78
Population of MA's and MUA's in southern Ontario	2,480,912	3,586,347	+ 44.56
Population of MA's and MUA's as per cent of southern Ontario	61.50	65.41	+ 6.36
Population of Small Urban Centres in southern Ontario [b]	562,908	756,157	+ 34.33
Population of Small Urban Centres as per cent of southern Ontario	13.95	13.78	- 1.20
Rural population in Southern Ontario [c]	989,957	1,141,782	+ 15.34
Rural population as per cent of southern Ontario	24.54	20.82	- 15.17

[a] The region considered as southern Ontario includes the counties of Haliburton, Muskoka, Hastings, Renfrew, and all counties to the south.

[b] Small Urban Centres are all incorporated centres larger than 1,000 in 1961 which are not part;of Metropolitan or Major Urban Areas in 1961.

[c] Rural population is derived by subtracting the population of MA's and MUA's and Small Urban Centres from the total county populations.

relationship between city populations and their ranks is log-linear: [4]

$$Log \ r = -q \ Log \ P + C$$

where: q and C are constants and
r is a city's rank and P is its population.

[4] For another discussion and list of references on the rank-size role see Paper 3 by Davies in this volume.

Curry (1964) has recently attempted to provide such a basis, and it is within this framework that we consider the growth characteristics of Ontario's small urban centres. Curry suggests that if growth is the result of an unrestrained random process, the distribution of towns by size would show zero order, or maximum entropy. Such a situation would be characterized by an exponential relationship between population and rank which would be best represented by the Pareto distribution of the rank-size rule. Deviations from this regularity would be indicative of certain forces operating upon the system and acting as "barriers" to normal growth processes. It is with an investigation of this point in mind that the rank-size relationships among the 165 urban places in southern Ontario are examined.

Davies in Paper 3 of this volume suggests that the existence of rank-size regularities indicates the "systematic nature" of a group of cities. It is argued that if the slope of the regression lines were significantly different for the groups of large and small centres, it could be taken as evidence of different systematic characteristics within each group. The results of the six consequent rank-size regressions are given in Table 10.2.

Although rank-size regressions normally provide good fits, each of those in Table 10.2 is more significant than those of Davies in representing the existence of "systematic relations" within the group of larger urban places. This result may be taken, by Curry's reasoning, to indicate that the growth within the system and its two subsystems is "progressing normally," or that there are no artificial barriers to growth processes. Although slight differences are apparent, in neither year are the slopes of any of the lines significantly different from any of the others, indicating that the same systematic characteristics operate within each group. On this basis we now turn to an examination of the spatial patterning of the growth of southern Ontario's small urban centres, to test the hypothesis that growth is a regional phenomenon, that is whether growth tends to be clustered rather than dispersed.

Spatial Autocorrelation of Growth of Small Ontario Centres
The following analysis has been undertaken to test for the existence of "growth regions" or clusters among the centres under consideration. If growth is a regional phenomenon, we may feel justified in searching for explicit spatial variables to ac-

TABLE 10.2 RANK-SIZE REGRESSION STATISTICS FOR SMALL AND
LARGE URBAN CENTRES, SOUTHERN ONTARIO, 1951 and 1961.

No. and Type of Centres	Regression Equation	Standard Error of Regression Coefficient	Coefficient of Determination
	1951		
MA & MUA 14	Y = 4.393 - .727 X	.0318	.977
Small 151	Y = 4.356 - .725 X	.0045	.994
Total 165	Y = 4.320 - .716 X	.0033	.996
	1961		
MA & MUA 14	Y = 4.430 - .714 X	.0286	.981
Small 151	Y = 4.277 - .682 X	.0033	.996
Total 165	Y = 4.294 - .687 X	.0027	.997

NOTE: Y is the log of a place's rank, X is the log of its population.

count for it. On the other hand, if growth occurs at random
points in space, such justification would be more difficult. A
151 x 151 matrix of distances from each centre to all others in
the sample is used. The first, second,...through to the 150th
nearest neighbour of each centre is identified. The growth rates
of these first, second,...etc., nearest neighbours are then
subjected to product-moment correlation analysis.

If urban growth is in fact a clustered phenomenon, one
would expect that the growth of a centre would be highly correlated with that of its nearest neighbours, such that a centre
would be growing or stagnating along with its neighbours, and
that the correlation would decrease with increasing distance.

The actual pattern of autocorrelation coefficients is depicted
in Figure 10.1. It seems to comprise cycles of decreasing
amplitude, as one progresses from immediate to distant neighbours. Although no attempt is made to test and analyze this
curve in detail, several simple and tentative conclusions may

137

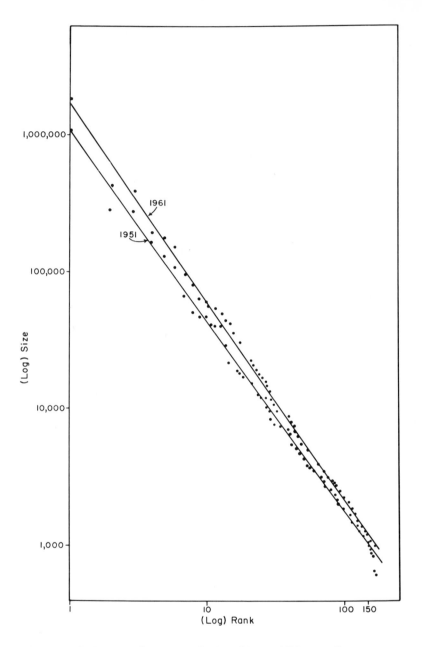

Figure 10.1   Rank-size relationships within southern
Ontario's urban centres

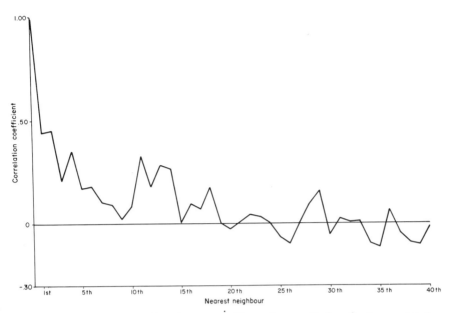

Figure 10.2 Spatial autocorrelation of growth for forty nearest neighbours: 151 Ontario small urban centres

be drawn from it. Growth would appear to be a regional phenomenon rather than a sporadic or dispersed one. Moreover, it seems to be a complex function of the distance between towns in a given urban system. The effect of this interrelationship however diminishes rapidly and is generally not significant beyond the 7th or 8th order of neighbouring centres. We therefore feel justified in searching for simple spatial variables to explain the growth of the small centres. In further work upon the distribution of growth patterns, an attempt to identify regions of growth or decline might be both interesting and fruitful.

Thus far, this paper has drawn several general conclusions about the growth variability of small urban centres within southern Ontario. It has been shown that although these centres are in relative decline they are still enjoying fairly high absolute growth rates. There do not appear to be grossly "unnatural" constraints upon the growth process within the southern Ontario region, and the smaller and larger centres within the entire urban system seem to share the same systematic characteristics. We have indicated that growth tends to be a regional phenomenon, and that we are justified in the search for spatial variables to explain it. A multiple regression model comprising simple population and spatial variables is now formulated in an attempt to provide some explanation of the growth processes within the system of small urban centres in southern Ontario.

A Model to Describe Small Centre Growth

Four variables, one from the census, and three spatial ones are introduced into a multiple regression framework as 'independent' variables to probe their relationship with variations in the growth of small urban centres. The dependent variable (Variable 1) was 1951-1961 GROWTH as defined above. The first independent variable is 1951 POPULATION SIZE. The tendency for the "rich (big) to get richer (bigger) and the poor (small) to get poorer (smaller)" is well documented in many areas of social and biological activity. The forces which are postulated as contributing to growth through size are primarily phenomena which correlate highly with size rather than population itself. Those variables might be categorized as: 1) economic variables such as employment opportunities, availability of capital, or general levels of economic activity; and 2) social variables such as the variety of recreational activities, sex-age ratios, levels of welfare payments, and so forth. In order to keep the model as simple as possible population size is used as a surrogate for all of these variables. These aspects of urban growth have been discussed in numerous studies, but in the context of places which are larger than those under study here. It is not clear whether the tendency will continue down the size spectrum, or whether there might be some minimum threshold value beneath which no centre could compete with the metropolitan areas and where its population would have no bearing upon its growth. In any case, population is introduced at the beginning of the time period as a predictor variable.

Accessibility is introduced as the major spatial variable. It is assumed that the growth of a centre will be related positively to its accessibility to the larger population centres within the area of study. Accessibility to centres of capital, manufacturing or population will no doubt enhance a centre's attractiveness for new economic activity, a) because the centre is close to the market and suppliers; b) because it has similar accessibility characteristics as current economic centres; and c) because information about economic opportunities tends to decline as the distance from the major decision making centres increases.

140

Socially it is also to be expected, for again this variable measures the possibility of increased social contact. Centres of large
population are taken to be the centres which are larger than
those used in this study, namely the metropolitan and major
urban areas. There are 14 such areas within southern Ontario,
which as Table 10.1 indicated, contain over 65 per cent of the
area's population. One other metropolitan area, Montreal, is
also introduced into the accessibility measure, although there
is evidence to indicate that its effect might be less than its
population alone would suggest (Mackay 1958). The actual measure used is:

$$X_{3_i} = \sum_{j=1}^{15} \frac{P_j}{d_{ij}}$$

where:

X_{3_i} is the ACCESSIBILITY INDEX of small urban centre i.

P_j is the population in 1951 of the metropolitan or major
urban area j.

d_{ij} is the great circle distance between small centre i and
metropolitan or major urban area j.

This variable is basically the Stewart-Warntz measure of
population potential (Warntz and Stewart 1959), but with only
the metropolitan or major urban areas capable of contributing
to a centre's potential. It is of course subject to the same
criticisms and modifications. Population is again a surrogate
for the types of variables discussed in the above section, and
the use of great circle, rather than a more realistic effective
distance-decay measure may be criticized, although an attempt
is made to correct one of the problems inherent in this measure
by the introduction of variable 4. The assumption that a place's
"accessibility" is a simple inverse function with an exponent of
unity is also open to criticism, but since no 'correct' distance-
decay exponent is known the above simple measure seems acceptable.

Variable 4 measures the distance of each centre from the
Ontario transportation corridor. The contribution to a place's
accessibility made by a large centre will obviously depend to a
degree upon the type of transportation facility joining them. To
derive a measure of this factor in the above accessibility index
would be a difficult and tedious task, but we introduce variable

141

4 to compensate somewhat for its lack. The term HIGH-SPEED TRANSPORTATION CORRIDOR is used to describe the connected, four-lane highway network within the study area (Highways 401, 400 and the Queen Elizabeth Way). The distance measured is the shortest road distance to such highways and was measured from the 1968 Official Ontario Highways Map. Growth is expected to vary negatively with this measure.

The fifth variable included is called a COMMUTING FACTOR. A certain number of centres within Ontario, which are located within commuting distance of metropolitan areas have experienced extraordinary growth largely due to their becoming dormitories for the large areas. This variable represents an admittedly feeble attempt to control the growth model for this spill-over phenomenon. We might expect centres within commuting distance of a metropolitan area to grow more rapidly than otherwise, while those areas outside of such limits might be expected to undergo slow rates of growth. In operational terms, variable 5 is a dummy variable taking the value 1 if a centre is within 30 miles of a metropolitan or major urban area and 0 if it is not. In reality, such an arbitrary limit is quite unrealistic, since it is probable that the commuting radius of Toronto (distance from which the average commuter would be willing to travel to work) should be larger than that of Kingston. In the absence of Canadian census data on commuting, and because the above measure was easily derived by the computer from data already under analysis, the 30 mile limit was introduced to see what effect it might make upon the model.

Analysis of Regression Results
Table 10.3 contains the correlation coefficients for the five variables in the regression analysis. Examining the first row which indicates the correlations of growth with the other variables, we see that each of the specified independent variables has a relationship of expected sign with growth. The correlations between growth and the accessibility and distance to high speed corridor variables are significant at better than the .01 significance level; and between growth and 1951 population and the commuter factor, at between this level and the .05 level. Strong redundancy is evident, however, for both distance to corridor and the commuter factor are more strongly related to each other and to the accessibility index than to growth. The resulting regression models, based on different combinations

142

TABLE 10.3 SIMPLE CORRELATION COEFFICIENTS AMONG GROWTH VARIABLES

	X_1	X_2	X_3	X_4	X_5
X_1	1.00	.22	.56	-.24	.18
X_2		1.00	-.01	-.12	-.01
X_3			1.00	-.35	.43
X_4				1.00	-.35
X_5					1.00

WHERE: X_1 is 1951–1961 GROWTH of a Small Urban Centre

X_2 is 1951 POPULATION SIZE of that Centre

X_3 is ACCESSIBILITY INDEX of that Centre

X_4 is Distance of that Centre from the HIGH-SPEED TRANSPORTATION CORRIDOR

X_5 is COMMUTER FACTOR

TABLE 10.4 REGRESSION RESULTS FOR SMALL CENTRES

No. Equation	R	R^2
1. $X_1 = -29.96 + .0016X_2 + .0015X_3 - .0414*X_5$	.61	.37
F = 21.3 (4, 146 df)	.61	.37
2. $X_1 = -32.40 + .0017X_2 + .0015X_3 - 4.64*X_5$		
F = 28.5 (3, 147 df)	.61	.37
3. $X_1 = -31.78 + 0017X_2 + .0014X_3$		
F = 42.3 (2, 148 df)	.60	36

* Not significant at .05

of these variables, are given in Table 10.4.

The first equation in Table 10.4 reveals the effect of the redundancy in variables 4 and 5. The partial correlation coefficients show that within the model, the contributions of variables 1 (SIZE) and 2 (ACCESSIBILITY) are significant at better

143

than the .005 level. But DISTANCE TO CORRIDOR makes an insignificant contribution, while the contribution of the COMMUTER FACTOR is only significant at less than the .10 level, and then in the opposite direction from that which we would expect. The commuter factor is, of course, highly correlated with the accessibility index, for it arises with proximity to large centres, a situation which also enhances a centre's accessibility index. That it should make a negative contribution, however, shows that in its present form it is ill-conceived. It is quite probable that centres within thirty miles of all but the largest metropolitan areas might well be suffering population decline due to the effects of what we are calling metropolitanization. On the other hand, many small centres which are dormitory towns have already been absorbed into the census definition of metro-' politan areas and thus are omitted from consideration here. Some commuting factor should be of use in the explanation of the growth of small centres, but the simple spatial one used here is clearly not the relevant one. Distance to corridor makes an insignificant contribution to the explanation of growth, in part because of collinearity with other variables. Four-lane highways have been built in areas of existing high accessibility to population and thus are quite redundant in this analysis. This variable is dropped in the next regression run.

The second regression run serves to verify the above conclusions about the problems with the commuter factor variable. By dropping variable 4, distance to the corridor, the F-Value for the regression equation indicates that the significance level has decreased to the .01 level. The variable itself adds little to the analysis. The next run is made with only the first two independent variables.

The third and final regression model represents the best explanation of the growth of small urban centres from the above variables. In dropping variables 4 and 5 we have experienced a drop of only .0055 (.3690 - .3635) in the coefficient of determination, while dropping a variable which contributed to variance explanation in the opposite way to that hypothesized.

The regression indicates that of the four variables introduced as "independent," accessibility is the most significant, while 1951 population makes a significant contribution. The most important result, however, is perhaps that the two simple variables of existing population and relative location are significantly related to the growth of small urban places, and that

at least two attempts to introduce more complicated variables
do not enhance the explanation of growth.

Conclusions

The paper noted that small urban centres are still growing
absolutely, but that relative to the metropolitan and major urban areas they are declining. Not all such centres are experiencing this relative decline, however; some of them experience
greater growth than any of the large centres. An examination
of the spatial pattern of growth, using simple nearest neighbour
statistics, suggests that the growth of small urban places in
Ontario could be considered to be at least in part a clustered or
regional phenomenon.

An attempt to explain growth using simple population and
spatial variables and multiple regression analysis has proved
to be modestly fruitful. The variables which contribute significantly to the explanation of growth variation are 1951 population
and an accessibility index which acted as a measure of potential.
The first of these indicates that the growth-size relationship
noted among larger centres continues to a certain extent down
through the spectrum of centres included here. The second
variable contributes most to the explanation of growth. Although
much higher variance explanations have been achieved in other
studies, most of these seem to introduce artificial explanations
by relating potential to absolute measures which are of course
even more highly related to population. We mention some of
the difficulties with each of these variables and indicate what
type of more complex variables they actually represent.

It is probable that the explanation of growth could be height-
ened by the use of other variables for which population is used
as a surrogate, or by modifying the form of the accessibility
index. The purpose of this paper, however, has been not to
achieve the highest possible explanation of variance, but to
explore the possibilities of the existence of such an explanation
using simply and direct variables, and to suggest further ave-
nues of exploration.

Refinements which might be made to the accessibility and
population variables have also been mentioned. Also deserving
of some mention is the insignificance of the commuter factor
as measured here. The mercuric growth of such centres as
Bolton, Aurora, and Richmond Hill, not to mention other small
centres already absorbed into the metropolitan areas, suggests

that it cannot be ignored. This points strongly to the need for adequate commuting data in the Canadian census. The final regression model accounts for only about one-third of the variation in the growth of small urban centres, and thus does not provide a solution to the problem of explaining growth. What is perhaps significant, however, is that small centres are not declining rapidly, and that there are recognizable regularities in their growth.

References

CURRY, L. 1964. Random spatial economy: explorations in settlement theory. Annals American Association of Geographers 54:138-46.

HARRIS, C. D. and E. L. ULLMAN. 1959. The nature of cities. In H. M. Mayer and C. F. Kohn, eds Readings in Urban Geography. Chicago: University of Chicago Press, pp. 277-78.

HODGE, G. 1966. The Identification of 'Growth Poles' in Eastern Ontario. Report to the Ontario Department of Economics and Development. Toronto, p. 2.

HOOVER, E. M. 1963. The Location of Economic Activity. New York: McGraw-Hill.

MACKAY, J. R. 1958. The interactance hypothesis and boundaries in Canada: a preliminary study. Canadian Geographer 11:1-8.

WARNTZ, W. and J. Q. STEWART. 1959. Some parameters of the geographical distribution of population. Geographical Review 49:270-72.

11

Growth determinants in the Central Canada urban system

G. Barber

One of the most perplexing problems in urban research is to account for the differential growth rates of cities and towns within one urban system or between several regional sub-systems. One approach to this problem has been the construction of elaborate general models tracing growth and development of an urban system over space and through time. On the other hand, specific empirical investigation into the relationship between the growth of a city and its locational, demographic, and economic characteristics provides a viable alternative. This study represents one part of a continuing inquiry into the second problem, namely the identification of the key factors influencing the differential growth rates of urban centres in Central Canada. Specifically, this research is directed towards the use of discriminatory techniques to identify the key variables distinguishing groups of cities with similar growth histories in Ontario and Quebec.

Measurement Problems

The recognition of key variables influencing urban growth rates by use of discriminant analysis is not without precedent. King (1967), in a study of this same Ontario-Quebec urban system, concludes that interprovincial contrasts are more pronounced than contrasts among his selection of city growth groups. The selection and definition of cities however handicaps his analysis. Though he includes all cities whose population in 1951 is greater than 10,000, these cities represent a mixture of statistical entities. They include both clearly distinct urban centres, such as Chatham, London, or Peterborough, as well as suburban and inner city districts of metropolitan areas, such as Forest Hill and Mimico, which are logically part of Metropolitan Toronto.

147

The sample thus reflects both intra- and inter-urban growth patterns, and the results are somewhat ambiguous.

In order to improve definitional conformity here, available urban data are aggregated to obtain more compatible and representative definitions of urban areas. Where possible, census metropolitan area and major urban area data are used. Several other aggregations are made, often to reflect recent annexations.[1] All economic locational, and demographic characteristics are computed on the basis of these revised urban units. The justification for these aggregations is that the growth characteristics of municipal cities could not be analyzed independently. In all cases of aggregation, the strength of linkages between the cities is considered   sufficiently strong such that their recognition as a single unit is warranted.

Urban Growth Characteristics

Thompson (1965), in an overview of the urban growth process, has introduced the concept of the 'urban size ratchet.' The essence of this concept is that once a city attains a certain critical threshold population, which he sets at approximately 250,000 in the United States, certain processes take effect to ensure further growth. The larger the city the closer its average growth rate to the national or regional average.

Rationalizations of this concept include the following factors: 1) greater labour productivity due to increased use of capital in large scale production, 2) cost reductions in the provision of public sector services, 3) production externalities of firms when indivisibilities require a large market for individual producing units, 4) similar indivisibilities within the consumption sector, and 5) the ability to achieve further economic returns from the fixed social overhead investments that already exist within the city.

A graph of city percentage growth rates as a function of city size reveals several important scalar properties (see Figure 11.1). All cities in this analysis have experienced positive growth rates over the ten year period, though it should be noted that the size hierarchy has been truncated at a population of 10,000 (as of 1956), thereby neglecting the smaller

[1] The resultant aggregations: 1) Thunder Bay (Fort William and Port Arthur, recently amalgamated), 2) Lac St. Jean (Arvida, Chicoutimi, Chicoutimi-Nord, and Jonquière), 3) Oshawa and Whitby, 4) Welland and Port Colborne, 5) Trois Rivières and Cap de la Madeleine, and 6) Shawinigan, Shawinigan-Sud, Grand Mère.

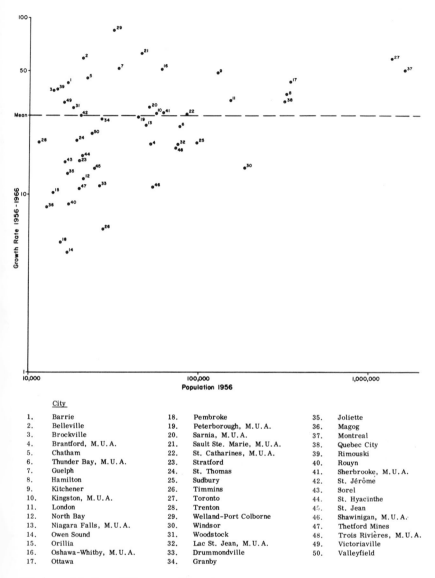

Figure 11.1   City growth rates versus city size

urban centres, a few of which did decline in population over the
study period.   Cities over 10,000 in 1966 but under 10,000 in
1956 were not included in this study due to data inconsistency
and unavailability.   In general, as city size increases the range
and variance of growth rates decreases steadily.   Interestingly,
no city above 200,000 population has a growth rate below the

149

TABLE 11.1 COMPARATIVE PERCENTAGE GROWTH RATES
FOR THE URBAN SYSTEM

Period	Ontario-Quebec	Quebec	Ontario
1956-1961	17.1	12.9	19.7
1961-1966	9.2	7.7	10.3
1956-1966	28.2	21.5	32.3

mean; in fact, only Windsor, of all the cities whose populations
exceed 100,000, has a growth rate below the mean. In addition,
all of the slowest growing centres illustrated in Figure 11.1
have peripheral locations: Windsor (30), Shawinigan (46),
Timmins (26), Pembroke (18), Owen Sound (14).

An effect similar to Thompson's ratchet would seem to be
applicable in Ontario and Quebec. Graphically, this effect takes
the form of a funnel with a broad base (wide variation of growth
rates of smaller cities and towns) and tapering to a narrow
point on or above the mean. As a test of the importance of the
influence of economies of scale on growth rates, variables measuring both urban and hinterland population are included in the
discriminant analysis.

Inter-provincial contrasts are also reflected in this sample
of cities. In Table 11.1 comparative growth rates between
Ontario and Quebec cities for three time periods are illustrated.
In each time period, Ontario cities have markedly higher growth
rates than Quebec cities. This is consistent with the findings
of King (1967).

Employment Mix
Certain economic activities are growing faster than others. In
general, cities or regions with a relatively high proportion of
rapidly growing activities are most likely to experience high
levels of growth. In Ontario-Quebec over the 1956-66 period,
high growth rates are recorded in the manufacturing sector,
particularly within the electrical products, transportation equipment, and non-metallic mineral industries. It is to be expected
that the selected growth categories will be highly responsive to
variations in employment among these industry groups.

The presence of slow growth activities however does not
necessarily imply that a city cannot achieve sustained economic
growth. For instance, a city may be able to achieve a moder-
ately high rate of growth by attracting a larger share of slow

growth or even declining industries. The example of rapid
growth among smaller cities in the American South based on
the migration of textile industries from New England is one
illustration.

Differential Accessibility

Each city within any urban system has a distinct position in a
broader system of cities, and as a result has a different level
of accessibility to other cities in the system; to regions outside
the system; and to known natural resources. Changes in the
relative accessibility of an urban centre may be reflected in its
growth. Several measures have been computed for use here,
each of which accounts for one dimension of a city's accessibility.

The first such measure is metropolitan accessibility. A
city might have a high rate of growth because of its proximity
to a metropolitan area for a number of reasons. First, it might
be a dormitory town for a large, rapidly growing metropolitan
area. In the Ontario-Quebec urban system, Oshawa-Whitby,
Guelph and Barrie, all within the commuting range of Metropolitan Toronto, are notable examples. Alternatively, a city
in close proximity will be able to take advantage of the innovations, services, and externalities provided by a large metropolitan area more effectivly. In either case rapid growth might
well be the outcome.

Any urban area which is itself not large enough to achieve
economies of scale, nor in close proximity to a metropolitan
area, might overcome such a disadvantage by being in close
proximity to a group of urban centres whose aggregate population allows each to achieve some partial economies of scale.
A variable measuring hinterland population, the total population
within fifty miles (excluding the city itself) is used here to identify cities with such advantages.

Changes in the relative accessibility of cities within an urban
system through the development of transportation and communications networks can thus directly affect the growth of each city.
One outcome of such change is the alteration of the production
and consumption patterns in the entire system. Such changes
will undoubtedly place some cities in distinctly advantageous
positions relative to the rest of the system.

Foreign Immigration

Another source of both urban and regional population growth is

foreign immigration. While the larger cities, particularly
Montreal and Toronto, have been the major beneficiaries of such
immigrants, other smaller centres (especially in Ontario) have
attracted significant numbers. The available immigration data
consists of the number of immigrants entering the urban area
from 1945 to 1961. These numbers have been standardized and
expressed as percentages of the total population.

Government Investment

Government institutions have a variety of policy instruments
which can be used directly or indirectly to affect the growth
possibilities of regions. Direct capital investments, subsidies,
or tax concessions can both stimulate growth as well as attract
private capital which further aids the economic growth effort.
As well, both types of investments will benefit from the multi-
plier effect. However, data concerning government financial
policies are generally not readily available, and it is unlikely
that they could be disaggregated to the level required here, in
any case. One available proxy for such government investment
is provided by federal and provincial employment data. It is
not true that all government policy instruments are directed
towards employment in the public sector; nevertheless employment data are used as a surrogate of investment in this inquiry.

Basis of Group Classification

Cities are classified into three groups based on their growth
characteristics during the 1956–66 decade. Group I contains
all cities which grew faster than the mean growth rate for all
cities in the system for both the 1956-61 and 1961-66 periods.
These cities are termed growth centres. Those centres which
grew faster than the mean system rate for either the 1956–61 or
the 1961-66 periods but not both are assigned to Group II. Because they exhibit both above average and below average growth
rates in consecutive time periods, these cities are labelled
unstable. Group III contains all cities which grew at a rate
below the average for both time periods; these centres are
designated in relative terms as declining centres. The graphical basis for this classification is depicted in Figure 11.2 and
the resultant classification of cities is summarized in Table 11.2
Although this classification is obviously crude, the relatively
small sample of cities involved precludes a more refined subdivision.

    An initial test of the ability of this grouping to discriminate

TABLE 11.2 DISCRIMINANT ANALYSIS GROUP CLASSIFICATIONS

Group I - n = 13	Group III - n = 20
1. Barrie	1. Thunder Bay (Port Arthur - Fort William)
2. Guelph	2. North Bay
3. Hamilton	3. Niagara Falls
4. Kitchener	4. Owen Sound
5. London	5. Orillia
6. Oshawa-Whitby	6. Pembroke
7. Ottawa	7. Sudbury
8. Sarnia	8. Timmins
9. Sault Ste. Marie	9. Trenton
10. St. Catharines	10. Lac St. Jean (Arvida-Chicoutimi-
11. Toronto	11. Drummondville Chicoutimi-Nord-
12. Welland-Port Colborne	12. Joliette Jonquière)
13. Montreal	13. Magog
	14. Rouyn
Group II - n = 16	15. St. Hyacinthe
	16. St. Jean
1. Belleville	17. Shawinigan-Shawinigan Sud-Grand Mère
2. Brockville	18. Thetford Mines
3. Brantford	19. Trois Rivières-Cap de la Madeleine
4. Chatham	20. Valleyfield
5. Kingston	
6. Peterborough	
7. Stratford	
8. St. Thomas	TOTAL SAMPLE SIZE = 49
9. Windsor	
10. Woodstock	
11. Granby	
12. Quebec City	
13. Sherbrooke	
14. St. Jérôme	
15. Sorel	
16. Victoriaville	

among growth groups is a direct comparison of the average growth rates for these three groups for various time periods. A brief examination of these figures suggests the classificatory basis used here provides a significant grouping framework for this set of cities (see Table 11.3).

A Discriminant Analysis Formulation

The development of discriminant analysis stems from the need for a statistical technique which would insure not only maximum discrimination between 2 or more populations, but also to minimize error probability in classifying new observations into these previously defined population groups. Various approaches to

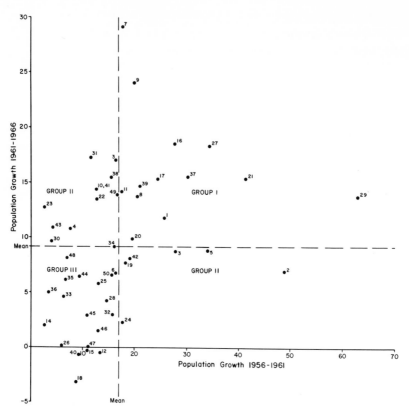

Figure 11.2   Graphic base of group classification

TABLE 11.3   PERCENTAGE GROWTH RATES OF
DIFFERENT GROUPS OF CITIES

Period	Group I Growth Centres	Group II Unstable	Group III Declining Centres
1956–61	27.3	16.8	10.5
1956–66	48.1	29.1	14.1
1961–66	16.5	10.7	3.3
No. of cities	13	16	20

this problem have been presented by Rao (1952; 1965), Kendall (1957), Anderson (1958), and Casetti (1964a; 1964b). The approach used here follows that of Anderson.

    This discriminant analysis program directs the calculation of K linear discriminant functions of the n variables measured

Empirical Example: Central Canada Cities

Twenty-four variables are included in this analysis, for each of forty-nine cities (see Table 11.4). These variables include measures of immigration, employment mix, age structure, urban accessibility, and government investment; each of these variables is selected in order to test the effectiveness of the hypotheses outlined in the previous section. Within the employment mix variables, distinctions are made between gross industry groups, such as financial, insurance, real estate employment; construction employment; manufacturing employment; and also within the manufacturing sector itself, that is, between electrical apparatus industries versus rubber, chemical, and transportation equipment industries.

In Table 11.5, the computed means of all variables for each of the three growth groups are listed. Three general groupings of variables seem to be present. One set of variables (1, 2, 4, 6, 10, 14, 17) seem to be particularly responsive to the growth for each observation of the form:

$$Y = \propto_1 + \lambda_1 X_1 + \lambda_2 X_2 + , \ldots, \lambda_n X_n .$$

Here there are K groups and n variables. These discriminant functions optimally divide the n variate space into K classificatory regions. Various test statistics can be used to test the validity of the discrimination, the most common being the generalized Mahalanbois statistic D^2 which is tested as a Chi-square statistic, and the F-test. Both tests can be used to test the hypothesis that the mean values are the same in all K groups (or any 2 of three K groups) for these n variables. In addition to these significance tests, a classification matrix of the original observations is derived. The data for each original observation are evaluated on each discriminant function, and each observation is assigned to that group for which the value is the highest.

In this study, the identification of the key growth determinants in the Ontario-Quebec urban system is achieved through the application of multiple discriminant analysis in a step-wise manner. At each step, a single variable is entered into the set of discriminatory variables according to any specified criterion. That single variable which results in the greatest decrease in the ratio of within to total generalized variances is the criterion for each variable chosen in this analysis.

155

TABLE 11.4. DISCRIMINANT ANALYSIS VARIABLES

No.	Description
1.	Per cent immigration 1945-1961
2.	Per cent total employment in manufacturing industries
3.	Per cent employment in construction industries
4.	Per cent employment in transportation industries
5.	Per cent total employment in trade industries
6.	Per cent total employment in finance, insurance, real estate
7.	Per cent total employment in community, business, personal service
8.	Per cent total employment in public administration and defense
9.	Per cent population less than 14 years old
10.	Total population 1961
11.	Metropolitan accessibility--miles from either Toronto or Montreal
12.	Nodality index--no. of major highways entering urban boundary
13.	Urban situation--no. of urban areas greater than 5,000 population within 50 miles
14.	Hinterland population--population in urban areas greater than 5,000 within 50 miles
15.	Per cent of total manufacturing employment in chemicals
16.	Per cent of total manufacturing employment in printing and publishing
17.	Per cent of total manufacturing employment in metal fabricating
18.	Per cent of total manufacturing employment in transportation equipment
19.	Per cent of total manufacturing employment in electrical products
20.	Per cent of total manufacturing employment in non-metallic minerals
21.	Per cent of total manufacturing employment in rubber
22.	Per cent of total manufacturing employment in machinery
23.	Per cent of public administration employment in federal service
24.	Per cent of public administration employment in provincial service

categories, having a high positive association with the growth centres (Group I), a lower association with the unstable centres (Group II), and lowest correlation with the declining centres (Group III). Another set of variables (9, 18, 19, 21) seem to differentiate the growing and unstable centres from the declining centres. The remaining variables either have similar means for all growth groups, or fail to reveal any generalized pattern of variation with respect to the three growth categories.

Validity of the Discriminatory Analysis

Analysis of the results of both the simple and step-wise multiple discriminant analyses indicates a significant statistical discrimination among the growth categories has been achieved.

The first analysis includes all twenty-four variables and is used to test the ability of the complete set of variables to discriminate among the three growth categories. The calculated D^2 statistic, 219.5, is significant at the .01 level with 48 degrees of freedom, allowing a rejection of the hypotheses that the mean

156

TABLE 11.5   VARIABLE MEANS BY GROUP CLASSIFICATION

Variable No.	Group I	Group II	Group III
1.	13.2	5.8	4.8
2.	35.1	34.1	25.7
3.	6.6	6.0	6.4
4.	7.4	8.3	8.3
5.	15.4	15.9	15.4
6.	3.9	3.2	2.7
7.	20.3	23.4	21.0
8.	7.9	5.9	7.7
9.	32.0	32.0	34.1
10.	423550.0	64091.0	38883.0
11.	82.5	98.6	148.7
12.	6.5	4.9	3.7
13.	7.1	5.9	3.5
14.	1172529.0	691771.0	609058.0
15	6.5	4.1	6.8
16.	5.4	3.9	6.0
17.	8.1	5.7	4.2
18.	10.7	11.7	2.8
19.	9.6	10.1	5.2
20.	2.9	2.7	3.2
21.	2.6	3.4	0.2
22.	4.5	7.1	4.3
23.	43.5	35.4	39.3
24.	12.9	19.0	16.8

values of these 24 variables are the same in all three growth groups.

The classification matrix of cities according to the three discriminant functions obtained in the analysis is shown in Table 11.6.   All 13 growth centres are correctly classified by the discriminant function corresponding to the first group.   As well, all 16 unstable centres are correctly identified as being in Group II by the second discriminant function.   Eighteen of the twenty declining centres are also classified correctly, the remaining two cities being classified as unstable centres.   The two misclassifications, it might be added, are marginal.   The probability that these two unstable centres are in the rapidly declining category exceeds forty-three per cent in each case.   In all, 47 out of the original 49 cities are correctly designated.   The two misclassifications, Orillia (1966 population 17,769) and Drummondville (1966 population 29,216), are both small regional centres whose populations have recently been affected by annexations.

The results of the step-wise analyses are equally encourag-

TABLE 11.6. CLASSIFICATION MATRIX

	Discrimination Function Number			
	I	II	III	Total Cities
Group I	13	0	0	13
Group II	0	16 |	0	16
Group III	0	2	18	20

TABLE 11.7. SUMMARY OF SIGNIFICANT STEP-WISE ITERATIONS

Step Number	Variable Entered	F-Value to Enter	Variable Description
1	12	15.95*	Nodality index
2	2	3.83**	Per cent manufacturing employed
3	7	4.61**	Per cent community business personal service
4	14	3.40**	Hinterland population
5	21	2.96***	Per cent manufacturing employed in rubber
6	3	3.02***	Per cent construction employed

NOTE: *Significant at .01
        **Significant at .05
       ***Significant at .10

ing. Six variables enter the set of discriminatory variables above the 90 per cent confidence limit, of these 4 entered above the 95 per cent confidence level[2] (see Table 11.7). The results of this step-wise analysis suggest that the key growth determinants within the Ontario-Quebec urban system are the employment mix, especially the percentage of manufacturing employment, and the accessibility of the city to road network and the surrounding population. The six significant variables include two measures of urban accessibility and four measures of the employment mix. The inclusion of these six variables alone

[2]The F-test to enter the set of discriminating variables is a likelihood ratio test, which when significant, allows rejection of the hypothesis of the equality of the group means over the three groups, given the remaining entered variables.

158

TABLE 11.8 CLASSIFICATION MATRIX,
STEP-WISE ANALYSIS

| | Discriminant Function Number | | | |
	I	II	III	Total Cities
Group I	12	1	0	13
Group II	1	12	3	16
Group III	1	6	13	20

resulted in the correct classification of 37 out of the original
49 cities (Table 11.8). Again the major difficulty is the correct
classification of the smaller declining centres. Using an F-
statistic, the hypothesis of the equality of the group means for
the set of six variables can be tested. All F-statistics proved
to be significant at the 95 per cent confidence limit allowing
rejection of the null hypothesis.

Interpretations; Conclusions

Several additional comments pertaining to the validity of the use
of discriminant analysis procedures to identify key growth determinants seem warranted. First, it is obvious that inferences
to be drawn from these statistical analyses presuppose the legit-
imacy of the initial classificatory basis. In this inquiry, cities
are classified on the basis of their relative growth rates over
only two consecutive five year periods. As illustrated in Figure
11.2 this classificatory basis does not readily divide the set of
observations into distinct clusters of observations. An initial
test of the grouping procedure did, however, indicate that the
means were significantly different among the three growth groups:
growth centres, unstable centres, and declining centres.

In the absence of a well-developed theory of urban and
regional growth, it is also possible that several important growth
determinants have been excluded from this inquiry. As well, it
is difficult to isolate variables which can be unambiguously proposed as growth determinants, and are not merely the outcome
of the growth process. However, it can be argued that the
hypotheses presented earlier in this paper have been tested
elsewhere with similar success, lending some support to these
arguments.

159

Growth in urban and regional systems is undoubtedly a continuous process. The discrete additions and subtractions of population approximate a continuous function. As the unit of time measurement becomes larger, the validity of the approximation also increases. A discriminant analysis approach neglects this characteristic of the urban growth process. It presumes that characteristics and determinants of this growth process can be differentiated by measurements taken at discrete intervals of time. Cyclical or other temporal variations in both the growth process and the variables used to identify the causal factors are ignored.

The success of both discriminant analyses suggests that the processes influencing the differential growth of urban centres in the Ontario-Quebec urban system are related to the variables employed in this analysis. In particular, the step-wise multiple discriminant analysis suggests the key growth determinants to be differential accessibility and employment mix, especially the amount of manufacturing activity. Other studies using different techniques, (e.g., Thompson 1965), have produced similar results, offering additional support for these conclusions.

References

ANDERSON, T. W. 1958. Introduction to Multivariate Statistical Analysis. New York: John Wiley and Sons.

CASETTI, E. 1964a. Multiple Discriminant Functions. Technical Report No. 11, Department of Geography, Northwestern University, Evanston, Ill.

--------. 1964b. Classificatory and Regional Analysis by Discriminant Iterations. Technical Report No. 12, Office of Naval Research Task No. 389-135, Geography Branch. Washington: GPO.

COCHRAN, N. G. 1962. On the performance of the linear discriminant function. Bulletin de L'Institut Internationale de Statistique 39:435-47.

KENDALL, M. G. 1957. A Course in Multivariate Analysis. London: Griffin Co. Ltd.

KING, L. J. 1966. Cross sectional analysis of Canadian urban dimensions, 1951-1961. Canadian Geographer 10:205-24.

--------. 1967. Discriminatory analysis of urban growth patterns in Ontario and Quebec. Annals American Association of Geographers 57:566-78.

--------. 1969. Statistical Analysis in Geography. Englewood Cliffs, N.J.: Prentice-Hall.

--------. 1970. Discriminant analysis: A review of recent theoretical contributions and applications. Economic Geography 46:2:Supplement.

RAO, C. R. 1952. Advanced Statistical Methods in Biometric Research. New York: John Wiley and Sons.

--------. 1965. Linear Statistical Inference and Its Applications. New York: John Wiley and Sons.

THOMPSON, W. R. 1965. A Preface to Urban Economics. Baltimore: The Johns Hopkins Press.

IV

Transportation Networks and Interaction Within the Urban System

12

Editors' comments

Transportation and communication services are extremely important both in facilitating the operation and shaping the form of a system of cities. The spatial networks of transportation and communication are the channels through which the urban centres interact with one another, thereby giving order and cohesiveness to the system. Indeed without intercity transportation and communication networks, it is doubtful whether any set of cities could be called with any justification an urban system.

The southern Ontario and Quebec region contains a multi-nodal complex of transportation facilities and services similar to that in other highly urbanized and industrial areas of the world. Transportation has played a strategic role in shaping the development of this region as it has for the rest of Canada. Even today approximately 20 per cent of the Canadian Gross National Product is accounted for by transportation activities.

At the regional level, one can identify four functional types of transportation routes or services. First, it is the function of many facilities to move people and goods between the major urban centres of the region (e.g., Highway 401, the Queen Elizabeth Way, North Shore Highway, CN-CP Montreal-Toronto lines, etc.). Secondly, recreational routes give people the capability to move from urbanized areas primarily in the south to the lakes and ski slopes to the north (Highway 400 and the Laurentian Autoroute, for example). Thirdly, many routeways (roads and rails) exist to service the rich and extensive agricultural hinterlands of the region--to provide personal accessibility to the farmer as well as a system by which his agricultural products can reach the market place. Finally, other facilities exist to connect points within the region to other centres in western Canada and the Atlantic Provinces, in the U.S., or in the rest of the world (e.g., CN-CP main lines, the seaports and airports). Of course some facilities may perform more than one of these functions, but it is useful to bear in mind that any routeway or service is responsive to at least one of these types of demand.

The most striking geographical characteristic of the transportation network of Central Canada is a strong spatial linearity. A median great circle line fitted to the set of 28 metropolitan centres and major urban areas in southern Ontario and Quebec has an average deviation of only 21 miles! Thus a single linear transportation facility could be on the average only 21 miles away from the set of cities and only 47 miles from the most distant city. Extending out from the linear trend of major cities and transportation trunk lines are important land transportation feeder lines into the U.S., the Canadian Shield for recreation, forestry, and mining, and into the hinterlands of western and eastern Canada. And superimposed on these major transportation arteries is a dense network of rural service routes.

In Paper 13, MacKinnon, Hodgson and Bushell attempt to synthesize the characteristics of the multilane highway networks of southern Ontario and Quebec using very simple principles of spatial organization. Various networks are generated and compared to the existing highway networks. It appears that much of the spatial structure of these intra-regional transportation networks may be "explained" by the relative location of larger urban centres as well as the spatial distribution of travel demands. Assuming that the decision rules on highway construction have been identified, some predictions about future highway link additions are made for both Ontario and Quebec.

Paper 14, by MacKinnon, describes vehicular flows along one link of these networks, the major road route in Ontario (Highway 401), as a function of distance from the Toronto metropolis. An extremely good statistical fit is obtained. In addition, the changes in this spatial pattern are described by simple linear trend analysis. Also in this paper the influence of the lesser centres of London and Kitchener-Waterloo is identified as well

164

as the external impacts of Montreal on eastern Ontario traffic.
This paper illustrates the intimate relationship between the distribution of population and transportation flows and suggests
that traffic flow may be used as a surrogate measure of population distribution.

Given the analyses of transportation networks provided above,
Paper 15, the final paper in this section, by Simmons, examines
the spatial patterns of interaction and flows between cities in
Central Canada. Using business and residential telephone communication statistics, airline traffic and commodity flow data,
Simmons identifies an explicit pattern of regional urban hierar-
chies--each articulated by networks of urban influence or dominance centred on Toronto and Montreal. Using factor analytic
techniques, various flow patterns are compared and a high degree of integration within the Ontario system is documented.

13

Transportation network models for the southern Ontario and Quebec system of cities[1]

R. D. MacKinnon, M. J. Hodgson and G. E. Bushell

Transportation services both condition and are conditioned by
the spatial pattern of population and activities within a region.
In recent years various methods of analyzing and synthesizing
transportation networks have been developed. In this paper,
some optimizing methods are applied within the context of the
system of cities of Central Canada.

All of these models may be interpreted from two points of

[1]This paper is adapted from MacKinnon and Hodgson (1969), MacKinnon and Hodgson
(1970), and Bushell (1970). The first two papers derive from projects supported by Bell
Canada, the latter is jointly supported by the Canadian Transportation Commission
(C. T. C.) and Bell Canada.

view. First they may be viewed as planning models, that is, models which generate normative transportation networks insofar as they maximize the attainment of a set of objectives subject to certain constraints.

These models may also be used as descriptive models. It may be assumed that the spatial configuration of a system of cities places severe restraints on the spatial structure of a transportation system whose function is to provide a mechanism by which cities may interact with one another. It may be hypothesized that certain fundamental principles of spatial organization are at work in determining network structure. Insofar as the models based on these principles yield results which are similar to actual network structures, the hypothesis about underlying organizational principles may be justified. In this respect, optimizing models may have the same function as statistical modes of analysis; that is, to describe, replicate, and/or predict actual patterns by using certain principles and relationships.

Taking even a broader interpretation of this descriptive function, network synthesis approaches identify linkage patterns and physical facilities which could optimally service these linkages between urban centres. Thus even if discrepancies exist between actual and generated networks, the "optimal" networks may provide insights into the spatial organization of the system of cities. The discrepancies may be interesting in the same way that residuals from regression lines are interesting--suggesting variables and principles which have not been incorporated in the model.

The Highway Network

The network of reference for this study is the multilane highway system of southern Ontario and Quebec (Figure 13.1). This system has the advantage that it is relatively simple and manageable within the context of the network models considered. Moreover, it is an extremely important element in the transportation system of the region. A large proportion of the regional intercity movement of goods and persons occurs over this network. Almost all of the major urban centres are located on or near this network.

Because of the limitations of the current methods of network generation, this network, while relatively uncomplicated, must be simplified. Few network synthesis procedures can generate networks with intersections at points other than the original

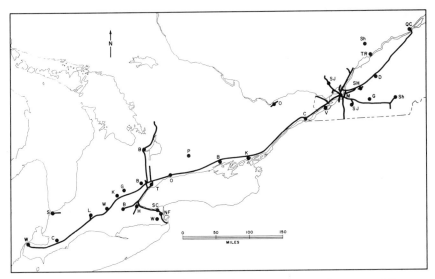

Figure 13.1 Existing multi-lane highway network -- southern Ontario and Quebec

input nodes (cities). All of the nodes of the network must be specified in advance. For the purposes of this study, then, where the actual network passes within ten miles of a city, it is assumed that the simplified network passes through the city. From the point of view of the intercity traveller, this would seem to be a reasonable approximation.

Because of computational limitations of our models, only the 32 largest centres are included in the analysis. These have been selected because they are the group of largest urban centres which appear to be associated with the multilane highway network. The simplified network is shown in Figure 13.2.

The problem can now be stated as follows: given the set of 32 largest cities, their locations, and other readily obtainable information, generate a transportation network which reasonably approximates the network shown in Figure 13.2 by optimizing a spatial efficiency criterion function subject to certain constraints.

By attempting to provide solutions to this problem it is hoped that some aspects of the spatial investment decisions are introduced and clarified within the context of the southern Ontario and Quebec system(s) of cities. That is, in part these models should be looked at from a transportation planner's point-of-view indicating which links should have been (or should

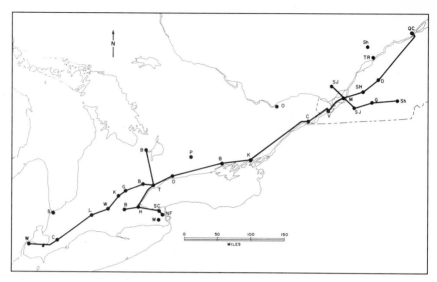

Figure 13.2   Simplified existing highway network -- southern
Ontario and Quebec

be) constructed according to an explicit set of decision rules.
Perhaps more important, however, are the insights which these
models may give into the apparent strength of spatial ties and
the pattern of spatial structure as indicated by the networks
which are generated.

Minimal Spanning Trees

In the first three categories of models considered, the models
are formulated so that data requirements are minimal. Only
the locations and populations of the cities are utilized. In the
first and simplest of models, only the locations of the 32 cities
are assumed to be given.

        In graph theoretic terminology, a "tree" is simply a network
of links and nodes such that there is exactly one path connecting
any two nodes. A minimal spanning tree is the shortest possible
network which joins all of the nodes so that one and only one path
or set of links exists between any pair of nodes. Minimal spanning trees or shortest connection networks are probably the
simplest of any optimal network configuration. Such a network
provides a lower bound on total network length, assuming that
all nodes are to be linked to the network. This planning criterion assumes that the decision maker wishes to minimize total
network length subject to the constraint that all points are to be
joined in a single network.

168

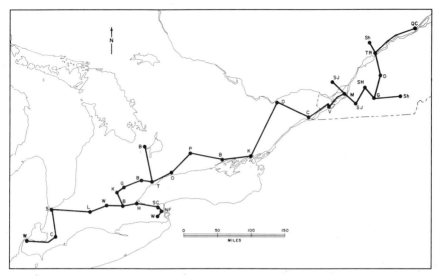

Figure 13.3   Minimal-spanning-tree network -- southern
Ontario and Quebec

Prim (1957) and others have developed very simple algorithms which generate the minimal spanning tree for any set of
points. For the set of 32 largest cities in the southern Ontario
and Quebec region, the minimal spanning tree is the network
shown in Figure 13.3.   There are certainly some similarities
between Figures 13.2 and 13.3.   Some of the same spatial
structure appears to be captured using this extremely simple
decision rule.   Upon closer examination, however, it appears
that several "mistakes" are made.   Seventeen links are correctly predicted.   The value of the $r_\emptyset$ coefficient, is 0.58,
correlating the existing network with the minimal spanning tree. [2]

It is not surprising that this simple model does not closely
approximate the actual transportation network.   Assuming link
length is highly correlated with construction costs, this model
hypothesizes that planners minimize highway construction costs
regardless of the travel costs implied by the spatial structure
of the generated network.   Thus many travellers could be forced
to make very circuitous journeys.   The fit between existing and
predicted network structure is remarkable considering the sim-
plicity of the model.   This good fit is perhaps a result of the

[2] The $r_\emptyset$ coefficient is a measure of correspondence between observations on two binary
variables where $r_\emptyset$ = 0.0 indicates no correspondence and $r_\emptyset$ = 1.0 indicates a perfect
one-to-one correspondence.

linear nature of the system of cities of the region. This linearity effectively restricts the range of feasible network configurations.

"Shimbel Networks"

An alternative approach to optimal network generation is to maximize some measure of accessibility i.e., the ease with which it is possible to move between different parts of the region. Algorithms which allow such networks to be generated have only recently been developed. Enormous computational problems are encountered because of the very large number of possible combinations of links which constitute potential network configurations. For example, an N-node network can have a total of $2^{1/2N(N-1)}$ possible distinct configurations. A system of 32 cities can be connected in 2^{496} different ways. Clearly an optimal solution cannot be obtained by direct enumeration. In fact, the computational difficulties are of such a magnitude that approximation algorithms must still be used to solve most empirically relevant combinatorial problems. Such an algorithm as adapted from Scott (1969) is utilized in this study. In addition, our system of cities must be partitioned into two subsystems in order to make the problem computationally feasible. Thus the 15 cities of Quebec and eastern Ontario are included in the "Quebec" subregion and the 19 cities of the rest of Ontario constitute the "Ontario" subsystem of cities. Kingston and Belleville are included in both regions.

The first model to be considered attempts to minimize the sum of shortest path distances between every pair of nodes subject to the constraints that a predetermined total "construction mileage budget" T is not exceeded and the resulting network is a connected graph.

The only additional parameter which this model requires is T the mileage construction restraint. The value of any parameter must be either established empirically or based on theoretical reasons. For our purposes, a reasonable value of T is the actual existing network length.

Figure 13.4 answers the first question for the Ontario and Quebec subregions. The $r_\emptyset$ coefficients are equal to .635 and .634 for Ontario and Quebec respectively.

Comparison of the spatial configuration of networks or indeed of maps in general, has not advanced far beyond simple visual examinations. Lost in statistics such as the $r_\emptyset$ coeffi-

170

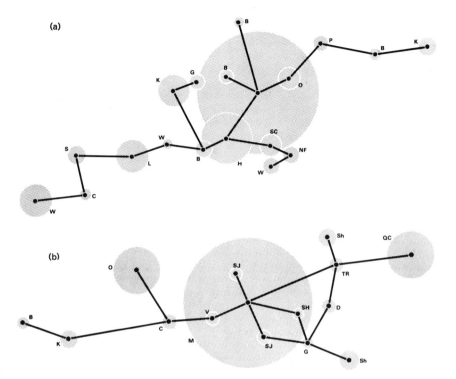

Figure 13.4 'Shimbel' network: (a) southern Ontario (b) southern Quebec

cient are any measures of systematic spatial biases as well as any indications of the importance of the links in the network.

Although this model is in many ways more satisfactory than the preceding one, it does not take into account the differential trip generation rates of cities of different sizes. All cities have equal weight in this model.

Gravity Generated Networks
It may be assumed that flows between any two cities are directly proportional to the product of the populations and inversely proportional to the "costs" of travel between them; that is,

$$F_{ij} = k \ \frac{P_i P_j}{D_{ij}^b}$$

where k and b are parameters. This simplest of gravity model formulations may be used to obtain a gross estimate of trip generation and distribution for an intercity travel pattern which is a function of the network configuration as incorporated in the D_{ij} component of the model.

This network generation procedure selects the binary variable values λ_{ij} (the existence of non-existence of a direct link between i and j) so that

$$\sum_{i=1}^{N} \sum_{j=1}^{N} P_i P_j D_{ij}^{-b} \quad \text{is maximized}$$

where

$$D_{ij} = \min_{j_1, \ldots, j_r} [\lambda_{ij_1} d_{ij_1} + \lambda_{j_1 j_2} d_{j_1 j_2} + \cdots + \lambda_{j_r j} d_{j_r j}] \leqslant \infty$$

and

$$\sum_{i=1}^{N} \sum_{j=1}^{N} \lambda_{ij} d_{ij} \leqslant T.$$

The problem is thus to construct those links which maximize expected usage (or an accessibility measure) subject to the constraint that total construction mileage is less than a predetermined value. Parameters T and b must be specified. The values of decision variable λ are determined by an approximation procedure used in the previous model. Somewhat arbitrarily b is set equal to 1.5 and T = 582 for the Ontario system and the resulting network and the assigned traffic flow pattern are shown in Figure 13.5.

One serious problem with the proposed model is immediately apparent. The two regional systems are assumed to be closed to traffic from other regions, including each other. Thus Ontario-Quebec traffic, as well as U.S.-Ontario, U.S.-Quebec, and other linkages, are excluded from the analysis. These exclusions can result in poor performance of the model near the regional boundaries. For example, a Chatham-London link is excluded in favour of Chatham-Sarnia-London links. It would seem that the southerly route might be preferable because of the heavy U.S. traffic crossing at Windsor.

By not 'constructing' links to the north or east, other links near the centre of the region can be constructed. Here, major urban centres are close together and there is greater opportunity to increase the gravity values of the system. The model

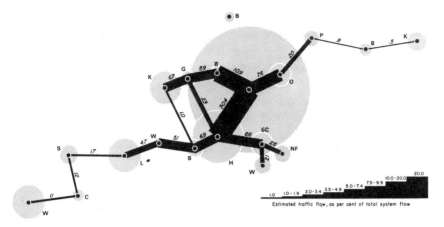

Figure 13.5   Gravity-generated network and flows -- southern Ontario

tends to favour shorter links connecting major population centres. Thus, 'over-investment' connecting, for instance, Brantford-Kitchener, Guelph-Hamilton, Welland-St. Catharines, and Welland-Niagara Falls, is predicted.

An additional shortcoming of the model is apparent. Infinite capacity and zero congestion costs are assumed. Thus, all southwestern Ontario-Toronto traffic is routed through Hamilton, ignoring the fact that the Hamilton-Toronto link is intensively used by other traffic. The dominance of the subregion centred on Toronto and Hamilton is remarkable. For example, 48.9 per cent of all link flows are centred on Toronto, with over 30 per cent on the Toronto-Hamilton link alone.

It is interesting that this formulation does not appear significantly to improve the replicative performance of the model over the simple Shimbel formulation. Indeed, $r_\phi = 0.635$ for the Shimbel model and $r_\phi = 0.614$ for the gravity model. Moreover, $r_\phi = 0.610$ for the minimal spanning tree model for the Ontario system of cities. Of course the r_ϕ coefficient is not a very sophisticated measure of network similarities, for spatial biases are not detected. In addition, all links are weighted equally--thus the exclusion of the Toronto-Hamilton link by the minimal spanning tree model is not weighted more heavily than the exclusion of a Chatham-London link for example.

Comparing the gravity network with the existing network, one generalization could be made: the highway network structure

173

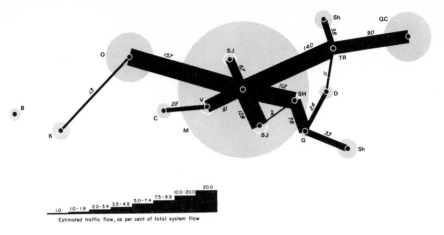

Figure 13.6   Gravity-generated network and flows -- southern Quebec

of southern Ontario would seem to be determined more by the relative location of cities in the region than by the relative size of the cities. The Shimbel Index model which takes only inter-nodal distances into account seems to provide, in some respects at least, as good a replication of the existing network as a gravity-model formulation which includes both distances and populations in the analysis. This certainly does not imply that in general network generation models need not consider popu-lation and expected flows. It may be that the network in south-ern Ontario is so simple that relative location can account for much of its spatial structure. Again, however, the importance of links omitted or included is not incorporated into this simple statistical measure of correspondence.

Using b = 1.5, a network has been generated for the Quebec region, and is shown in Figure 13.6. A mileage budget of 674 (the length of the existing network plus the already committed Ottawa-Montreal and Montreal-Trois Rivières links) is specified. The model generates a network which is not strikingly similar to the actual Quebec system (r_ϕ = 0.331). The high nodality of Montreal is predicted by the Shimbel Index model (Figure 13.4) and somewhat over-predicted by the gravity model. It appears that Ottawa 'should be' connected to the network in spite of its somewhat eccentric location. Trois Rivières should also be connected to the system. Neither the gravity nor the Shimbel Model predicts a southerly Montreal-Quebec City route. It would appear that such a route would have to be justified on

174

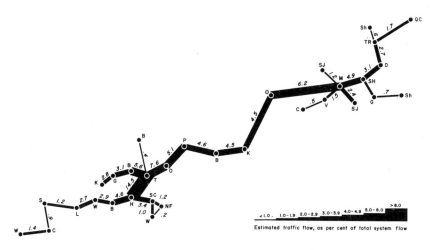

Figure 13.7 Gravity-generated network and flows -- southern Ontario and Quebec

grounds other than simple intercity spatial efficiency.

The partitioning of the region has been necessitated by the model's computational demands; the results so achieved are unsatisfactory in that the flows between the two dominant centres in the Ontario-Quebec system are ignored. In the Quebec run, for instance (Figure 13.6), the Belleville-Kingston link, a portion of the Toronto-Montreal four-lane route, is not constructed, while the mileage so released is used to increase gravity values by 'over-investment' in the central area. One run of the 32-node network was performed with distance-decay exponent b = 1.50 and budget 1233. The generated network is illustrated in Figure 13.7, and it is clear from both its configuration and the flow values associated with its links that the problems due to the absence of Toronto-Montreal flows are alleviated.

The generated network itself is of some interest. Note that the basic trunk line between Toronto and Montreal does not take the shortest path. Instead it takes a circuitous path 'picking up' such centres as Ottawa and Peterborough. These results, however crude, throw some doubt on the appropriateness of the present alignment which has isolated these centres from the multilane highway system. There is some indication that the locations of major trip generators slightly displaced from the strongly linear pattern should have had some effect on the alignment of this trunk highway.

175

Optimal Link Addition Models

From the point of view of a planner or forecaster, the preceding network generation models are somewhat irrelevant. Seldom is the decision-maker faced with the problem of generating a network in its entirety. More usually, an existing network is given and it must be decided which links to add to this so that the resulting network is in some sense optimal. The history of network development and its derivations from optimality is irrelevant. "Bygones are bygones" and a decision must be made irrespective of how the present stage was attained.

Given the existing inter-city multilane highway network, which links should be added so that the increase in expected flows is maximized subject to the constraint that the budgeted construction mileage is not exceeded?

There are again two parameters: the distance exponent and ΔT, increase in mileage. A distance exponent of $b = 1.5$ is again used. ΔT is set equal to 50, so that for the first stage of the link addition process up to 50 miles can be added. The second maximal additions are:

$$\Delta T_2 = 50 + \Delta T_1 - \Delta L_1 = 100 - \Delta L_1,$$

where ΔL_1 is the number of miles constructed during the first stage. This permits unused portions of the budget to be used in subsequent stages. In general then,

$$\Delta T_i = 50 + \Delta T_{i-1} - \Delta L_{i-1} \qquad i = 2, 3, \ldots, N$$

$$\Delta T_1 = \Delta T = 50$$

The results of this model for six stages for southern Quebec are shown in Figure 13.8, assuming that Ottawa-Montreal and Montreal-Trois Rivières links, which are under construction have already been built.

Note that the southern portion of the planned Trans-Quebec Highway is built in the first two stages. Next, the Ottawa-Cornwall link is built closely approximating the contemplated Ottawa-Prescott link. When ΔT is small, long links such as the Trois Rivières-Quebec City link cannot be considered until shorter ones have been added. Transportation budgets and investments are obviously not this lumpy in reality. Partial links may be added over two or more stages and budgets can be

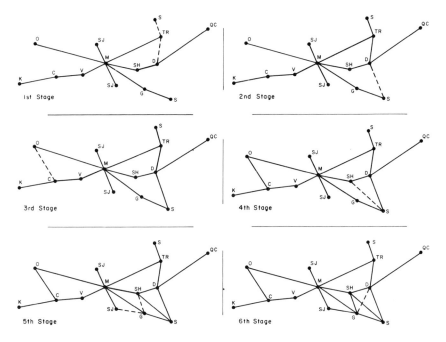

- - - - - Link added during current stage

Figure 13.8   Gravity link-addition. Extension of present Quebec network. Six 50-mile increments

shifted forward and backward in time and in response to investment priorities. The results of the model can thus be extremely sensitive to the choice of the Δ T parameter.

The same model has been run for the Ontario system and Peterborough-Oshawa, Niagara Falls-Welland, Welland-St. Catharines, Kitchener-Brantford, Guelph-Brantford, Sarnia-London, and Woodstock-Brantford links have been generated by one or both Δ T = 50 and Δ T = 100 assumptions.

Network Growth Model for Southern Quebec
One final special case of the link addition model is formulated by setting $T_o = 0$, $\Delta T_1 = 50$, N = 10.   That is, it is assumed that no links exist at the outset and that links are added over ten stages so that increases in expected flows over the network are maximized and increments are limited to fifty miles plus unexpended mileage from past periods. The results of this model are shown in Figure 13.9. Note that the model obviously discriminates against links longer than fifty miles. This

177

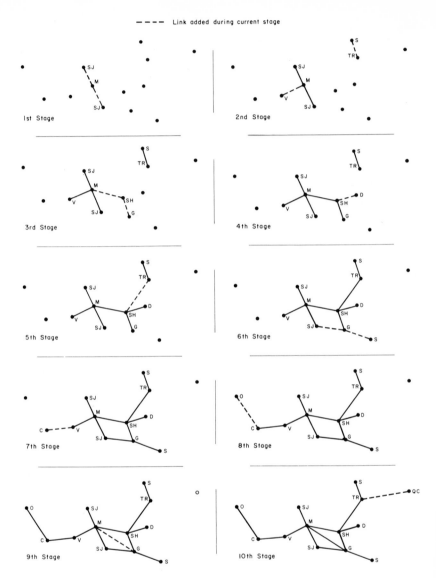

Figure 13.9 Gravity network evolution. Ten 50-mile increments -- southern Quebec

discrimination has spatial and temporal consequences. Thus one long link (for instance, Montreal-Trois Rivières) can be replaced by shorter ones (Montreal-St. Hyacinthe-Drummondville-Trois Rivières). Alternatively, links significantly longer than fifty miles are not added until late in the process. (Ottawa and

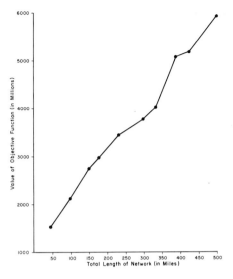

Figure 13.10 Improvement of objective function with network growth -- southern Ontario

Quebec City are not connected to the network until the eighth and tenth stages of the process.) The model would have much more relevance if all the potential links were almost the same length.

The rate of increase of the objective function with increased network length $\Delta F / \Delta T$ is fairly constant (see Figure 13.10). Increases in this rate occur only when large cities such as Ottawa and Quebec City are added to the generated network. Decreases in the rate tend to occur when only small link additions may be made and all of the more beneficial small links have already been added (for example, Montreal-Granby link in the ninth stage). Over the range of the network simulation, there is no tendency for the rate of increase to decline. However, at the tenth stage all of the cities have been connected, and therefore the rate of increase could be expected to decline as links are added which increase the redundancy of the network.

The objective of such network growth models could be to replicate descriptively the evolution of the highway network in a region. Alternately, it could be to provide planners with tools which specify the optimal temporal staging as well as the spatial layout of a new transportation system. For either purpose, it is clear that the model should be far more elaborate than the one presented.

179

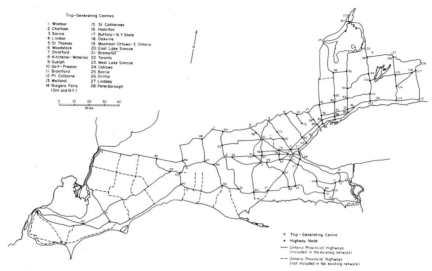

Figure 13.11   The existing highway network -- southwestern Ontario

A Traffic Assignment and Network Improvement Model for the Highway System of Southern Ontario

The previous models can be criticized on several counts. First, a very simple model of trip generation is utilized and no provision is made for inclusion of more reliable estimates of transportation demands. Secondly, no congestion costs are included in the models and all traffic is assigned to shortest distance paths. Thirdly, the existing two lane highway is assumed not to exist; thus the spatial configuration of the existing network is assumed to have no influence on the optimal investment decision for the multilane network. Many other criticisms could be made, but this final model addresses itself to these undesirable characteristics.

First then this model uses exogenously predicted estimates of traffic flow which have been generated by the Ontario Department of Highways based on extensive origin-destination surveys. Second, travel times are assumed to be an increasing function of traffic on any link and traffic is assigned using a separable linear programming approach so that total transportation costs are minimized subject to the fact that travel demands must be satisfied. Finally, major elements of the existing highway system are included as possible routes to accomodate the specified demands.

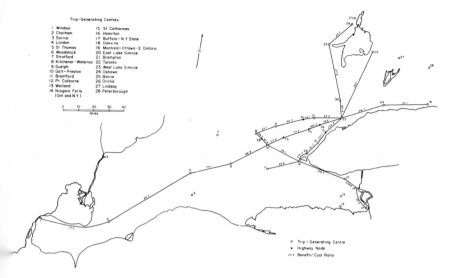

Figure 13.12   Freeway network generated using 1964 origin -
destination flow estimates

The problem then is to add multilane highway links (which
have different volume-travel time relationships) such that specified travel demands are all satisfied, highway construction
budget is not exceeded, and total system travel costs are maximized. The network generation (or link addition), decisions
are identified using an approximation algorithm described elsewhere.[3]

The "existing, " pre-freeway, highway network for the study
area and the cities and nodes are shown in Figure 13.11 . For
computational reasons, some less important links have been
omitted as possible paths.

Generation of a 1964 Freeway Network
Figure 13.12 shows the freeway network generated using 1964
travel demands. Links have been discarded or kept according
to a benefit-cost ratio; the resulting network bears a remarkable
similarity to the existing and certain elements of the planned
freeway system.

Highways 400, 401, the Queen Elizabeth Way and part of 403
(Brantford-Hamilton) are introduced. A link from Toronto to
the eastern side of Lake Simcoe is also retained at this level of

[3] See Bushell (1970).

181

freeway development. The Ontario Department of Highways is planning a freeway link to serve the resort area to the north-east of Toronto. The traffic flow in the Kitchener-Hamilton corridor appears quite heavy and as a consequence the model has retained freeway links joining Kitchener, Galt and Hamilton. Given the level of network development shown in Figure 13.12 and the 1964 origin-destination values used here, the Galt-Hamilton section of this route has a relatively high B/C ratio while the B/C ratio for the Kitchener-Galt link is even higher. Because the Ontario Department of Highways has only started a planning study for the Kitchener area, no comparisons can be made between the heuristic model's recommendations and those of the Ontario Department of Highways in this region of southern Ontario.

The inclusion of two almost parallel freeway routes, one between Toronto and Galt (the present route of Highway 401) and the other between Toronto and Kitchener (through Brampton, Georgetown, Acton and Guelph), may appear to be somewhat illogical although the following points may help to explain why the model includes both of them. Toronto has a dominating influence on the trip pattern of the study region. Trips between the western centres of the study region and Toronto can justify the construction of a freeway link between Galt and Toronto because of both high volume and the high travel times on alternative existing routes. A section of the northern route between Guelph and Georgetown does not have high volume so much as it has high travel time on the alternative existing route represented by Highway 7 which is narrow, winding, and passes through a number of villages and towns in this area. Thus, the link between Guelph and Georgetown may not require the increased capacity of freeway system as much as it requires the improvement of the existing two-lane highway. The Toronto Area Highway Planning Study, Western Section (1970) does recommend that a freeway be built from Georgetown through Brampton to Toronto.

Generation of 1986 Freeway Network

This application of the model uses 1986 origin-destination estimates and results in the network shown in Figure 13.13. The generated freeway system is basically the same as before, except that a few extra links are now included. The proposed link between London and St. Thomas is constructed as is the planned route between Port Colborne and St. Catharines. The

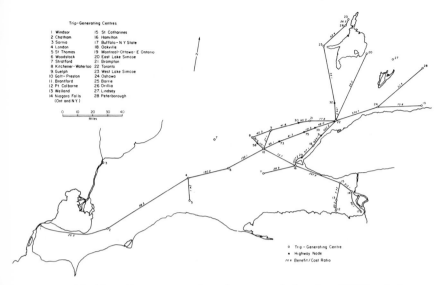

Figure 13.13   Freeway network generated using 1986 origin - destination flow estimates

1986 trip estimates appear to justify the inclusion of these highways whereas the 1964 figures did not. A link between Galt and Guelph is also included in this solution. The seemingly dense system of freeway links in the Kitchener-Guelph-Galt-Preston-Hespeler area could reflect the anticipated growth of this region. One other additional link, between Oshawa and Peterborough is included in this solution. Another more direct link between Highway 401 and Peterborough is also retained in the freeway network if the Oshawa-Peterborough link is removed, although the direct link between Port Hope and Peterborough has a lower benefit-cost ratio. Since estimates of trip flow between Peterborough and centres east of the study region are not included in this analysis, the Port Hope link could actually have the higher benefit-cost ratio. In any event it appears as if an improved connection between Highway 401 and Peterborough is needed.

The freeway network shown in Figure 13.13 still does not include the proposed Sarnia-London route or the Woodstock-Brantford section of the planned Highway 403. The London Area Highway Planning Study (Department of Highways, Ontario), does show the Sarnia-London link to have a lower priority than the London-St. Thomas connection but the Brantford Area Highway Planning Study shows the Woodstock-Brantford link to be of first priority.

183

The nature of the origin-destination estimates used in this study may well help to provide a reason for the omission of these two links, as well as explain why the Windsor-Chatham and the Brantford-Hamilton links have relatively low benefit-cost ratios. Although internal-to-external flow estimates for the Toronto-North, Toronto-East and Toronto-New York State corridors are included in the origin-destination tables, no estimate of the external-to-internal flows between Michigan and the study area are included in the tables as such estimates are not readily available from any of the Highway Planning Studies. If these flows could be obtained the benefit-cost ratios might be increased somewhat. One might even justify the construction of the Woodstock-Brantford link, the Sarnia-London connection and especially the Windsor-Chatham arc on the grounds that they are needed to complete a larger overall freeway system connecting not only the major centres in the study region but many external points as well.

Concluding Remarks

This paper has summarized some of the results of recent studies which have applied optimal network generation models to the highway system of southern Ontario and Quebec. These models have been used to attempt to gain an understanding of the under-lying principles of network structure and change as they manifest themselves in the study region. In addition, the results identify some of the more likely additions to the highway networks in the region. Future studies will attempt to identify the consequences of changing spatial network configurations on the distribution of population and socio-economic activities and incorporate them into more comprehensive network generation models.

References

BUSHELL, G. E. 1970. An optimization traffic assignment and network improvement model for the freeway system of southern Ontario. Research Paper No. 40, Centre for Urban and Community Studies, University of Toronto.

Highway Area Planning Studies. Various years. Ontario Department of Highways. Downsview, Ont.

MACKINNON, R. D. and M. J. HODGSON. 1969. The highway system of southern Ontario and Quebec: some simple network generation models. Research Paper No. 18, Centre for Urban and Community Studies, University of Toronto.

--------. 1970. Optimal transportation networks: A case study of highway systems. Environment and Planning 2:267-84.

PRIM, R. C. 1957. Shortest connection networks and some generalizations. Bell System Technical Journal 36:1389-1401.

SCOTT, A. J. 1969. The optimal network problem: some computational procedures. Transportation Research 3:201-10.

14

A note on the changing spatial pattern of traffic flow on Highway 401, Ontario [1]

R. D. MacKinnon

Geographical studies are frequently concerned with the description or explanation of two dimensional spatial patterns. Often, however, a one dimensional traverse of a region is studied, sometimes because it is believed that the variable in question varies more significantly along this traverse than within the region as a whole. More often however, traverses are studied because one dimensional spatial processes are far more easy to analyze quantitatively than those in two dimensions.

In this study, the major component of the Ontario highway system is chosen as the traverse. [2] Vehicular traffic flow is analyzed as a one dimensional spatial process using simple statistical techniques. The objectives of this project are to

---

[1] This paper has been adapted from MacKinnon (1970).

[2] In a similar vein, Tobler (1969) chooses U.S. 40 running from Baltimore to San Francisco as his traverse and analyzes the variation in population density as a one dimensional spatial process.

quantify this spatial process in terms of statistical relationships, to rationalize the residuals from these relationships quantitatively and/or verbally, and to study the parameter shifts of the relationships with a view to provide projections into the future.

The Data

The dependent variable used in this analysis is the "Annual Average Daily Traffic" (A.A.D.T) counts made by the Department of Highways of Ontario. These data are published for virtually every section of road under the Department's jurisdiction. In most cases, these data are based on statistical samples at various times in the year, although in some instances less formal estimating procedures are employed. The variable is an annual daily average and thus seasonal and daily cycles are obscured.[3] These data have only become available in their present form during the 1960's, but are now published formally on an annual basis.

Highway 401 has been chosen for analysis because of its central importance as the trunk line of the highway system of Ontario. It closely follows the main axis of principal cities and towns of southern Ontario. The highway has three principal functions: to provide the major intercity highway route for the region, to facilitate the inflow and outflow trips from and to other regions, and to aid in the movement of local, short distance traffic.

The Department of Highways indicates that there is on the average a 5 per cent annual increase in traffic flow over all Ontario roads. Traffic on Highway 401 is increasing more rapidly than traffic on the highway system as a whole and variation in growth rates from one segment to another is very high. The question arises then as to whether the spatial pattern of highway traffic has changed along Highway 401 in any systematic way. The strategy employed here is to identify spatial patterns cross-sectionally and analyze the shifts in parameters over time as well as between regions. A systematic sample of traffic counts has been made. The average numbers of vehicles per day passing points at 5 mile intervals are analyzed.

Selecting the Functional Form of the Model

There are perhaps three significant characteristics of the plots

---

[3]Summer Daily Average Traffic counts, although not published, are available from the Department of Highways and may be used in subsequent analyses.

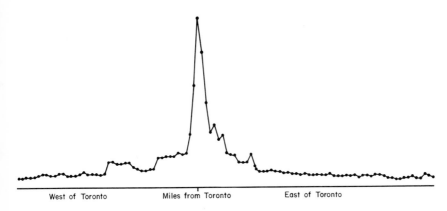

Figure 14.1   Annual average daily traffic flow on Highway 401, 1965. Source: DHO, AADT Volumes, 1966

of traffic flow. First there is an apparent regularity of the data for any given year. (Figure 14.1 shows the plot of points for 1965). This indicates that if an appropriate function is chosen, a very good fit should be obtained. Secondly, the plot of points appears to have the same general shape for all years. This indicates that the same functional form should be capable of summarizing the traffic patterns of all of the years for which data are available. The parameters of the function will vary in response to changes in traffic flow patterns from one year to the next. Finally, the plot of points is highly peaked and appears to have left and right asymptotes corresponding respectively to west and east ends of Highway 401.

     It is not possible to transform the data so that linear regression methods can be used. After some experimentation, the function form

$$Y_i = a + \frac{1}{b + cX_i}$$

has been selected to fit the data where:

Y_i = annual average daily traffic passing sample point i,

X_i = distance (in highway miles) of sample point i from the Toronto peak,

and a, b, and c are parameters to be estimated so that the sum of squared derivations of the data from the curve are minimized.

187

In fitting the data, a final option presents itself. For any given year, either a single curve $Y = a + \dfrac{1}{b + cX}$ may be fitted or two curves may be fitted independently: $Y = a_w + \dfrac{1}{b_w + c_w X}$ for all points to the west of the Toronto peak and $Y = a_E + \dfrac{1}{b_E + c_E X}$ for all points to the east of the Toronto peak. The latter option has been selected since the directional differences in the traffic patterns are not obscured.

Theoretical Rationale

To a considerable extent, this study is an empirical curve fitting exercise with a naive theoretical basis. The primary interest of the study is to make empirical observations, using quantitative analyses, about the changing spatial pattern of traffic flow along a particular transportation facility. The specific form of the function selected is based primarily on empirical considerations. As we shall see, however, the fit provided is so good, that it is perhaps appropriate to speculate about possible ways in which these results could be theoretically derived.

It is not difficult to give a loose verbal analysis of the explanatory factors involved in this pattern. Three factors suggest themselves. Traffic passing any one point is equal to the sum of three component parts:

1) "local traffic;"
2) traffic originating in the vicinity of the point and destined for more distant locations (and vice versa);
3) traffic which is passing by the point but which has an origin and a destination outside the local area.

On all three counts a Toronto peaked curve of traffic flow could be expected. Local traffic is higher because of the very large population which uses the facility for intra-urban commuting, social, recreation, and business trips. Moreover, a general decline of the intensity of economic activity and population density with distance from the metropolis may be observed. Thus, fewer local trips are generated at greater distances. The relationship of socio-economic activity with distance, however, is far more noisy or irregular than the traffic flow–distance relationship appears to be.

188

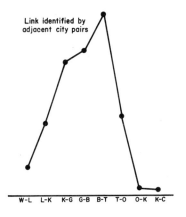

Link identified by
adjacent city pairs

W-L L-K K-G G-B B-T T-O O-K K-C

Figure 14.2   Profile of
traffic flow derived from
simple gravity and shortest
path assignment models

With respect to traffic of the second category, Toronto
attracts and generates many more intercity trips because of its
dominant role in the socio-economic systems of the region. The
decline of activity with distance from Toronto also would contribute to the peaked spatial pattern of this type.

Finally, even if all traffic generating centres were of equal
importance, highway segments near Toronto would have larger
counts than most other segments because of the central location
of Toronto within the linear region around the highway facility.
Toronto thus interposes itself between many pairs of potential
trip ends.

Ignoring the local traffic component, Figure 14.2 shows the
shape of a traffic distribution pattern derived from applying the
simplest gravity model formulation to the major urban areas on
or near Highway 401. From the west in particular, the pattern
is not nearly so peaked. Toronto's peak would be much higher
if local traffic were included in the derivation.

These general factors reflecting the spatial pattern of trip
distribution, trip generation, and socio-economic pattern of
activity, undoubtedly both contribute to the observed spatial
pattern of vehicle flow. It is impossible to identify the relative
importance of each factor however.

Model Calibration

The relationship $Y = a + \dfrac{1}{b + cX}$ is fitted to the data using
traditional least squares principles. The three normal equations,
one for each parameter, are, however, non-linear. They, therefore, are solved by using Newton's iterative method (Pennington

189

TABLE 14.1 PARAMETERS AND CORRELATION COEFFICIENTS FOR
HIGHWAY 401 TRAFFIC FLOW EQUATIONS

EAST OF TORONTO

Year	a_E	b_E	c_E	r
1962*	294	133E-07	144E-08	.984
1963	72	137R-07	111E-08	.985
1964	178	136E-07	109E-08	.986
1965	1153	122E-07	110E-08	.990
1966	1142	97E-07	105E-08	.988
1967	4512	91E-07	113E-08	.988
1968	1114	78E-07	92E-08	.991

WEST OF TORONTO

Year	a_W	b_W	c_W	r
1960*	2264	149E-07	318E-08	.974
1962**	2654	141E-07	230E-08	.979
1963	2548	149E-07	211E-08	.979
1964	3694	149E-07	222E-08	.977
1965	4940	130E-07	203E-08	.977
1966	5981	105E-07	254E-08	.981
1967	6536	94E-07	192E-08	.985
1968	6089	83E-07	171E-08	.987

NOTE: *N= 53 for this year as compared to N= 58 for other years.
      **N= 25 for this year as compared to N= 45 for all other years except 1962.
     ***N= 31 for this year as compared to N= 45 for all other years except 1960.

1965), whereby initial estimates of the parameters are made and
these estimates are improved upon until additional iterations
yield insignificant changes in the parameters. This convergence
will occur only if initial estimates are reasonably close to actual
values. If they are not, other estimates are made and the process continues until convergence occurs.

The results obtained by using this procedure are shown in
Table 14.1.

Perhaps the most remarkable feature of the results is the
extremely good fit obtained. Correlation coefficients are very
close to unity in all cases. Perhaps this observation should be
·tempered with the remark that the total variance in traffic flow
is heavily dominated by points close to Toronto; thus if a good
fit is obtained in this region, then very little variance in Y re-

mains to be "explained." Nevertheless, the fit is good and thus the choice of the functional form appears to be justified on empirical grounds.

Pattern of Residuals

Often a careful study of residuals from a regression model is revealing. The existence of a strong pattern in the residuals generally indicates that an incorrect functional form has been chosen or one of more significant variables has been omitted from the analysis, the latter being a special case of the first.

One of the primary reasons for undertaking this study initially, was to determine whether traffic flow (= trend + residuals) reflects the population distribution along the highway facility. Thus a quantitative analysis of the dynamics of residuals using simple autocorrelation techniques or spectral and cross spectral analysis could provide an indication of the changing spatial structure of social and economic activities within the Highway 401 region.

Without resorting to any formal statistical methods, one strong pattern manifests itself for all of the eight years. This appears to be the influence of London (105 miles to the southwest of Toronto) on the traffic flow pattern. Traffic flow appears to be higher than the general trend would indicate for approximately 40 miles around London (Figure 14.1). This in itself does not invalidate the basic trend relationship. One unfortunate result, however, is that these relatively large values of Y distort the apparent trend to the west of London; virtually all values are overpredicted. London's high values raise the curve not only at London but also farther to the west. This artificially induced autocorrelation can be eliminated by, somewhat arbitrarily, fitting the trend line only to points which are apparently not significantly influenced by London as a trip generator.[4] In general, this might be dependent on arbitrary judgments, but in this instance the decision is clear. At about 75 miles to the west of Toronto traffic volumes begin to rise and are well above the basic trend for 40 miles where an extremely sharp drop in traffic is encountered.

The model is calibrated for the smaller set of data points and the results are shown in Table 14.2 and in Figure 14.3. Using this procedure, the strong autocorrelation at the tail of

[4]This problem is closely related to Kruskal's (1960) discussion of dealing with wild or outlying observations.

TABLE 14.2 RESULTS FOR HIGHWAY 401 TRAFFIC FLOW WEST OF TORONTO
WITH LONDON'S INFLUENCE REMOVED

Year	a_W	b_W	c_W	r
1960	749	145E-07	290E-08	.965
1962	1552	139E-07	139E-07	.967
1963	1853	147E-07	205E-08	.968
1964	2958	147E-07	215E-08	.967
1965	4008	129E-07	196E-08	.971
1966	4916	104E-07	215E-08	.978
1967	5264	93E-07	184E-08	.980
1968	4952	82E-07	164E-08	.986

the curve has been eliminated.

The residuals for a sample year are plotted in Figure 14.4.
The London residuals from the curve calibrated without the London values are included.

Note that the pattern of residuals in the London area conforms with what would be expected. The urban influence field of London as indicated by traffic flows is skewed towards the east i.e., in the Toronto direction, dropping very quickly to the west. This is indicative of the larger population and secondary industry in this direction. Note also that the smaller positive residuals near the Kitchener-Waterloo urban complex are also skewed in this direction.

The regression assumption of homoscedasticity (constant error variance) is obviously violated. Variance in the vicinity of Toronto is much higher reflecting the enormously higher values of the data themselves in this region. Note, however, that the model is not biased over this range in that overpredictions are balanced with underpredictions.

Large negative residuals fifty miles east of Toronto reflect the rapidity with which economic activity and population levels decline in this direction. None of the urban centres in this direction have much of an impact on the basic Toronto distance decay pattern.

Note however that within 100 miles of Toronto there appears to be a slight increasing linear trend in the pattern of residuals towards the east. At least a portion of this apparent trend is undoubtedly due to the increasing influence of the Montreal metropolis in generating traffic in eastern Ontario.

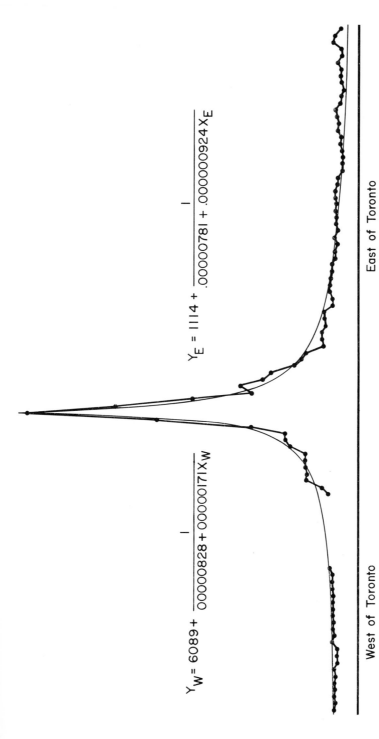

$$Y_W = 6089 + \dfrac{1}{.00000828 + .0000017IX_W}$$

$$Y_E = III4 + \dfrac{1}{.0000078I + .000000924X_E}$$

West of Toronto   East of Toronto

Figure 14.3   Annual average daily traffic flow on Highway 401 in 1968 with statistically fitted curve

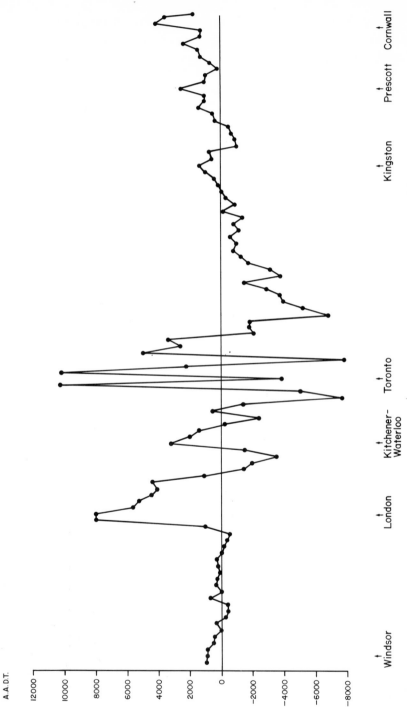

A.A.D.T.

Figure 14.4   Residuals from 1968 AADT trend functions, Highway 401, Ontario

This concludes a preliminary discussion of the pattern of residuals. Two broad alternatives present themselves for future studies. First, it should be possible and certainly desirable to introduce in a formal manner other variables into the analysis relating residuals to variation in population density, population potential, or some other surrogate for variation in socio-economic activity. Secondly, more sophisticated techniques could be employed to analyze the changing pattern of residuals.

Interpretation of Parameters

Each of the cross-sectional models has three parameters which are estimated from the data such that the sum of squared deviations from the resulting curve is minimized. The shape and position of the curve is responsive to changes in these parameters. Thus changes in the parameters should reflect the changing spatial trend in vehicular flow.

Figure 14.5 indicates that all three parameters tend to vary systematically with time. Parameter a tends to be an increasing function of time while b and c tend to be decreasing with respect to time. These generalizations tend to be true for traffic flow patterns in both directions.

If the parameter shifts of several cross-sectionally estimated relationships vary systematically with time, a simply dynamic model of the following form could be estimated:

$$Y_t = a_t + \frac{1}{b_t + c_t X}$$

where each parameter is now a variable and a function of time. By fitting a linear least squares regression equation for each of the six parameters $a_E^5, b_E, c_E, a_W, b_W$, and c_W, the following models are obtained:

$$_W Y_t = 498.9 + 636.7t + \frac{1}{(160.5 - 8.5t) + (303.5 - 21.2t)X_t}$$

$$_E Y_t = -287.6 + 199.1t + \frac{1}{(166.4 - 10.6t) + (140.0 - 5.6t)X_t}$$

where t = calendar year minus 1960.

[5] The value of a_E for 1967 is exceptionally large and apparently temporary. This shift is undoubtedly a response to Expo '67 held in Montreal during Canada's centennial year. It is therefore excluded in this regression model.

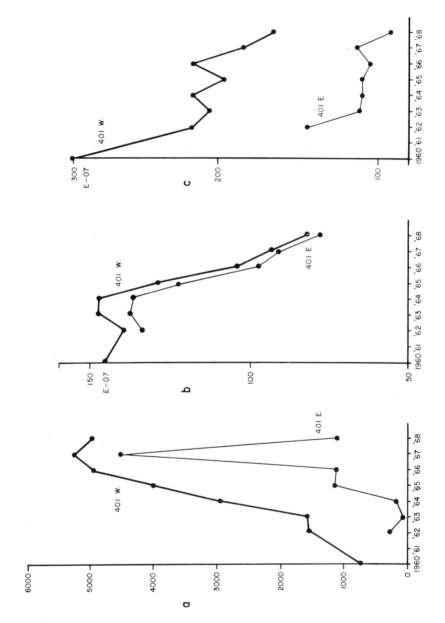

Figure 14.5 Trends in parameter values for annual average daily traffic flow curves

Although the trends in the parameters do not appear to be exceptionally regular nor is the sample size very large, it would be possible to use these two models as short term traffic flow forecasting models. Of course, it would be possible to achieve more reliable and longer term forecasts by using longer time series as they become available and/or by incorporating other factors such as population and economic growth and network change into the analysis.

Very roughly, similar trends are apparent for parameters of both sets of curves (Figure 14.5). The western parameter estimates for all years have greater values than eastern parameters. With respect to a, this implies that the western sector generates, attracts and processes more traffic than the eastern sector. This of course reflects the more intensive economic development of southwestern Ontario compared to eastern Ontario.

Somewhat surprising is the fact that $b_W > b_E$ and $c_W > c_E$ indicating that the eastern curve has larger traffic flow estimates for points which are short and intermediate distances from Toronto than does the western curve. It should be noted, however, that the western curve has been estimated by eliminating data which reflect a considerable portion of the activity of this sector--the traffic which appears to be strongly influenced by London. The results are still surprising, however, and only tentative factors can be advanced in an attempt to rationalize them.[6]

Summary
This paper has described a number of sets of spatial data using very simple curve fitting procedures. The resulting single equation models have been found to provide extremely good fits "accounting for" almost all of the variation in traffic flows along a major highway facility in terms of distance from the Toronto metropolis. Residuals from simple spatial trends have been discussed and informally related to the influence of other urban centres. The two sets of cross-sectional models have been united internally into two very simple growth models of traffic flow which could be used to forecast future traffic patterns along this facility. Finally, it may be possible to interpret traffic flow

[6] For example, some Toronto-Ottawa traffic uses Highway 401 over this range of distances and then moves northward to Highway 7. Alternatively, large negative residuals over part of this range may also indicate that the wrong functional relationship has been chosen.

as a surrogate for the intensity of socio-economic activity within
this linear band of cities.

References

DEPARTMENT OF HIGHWAYS ONTARIO. 1960-68. Annual Average Daily Traffic.
Traffic Planning Branch. Downsview, Ont.

KRUSKAL, W. H. 1960. Some remarks on wild observations. Technometrics 2:1-3.

MACKINNON, R. D. 1970. A note on the changing spatial pattern of traffic flow on a
major transportation facility:Highway 401, Ontario. Research Paper No. 39,
Centre for Urban and Community Studies, University of Toronto.

PENNINGTON, R. H. 1965. Introductory Computer Methods and Numerical Analysis.
New York: MacMillan.

TOBLER, W. 1969. The spectrum of U.S. 40. Papers, Regional Science Association
23:45-52.

15

Interaction among the cities of Ontario and Quebec[1]

J. W. Simmons

The urban "system" is defined in large part by the relationships
and interactions among its components, the cities. This paper
describes various aspects of the pattern of intercity contacts
within Central Canada, a view to identifying the degree to which

[1]This paper has been adapted from Simmons (1970b).

198

the cities of this region do indeed operate as a system, and of
specifying the role of the various media of interaction.

Data of this type are difficult to obtain, particularly in a
form suitable for comparison among different media. The most
complete data by far, and the main object of analysis herein,
are records of long distance calls among the telephone toll areas
of Ontario and Quebec. However rail freight, truck freight and
air passenger movements are also described briefly in order to
make some comparisons among the media. A single flow matrix
is no more valid in describing contacts within an urban system
than is a single variable in identifying the subtle variations among
a set of towns.

LONG DISTANCE TELEPHONE CALLS[2]

The most comprehensive information on contacts among cities
comes from records kept on long distance telephone calls. Bell
Canada has provided information on the number of long distance
telephone calls among toll centres in Ontario and Quebec on an
average business day in the spring quarter of 1967. The data
have been edited to provide measures of residence and business
originated calls, in addition data have been provided on the number of phones of various types in each toll area (Table 15.1).
Only the 61 toll areas of the southern parts of the two provinces
have been analyzed.

The areal boundaries of the toll areas were determined by
Bell Canada for economic and technical reasons. For larger
centres they approximate the metropolitan region; but for small
places, the town (e.g., Beaverton) is an arbitrary name and
location for a large region. The data describe the movement
of messages between regions. At the borders of the regions
small centres in different regions may well be closer to each
other spatially than to other centres within their own toll areas.
This will bias some of the results.

The arbitrary regional definitions and the peculiarities of
rate structure lead to great variation in the proportion of long
distance calls recorded within the toll centre (from 0.0 to over
50 per cent). These calls are recorded as long distance between

[2]Data were made available by Bell Canada, with the particular assistance of Mrs. Norma
Siddiqui and Mrs. Joan Marshall.

TABLE 15.1. TOLL CENTRES AND THEIR CHARACTERISTICS

	Name	Residential Phones	Business Phones	Total (000's)	Per cent Residential	Total In-Calls	Per cent Residential	Total Out-Calls	Per cent Residential	Total Within Calls	Per cent Residential	Per Cent Within
1.	Toronto	809593	385785	1205	62	62990	38	67407	36	19753	51	22.3
2.	Brampton	30748	9576	41	75	9616	46	9194	62	773	60	7.8
3.	Ft. Erie	9399	2386	13	72	1272	39	1527	46	1	0	0.0
4.	Windsor	86635	29269	117	74	4822	34	4634	34	3388	47	42.2
5.	Barrie	24581	8706	34	72	4469	43	4392	39	1344	41	23.4
6.	St. Thomas	14439	4424	19	76	3021	44	2976	42	641	51	17.7
7.	Woodstock	13536	4867	19	71	3102	42	2753	35	471	59	14.6
8.	London	85313	34652	121	71	12736	35	12341	37	3350	53	21.4
9.	Stratford	12654	4655	17	74	2809	40	2696	34	810	50	23.1
10.	Hamilton	154760	53938	210	74	19455	36	19839	41	6079	63	23.5
11.	Orangeville	8585	2106	11	78	2111	52	1819	52	209	62	10.3
12.	Peterborough	28682	11108	40	72	3822	41	3512	35	1282	47	26.7
13.	Simcoe	13898	3723	18	77	2336	45	2375	47	247	72	9.4
14.	Beaverton	3797	839	5	76	868	47	766	56	155	64	16.8
15.	Bracebridge	5829	1769	8	73	915	48	932	39	238	49	20.3
16.	Brantford	28540	9865	38	75	4817	39	5195	39	72	75	1.4
17.	Chatham	30847	9979	41	75	3369	36	3530	38	535	54	13.2
18.	Clinton	6263	2393	9	70	1320	43	1257	46	267	60	17.5
19.	Huntsville	5279	2226	8	66	920	42	876	36	288	39	24.7
20.	Kitchener	77709	29280	108	72	12014	35	12465	36	4561	43	26.8
21.	Lindsay	6537	2517	9	72	1835	48	1190	34	674	45	36.2
22.	Midland	6474	2577	9	72	1106	39	1234	37	342	56	21.7
23.	Newmarket	20599	5446	26	79	6004	51	4839	60	1153	53	19.2
24.	Niagara Falls	20549	9257	30	69	4320	42	4575	43	1	0	0.0
25.	Orillia	11251	4154	16	70	2224	43	1893	36	218	48	10.3
26.	Oshawa	48066	14912	63	76	7985	43	6872	46	1348	58	16.4
27.	Owen Sound	14476	4877	19	76	2052	42	2076	36	833	45	28.6
28.	Parry Sound	3281	1399	5	66	527	40	469	33	119	41	20.2
29.	Guelph	25927	9532	36	72	5572	41	5998	41	555	47	8.4
30.	Pt. Hope	10330	3354	14	74	1782	36	1671	41	201	63	10.7

31.	St. Catharines	44034	15628	60	73	8112	44	7842	40	41	71	5.2
32.	Sarnia	25427	10684	36	71	2817	39	2461	35	441	56	15.2
33.	Tillsonburg	6915	1971	9	77	1401	47	1701	47	250	66	12.7
34.	Walkerton	8357	2740	11	76	2220	46	1421	39	644	62	31.1
35.	Welland	24727	7132	32	77	4167	41	4356	46	282	68	6.1
36.	Montreal	875966	394334	1288	67	44798	37	48454	39	24903	62	34.0
37.	Trois Rivières	32496	12782	43	76	4206	42	3746	39	983	50	20.8
38.	Kingston	34632	15230	50	69	3669	41	3523	35	1972	50	36.0
39.	Thetford Mines	10767	3699	14	76	1296	38	1147	37	321	45	21.8
40.	Victoriaville	8563	3756	12	72	1837	38	1357	32	1008	52	43.9
41.	Drummondville	12399	5235	18	69	2118	38	2027	34	597	47	22.8
42.	St. Jérôme	27801	10399	39	71	5878	51	5560	50	1858	56	25.0
43.	Smith's Falls	15265	4651	20	76	2695	46	2505	43	1386	51	35.7
44.	St. Hyacinthe	12827	5486	18	71	3025	44	2274	41	396	55	14.9
45.	Joliette	24260	8773	33	74	3915	50	3324	47	1917	35	36.6
46.	Ste. Agathe	10062	5332	16	62	1902	50	1761	41	516	52	22.6
47.	St. Jean	21615	8347	30	72	4234	48	3891	49	1471	51	27.4
48.	Granby	22467	8410	31	73	3657	44	3668	42	2503	53	40.6
49.	Cornwall	22319	7703	30	74	2602	43	2778	40	1863	55	40.2
50.	Valleyfield	20177	6971	27	74	4360	51	3771	50	2629	50	41.0
51.	Belleville	35305	12770	48	74	3519	42	3403	41	3603	63	51.4
52.	Shawinigan	17312	5878	23	75	2073	45	1908	49	190	60	9.1
53.	Hawkesbury	6765	2373	9	75	1263	50	1272	46	421	61	24.9
54.	Renfrew	10804	3506	14	77	1846	44	1546	44	863	61	35.9
55.	Sorel	12324	5265	18	68	2052	46	1796	49	703	54	28.1
56.	Sherbrooke	50993	20116	72	71	4802	37	5141	35	2572	56	33.4
57.	Quebec	138040	68021	208	66	7416	31	8237	28	2061	52	20.0
58.	Pembroke	13453	5046	19	70	1476	42	1302	43	427	64	24.7
59.	Brockville	15783	5887	22	72	2019	42	2472	40	669	59	21.4
60.	Ottawa	196097	94909	293	67	13960	36	13614	41	7215	56	34.6
61.	Lac Mégantic	2829	1184	4	69	494	40	462	37	234		33.6
	Totals					335854	40	335854	40	119011	55	24.0

sub-areas of the centre such as Toronto and Oakville. The proportion is largest for isolated nodes (Walkerton, Smith Falls) where the total number of long distance calls to the rest of the system is small. Where a number of toll centres are located close together (Niagara Peninsula), the proportion of within toll centre calls is very small. The analyses reported here ignore the within area calls keeping in mind that the resultant spatial filter may have modified some of the results.

The other significant decision which affects the results of the analyses is the specification of system boundaries. By drawing a line around the southern Ontario-Quebec urban system all measures of system accessibility are affected. Places near the geographical centre of the system (so defined) appear to interact more intensely than peripheral places because a greater number of their links are within the system. By not considering Detroit, Windsor appears isolated; by eliminating locations north and east of Quebec City, the latter appears to be peripheral and poorly linked to the system.

The study area here is bounded by the U.S. border on the south and by the region of discontinuous settlement to the north. The effect of the border in reducing the degree of contact among places has been shown by MacKay (1958) using telephone data, and verified by the author, using air passenger movements. Cross border contacts are from 1/5 to 1/10 of what one would expect from the study of movements within Canada. The cities in the northern parts of the provinces have been eliminated for a variety of reasons; they are small, they are frequently another order of magnitude less accessible, and their economies tend to be highly specialized, operating at a national or international level.

The analysis focusses on three measures; matrices of residential messages, business messages, and total messages. Table 15.1 contains some summary data for the toll areas. Although the proportion of residential phones is fairly stable, ranging from 0.67 to 0.79, residential phones generate a smaller proportion (35 to 75 per cent) of within centre calls and only 28 to 62 per cent of the out-of-centre calls. Business phones generate a disproportional amount of long distance calls with the proportion increasing with distance. Cities acting as central places--regional centres--generate large numbers of business calls. Cities on the fringe of the metropolitan areas generate predominantly residential flows.

Previous studies (MacKay 1958 and Riddell 1965) describe
the patterns of intercity long distance calls using the parameters
of a gravity model. Although a large proportion of variance is
accounted for (70 to 80 per cent), the parameters show a great
deal of variation. Riddell shows, for instance, that the exponent of distance is largest for small places and isolated locations.
He is unable to find any association between the hierarchic links
of a postulated central place system and the flow measure.

Given the results of the previous studies the 61 x 61 flow
matrix has been approached in several ways: the gross flow
patterns are mapped and discussed, a hierarchic structure is
derived using maximum outflow and factor analytic techniques,
and patterns of indirect contacts are studied by a variety of
procedures.

Gross Flow Patterns

When the largest flows in the system are mapped (Figures 15.1
and 15.2) the complexity of the interaction pattern becomes
apparent. Both the residential and business call matrices are
highly symmetrical (the latter slightly less so) so that only the
largest of the two dyadic flows between points ($\max[f_{ij}, f_{ji}]$) are
indicated.

Flows among larger centres are very strong (Quebec-
Montreal, Ottawa-Montreal, Montreal-Toronto, Toronto-
Hamilton) indicating the 'main drag' effect mentioned earlier--
the tendency for larger, complex places to be linked by channels
of interaction. But smaller places of similar size which are
close together are also closely linked. Obviously a gravity
model describes much of the pattern.

The links between Ontario and Quebec cities are all through
Montreal, but the lack of large places in eastern Ontario makes
this pattern quite plausible. The southern Ontario cities are
much more highly interlinked, however, to nearby cities of the
same size.

The business and residential call patterns provide some
interesting contrasts. The latter appear to be more sensitive
to distance decay, the former more attracted to larger urban
places. When the proportion of residential cases are calculated
for the largest 25 routes (Table 15.2), this effect is clearly
seen. The proportion of residential calls is over 50 per cent
for nearby places (Toronto-Brampton) and drops to 20 per cent
for calls from Toronto to Montreal. The remaining discussion

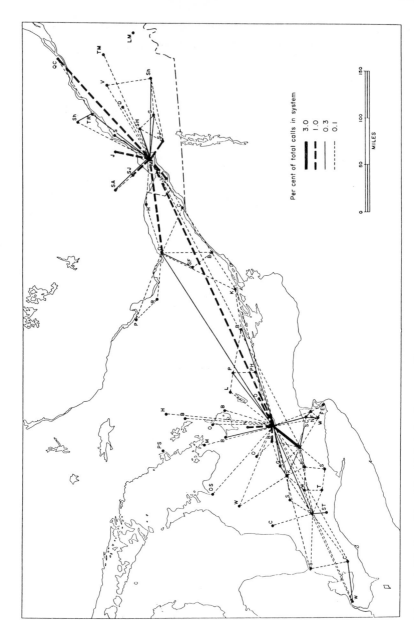

Figure 15.1   Residential telephone calls

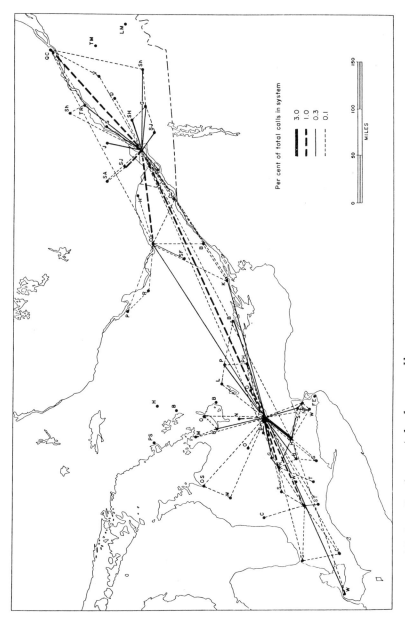

Figure 15.2 Business telephone calls

TABLE 15.2 MAJOR TELEPHONE ROUTES

Rank	Link	Total Messages	Per Cent Residential Origin	Distance in Miles
1.	Toronto-Hamilton	19013	38.0	33
2.	Toronto-Montreal	14238	21.6	314
3.	Toronto-Brampton	13269	54.8	19
4.	Toronto-Oshawa	10450	44.9	27
5.	Montreal-Quebec	9541	29.6	147
6.	Montreal-Ottawa	9152	35.7	102
7.	Montreal-St. Jérôme	8621	52.8	28
8.	Toronto-Newmarket	8524	56.5	24
9.	Toronto-Kitchener	7084	28.1	56
10.	Montreal-Valleyfield	6986	51.5	22
11.	Toronto-London	6434	27.1	103
12.	Montreal-St. Jean	5804	49.8	22
13.	Montreal-Joliette	5346	50.8	35
14.	Toronto-Ottawa	5105	28.8	219
15.	Montreal-Sherbrooke	4813	36.6	82
16.	Kitchener-Guelph	4447	39.9	16
17.	Toronto-Barrie	3912	44.0	53
18.	St. Catharines-Niagara Falls	3829	45.6	10
19.	Toronto-St. Catharines	3604	36.3	36
20.	Montreal-Granby	3565	43.7	44
21.	London-St. Thomas	3454	45.3	17
22.	Hamilton-St. Catharines	3017	40.6	27
23.	St. Catharines-Welland	2997	47.2	12
24.	Toronto-Windsor	2990	24.9	204
25.	Montreal-Trois Rivières	2975	39.0	75

TOTAL   169,081

NOTE: These 25 city pairs account for 50.4 per cent of total calls

will be primarily based on the business call matrix because of the greater proportion of long distance calls.

A variant of the map of gross flows plots the maximum outflow from each location, as suggested by Nystuen and Dacey (1961). Such a map (Figure 15.3) identifies the hierarchic structure of an urban system if such structure exists, since the largest flow from a place should be to a higher order place. It happens that in a spatial structure such as that of Central Canada, the positive effects of population size and the negative effects of distance decay balance each other so that this procedure generates a neatly connected hierarchic system, with each centre generating the maximum outflow to the nearest higher order place. The technique is useful in that it connects all points to at least one other point, and it eliminates most of the intense interconnections

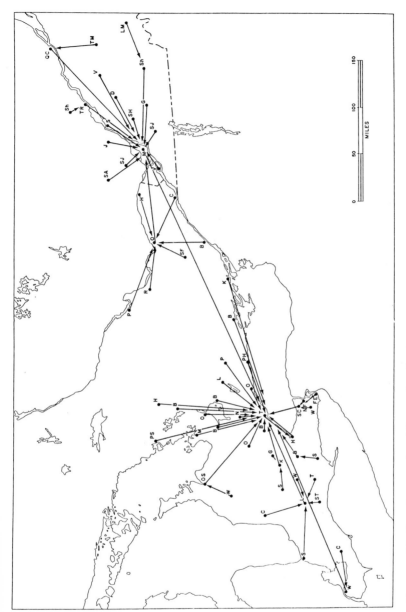

Figure 15.3   Largest outflow: business messages

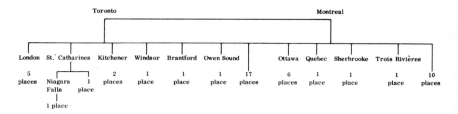

Figure 15.4   The commercial hierarchy

among larger places. One difficulty however, is that the proportion of out-calls in the largest outflow varies widely. Valleyfield sends 0.487 of its calls to Montreal, but Niagara Falls
sends only 0.189 of its calls to Toronto--its dominant destination (major outflows average 0.36 of total outflow for each place).
    The business calls define a more clear-cut hierarchy than
the residential graph which contains several unconnected sub-
graphs (Windsor, St. Catharines) because of the more rapid
distance decay. Figures 15.4 and 15.5 satisfy intuitive notions
of urban structure and appear to account for the main patterns
of commercial relationships in the study area. Notable features
are the irrelevance of Hamilton as a regional centre, and the
clear-cut dependence of Ottawa and its tributaries on Montreal.

Factor Analysis
This procedure provides a slightly different perspective to flow
matrix generalization. Correlations among the columns of the
flow matrix are used to group columns into components using a
variance maximizing procedure (Berry 1967). The procedure
uses the complete flow matrix but the statistical manipulation,
based on the correlation coefficients and variance, may be biased
by the skewness of the input data.
    Table 15.3 and Figure 15.4 describe output from analyses
of the residential, business and total calls matrices (using a
varimax rotation of all factors with eigenvalues greater than
1.0). Again the same basic structures are reproduced. Toronto,
Montreal, Ottawa, London and Kitchener are strong nodes, each
dominating their surrounding regions, and the Niagara penin-
sular cities are a closely interconnected subsystem.
    The factor analysis solutions for the residential and business
originated messages are almost identical. The business network
is slightly more far-flung--linking Windsor and Montreal, for
instance, to Toronto--and includes a very weak ninth component,

208

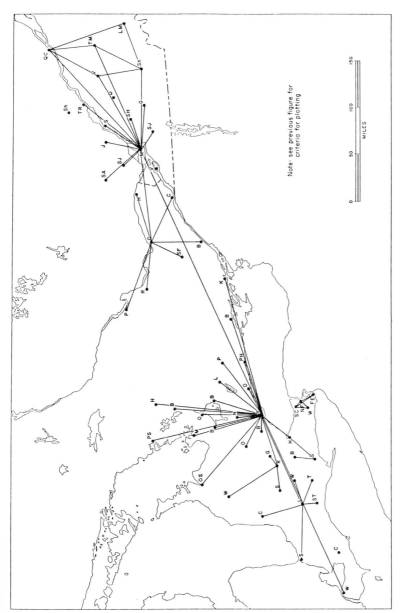

Note: see previous figure for criteria for plotting

MILES

0   50   100   150

Figure 15.5   Factor analysis: business messages

TABLE 15.3 FACTOR ANALYSIS RESULTS

Nodes Flow Matrix	Eigenvalues (Per Cent of Total)							
	Toronto	Montreal	Ottawa	London	Niagara	Kitchener	Hamilton	Eastern Townships	Barrie
Residential	27.3	22.5	7.8	7.3	4.5	4.3	3.6	2.6	–
Business	28.0	22.2	8.3	8.3	4.9	4.5	2.7	3.5	1.9
Total	28.3	22.4	8.2	7.8	4.7	4.5	3.1	3.2	–

NOTES: Eigenvalues are derived from interpretation of factor analyses of the 61 x 61 correlation matrices obtained by comparing columns of the flow matrices. Eigenvalues are the results of rotation of all the original factors which had eigenvalues greater than 1.0. The nodes are identified from the factor scores. The Niagara node includes both St. Catharines and Welland, and the Eastern Townships node, both Sherbrooke and Quebec City.

oriented to Barrie-Peterborough, which does not show on the map. Again there is a clear separation of the Montreal Group and the Toronto Group, with Ottawa clearly belonging to the former.

Details of the analysis show the ambiguities in the structure: St. Catharines is linked to both Hamilton and Toronto, Brantford to Toronto, Kitchener and Hamilton. The Eastern Townships cities generate a separate subsystem, but are also tied to Montreal.

Direct and Indirect Contact

The techniques used in the sections above to generalize the flow matrix are based on the direct (first-order) contact between two places, place i and place j. It can be argued, however, that indirect flows are also important: contacts can take place between i and j by way of k (second order) or by way of k, l, and m (higher order). In Ontario, for instance, a large amount of contact between cities takes place through Toronto.

These indirect linkages can be very important in planning physical channels of communication. The Toronto-Montreal link is the channel for practically all the communication between the cities of southern Ontario and Quebec. They can also be important in trying to predict direct flows (Britton [1970] discusses this problem in some detail),and in correlating different kinds of flow matrices as in diffusion models (Hudson 1969). Interpretations of indirect contact vary, however, according to the characteristics of the item which is moving. Studies of commodity flows raised to the second or third order contact would identify links between the primary producer (the cattle rancher) and the consumer through the processor. Studies of indirect information flows may also identify filters which could distort the message: Quebec communicates with the Prairies via Ontario.

The concern here is to measure and evaluate indirect contacts. The simplest approach is to generalize the flow matrix into a binary adjacency matrix where a link equals 1 and a nonlink equals 0. Nystuen and Dacey (1961) use an asymmetrical matrix defined by the largest outflow from each node. This has the advantage of tying every city into the system and as described in an earlier section, seems to identify a hierarchic structure. An alternative is the use of the 10 or 20 largest flows in a system. However, the binary representation eliminates much of the information in the original flow matrix by neglecting the scale of the origin and destination.

A similar problem exists when the mean first passage time is used (Beshers and Laumann 1967, Brown and Horton 1970). The use of a transition matrix eliminates the effect of size of origin and when the full set of indirect contacts are calculated the rows of the matrix are virtually identical.

A more satisfactory solution treats the whole flow matrix $(\bar{F})$. $\bar{T} = (K\bar{F}) + (\overline{KF}) + K(F)^3$ ...describes all possible direct and indirect contacts and the contacts made at various orders can be examined in detail. It is anticipated that second order flows such as London to Peterborough via Toronto will be significant because of the strength of Toronto; the third order flows--London to Toronto to Montreal to Sherbrooke--will be important because of the single link between southern Ontario and Quebec cities.

The selection of an appropriate weight (K) is difficult. If $K = 1.0$ then $(K\bar{F})^2$ has elements of the order of $(f_{ij})^2$ x 10 and $(K\bar{F})^3$ produces $((f_{ij})^2 \times 10)^2 = f_{ij}^4 \times 10^2$. If $K = 1/\max\Sigma_i f_{ij}$ (Nystuen and Dacey 1961) the order of magnitude of higher order contacts is similar to that of the original flow matrix, but also it means that the infinite series $\bar{T} = (\bar{I} - K\bar{F})^{-1} - \bar{I}$ exists.

The indirect flow matrices (Table 15.4) resemble the original matrix, but the effect of relative location is emphasized. Brampton, which is closely linked to Toronto, becomes proportionately better linked to all other places. Windsor, peripheral to begin with, appears to be even further isolated. When the full matrix of indirect contact is studied the most notable differences are the increased flows between Ontario and Quebec centres by means of the Toronto-Montreal link. The indirect contact matrix is, of course, senstive to the value of k. The very small value used in this study leaves the original flow matrix $\bar{F}$ as a a very influential component of $\sum_{i=1}^{\infty} (K\bar{F})^i$.

Measures of Scale and Accessibility
From the measures already established and those derived in the previous sections it is possible to estimate centrality in a variety of ways. Table 15.5 compares the places in the system. Notable features are the high degree of similarity among total inflows, the mean first passage time, and indirect contact; and the relation of these measures to the spatial structure of the province. Peripheral places, far from the major centres of population, do not generate or attract many long distance calls. Locations which are near to Toronto or Montreal have a high ratio of long

TABLE 15.4 INDIRECT CONTACTS

Place	1	2	3	4	5
1	0	6857	2247	1510	2007
2	6412	0	6	44	102
3	264	6	0	5	4
4	1480	48	4	0	17
5	1905	86	1	21	0

Total Messages $(\bar{F})$
$(X10^6)$

	1	2	3	4	5
1	303.3	11.0	2.5	7.6	5.4
2	11.0	4.2	1.8	9.8	12.4
3	2.5	1.8	0.4	0.5	0.5
4	7.6	9.8	0.5	4.0	2.9
5	5.4	12.5	0.5	2.9	4.2

NOTE: Each matrix is a 5 x 5 excerpt from the upper left hand corner of the full 61 x 61 matrix. (For full list of cities see Table 15.1)

$(\bar{F})^2$

	1	2	3	4	5
1	.220	.109	.007	.031	.034
2	.084	.121	.005	.029	.036
3	.113	.013	.001	.004	.005
4	.005	.001	.000	.000	.000
5	.028	.004	.000	.001	.001

$$\sum_{i=1}^{\infty} (\overline{KF})^i$$

distance calls per phone and appear to be highly connected to the rest of the system. Perhaps the most significant feature emerging from the telephone data is the isolation of eastern Ontario--apparently central, but in fact, too far from either Montreal or Toronto to be closely tied to these important linking nodes.

TABLE 15.5 MEASURES OF CENTRALITY
(30 largest places only)

City	Total Phones (000's)	Rank	In Messages	Rank	Out Messages	Rank	Average Mean First Passage Time	Rank	Indirect Contact	Rank
Montreal	1288	1	44798	2	48452	2	7.44	2	0.967	2
Toronto	1205	2	62990	1	67404	1	5.28	1	1.341	1
Ottawa	293	3	13960	4	13614	4	24.64	4	0.361	4
Hamilton	210	4	19455	3	19839	3	18.22	3	0.544	3
Quebec	208	5	7416	10	8237	8	45.76	10	0.198	10
London	121	6	12736	5	12341	6	26.62	5	0.293	7
Windsor	117	7	4822	14	4634	16	71.57	15	0.121	15
Kitchener	108	8	12014	6	12465	5	28.82	6	0.296	6
Sherbrooke	72	9	4802	16	5141	14	70.56	14	0.118	17
Oshawa	63	10	7985	9	6872	10	42.97	8	0.258	8
St. Catharines	60	11	8112	8	7842	9	45.50	9	0.190	11
Kingston	50	12	3669	25	3583	24	93.70	27	0.088	26
Belleville	48	13	3519	27	3403	27	93.67	26	0.088	26
Trois Rivières	43	14	4206	21	3746	22	78.25	18	0.096	23
Brampton	41	15	9616	7	9194	7	36.35	7	0.311	5
Chatham	41	16	3369	28	3530	25	99.19	28	0.074	28
Peterborough	40	17	3822	24	3512	26	82.62	20	0.100	21
St. Jérôme	39	18	5878	12	5560	12	59.76	12	0.165	12
Brantford	38	19	4817	15	5195	13	73.76	16	0.118	18
Sarnia	36	20	2817	29	2461	30	121.65	29	0.067	29
Guelph	36	21	5572	13	5998	11	62.55	13	0.138	13
Barrie	34	22	4469	17	4392	18	74.23	17	0.119	16
Joliette	33	23	3915	23	3324	28	89.29	24	0.109	20
Welland	32	24	4167	22	4356	19	87.90	23	0.093	24
Granby	31	25	3657	26	3668	23	93.06	25	0.091	25
Cornwall	30	26	2602	30	2778	29	134.78	30	0.062	30
St. Jean	30	27	4234	20	3891	20	82.87	21	0.117	19
Niagara Falls	30	28	4320	19	4575	17	84.37	22	0.097	22
Valleyfield	27	29	4360	18	3771	21	82.00	19	0.129	14
Newmarket	26	30	6004	11	4839	15	57.99	11	0.202	9

In summary the analysis of telephone contacts reveals that:

1. Toronto and Montreal completely dominate the system. Each city serves a large hinterland, and virtually all contact between the hinterlands takes place through the two places.

2. Ottawa is firmly fixed within the Montreal hinterland; Kingston is linked to Toronto.

3. The relative accessibility of any location to the system as a whole is determined by its distance to either one of the two major nodes. Peripheral places are found on the outskirts of the system (Quebec, Windsor), and also at the geographical centre of the system, midway between the two poles (Kingston, Belleville).

These generalizations have been derived from the intensive analysis of one mode of interaction. Confirmation is now sought from studies of interaction by other modes.

AIRLINE PASSENGERS

The second data set describes the annual origin-destination patterns of airline passengers among Department of Transport Airports in Canada. Within Ontario and Quebec there are 33 such airports, but only eight of these fall within the study area (Table 15.6).

The data matrix is symmetric and clearly shows the institutional pecularities of air travel--the effect of airport location, and the transport gap. Montreal dominates the system because of its international connections; Niagara Falls--too close to Toronto--sends most passengers to Montreal. Airline passenger data is not particularly suitable for puzzling out an urban system in Central Canada (Pearson [1969] discusses the idiosyncracies of air travel).

The strength of the links between Toronto and Montreal, two fundamentally similar places, stands out, but patterns of hinterlands are altered by the substitution of alternative travel nodes. Ottawa's major link is with Toronto; Niagara Falls' is with Montreal. Places which are closely connected by phone are peripheral by plane. The roles of Kitchener, London and Windsor are

TABLE 15.6 AIR PASSENGER ORIGIN - DESTINATION
(Passenger trips per year)

Airport	1	2	3	4	5	6	7	8
1. London	---	9505	0	5830	500	8220	0	280
2. Montreal	10055	---	870	18550	39770	290385	290	22705
3. Niagara Falls	0	1110	---	0	15	10	0	0
4. Ottawa	6060	18425	0	---	7150	101285	110	4570
5. Quebec	525	40365	10	7300	---	12820	10	535
6. Toronto	8480	289940	5	101440	12705	---	330	35885
7. Trois Rivières	0	230	0	90	60	230	---	10
8. Windsor	280	21790	0	4490	430	36295	0	---

reversed. Kitchener has no airport of its own, London has less
than half as many passengers as Windsor.

Conclusions

It becomes apparent that our concepts of relationships among
cities in an urban system are based on a very selective sample
of interaction patterns--primarily those in the tertiary economic
sector as represented by business messages. If one were to
examine other kinds of economic linkages--for instance primary
and secondary industrial flows as indicated by truck, rail, and
shipping flows, quite different patterns would emerge. Similarly
air passenger movements give a distorted picture of an urban
system of this size.

In an attempt to compare the flow patterns of differing modes
and commodities (rail, truck, bus, car), the 20 dyads of a 5 x 5
origin-destination matrix were compared. The nodes selected
were Toronto, Ottawa, London, Windsor, and Niagara, and all
stations within 50 miles of these places. The actual measures
of flows selected are shown in Table 15.7.

The resulting correlation matrix (Table 15.8) emphasizes
the points made above. Telephone calls, as well as trucking
movements and automobile flows are most sensitive to distance;
airline movements (at least within this system) correlate positively with distance. The same set of variables--phone calls,

TABLE 15.7   MEASURES OF DYADIC INTERACTION

No.	Code	Measure	Source of Data
1.	TOTTEL	Sum of measures 2 and 3	see text
2.	BUS TEL	Business Originated Telephone Calls	see text
3.	RES TEL	Residence Originated Telephone Calls	see text
4.	RAIL	Carloads/Year x 0.01	see Simmons 1970b
5.	TRUCK	Trucks per day	see Simmons 1970b
6.	AIR PASS	Passenger, 1967	see text
7.	DIST	Airline Distance	see text
8.	BUS/W	Busses/Week	Economic Atlas File
9.	TR/W	Passenger Trains/Week	Economic Atlas File
10.	AUTO	Cars/Day	Economic Atlas File
11.	TF	Trucking Firms licenced to operate between cities	Economic Atlas File

TABLE 15.8   CORRELATION MATRIX FOR TWENTY DYADS

	1	2	3	4	5	6	7	8	9	10	11
1.	–										
2.	0.093	–									
3.	0.096	0.985	–								
4.	0.475	0.470	0.454	–							
5.	0.942	0.931	0.946	0.673	–						
6.	0.153	0.170	0.097	0.193	0.017	–					
7.	-0.579	-0.568	-0.596	-0.373	-0.623	0.101	–				
8.	0.523	0.481	0.561	0.467	0.642	0.057	-0.370	–			
9.	0.634	0.640	0.600	0.331	0.559	0.027	-0.417	-0.073	–		
10.	0.931	0.929	0.920	0.714	0.977	0.075	-0.561	0.522	0.628	–	
11.	0.769	0.739	0.794	0.354	0.761	0.017	-0.639	0.673	0.102	0.690	–

217

automobile movements, trucking flows are closely related to each other. A significant complementarity may be indicated by the lack of association of bus service and rail service.

The one universal characteristic of the flow matrices is the high degree of integration of the southern Ontario urban system, in particular that area west of and including Kingston. The patterns of linkage differ, as various models of urban systems would suggest. Business-originated telephone calls describe hierarchic structure. Commodity flows describe a more widespread intercity exchange.

References

BERRY, J. L. 1966. Essays on Commodity Flows and the Spatial Structure of the Indian Economy. Department of Geography Research Paper No. 111. Chicago: University of Chicago.

BESHERS, J. M. and E. O. LAUMANN. 1967. Social distance: a network approach. American Sociological Review 32:255-36.

BRITTON, J. N. H. 1970. The interaction model and relative location variables. Private manuscript. Toronto.

BROWN, L. A. 1970. On the use of Markov chains in movement research. Economic Geography 46:393-403.

BROWN, L. A. and F. E. HORTON. 1970. Functional distance: A note on an operational approach. Geographical Analysis 2:76-83.

CASETTI, E. 1966. Optimal location of steel mills serving the Quebec and southern Ontario steel market. Canadian Geographer 10:27-39.

COLLINS, L. 1970. Markov chains and industrial migration: forecasting aspects of industrial activity in Ontario. Unpublished Ph.D. dissertation. Department of Geography, University of Toronto.

CURRY, L. 1969. Gravity flows and location: a discussion. Reading, England. Mimeographed.

DEAN, W. G. and G. J. MATTHEWS. 1969. The Economic Atlas of Ontario. Toronto: University of Toronto Press, Plates 84-96 "Transportation Facilities."

GARRISON, W. L. 1960. The connectivity of the interstate highway system. Papers and Proceedings of the Regional Science Association 6:121-38.

GARRISON, W. L. and D. F. MARBLE. 1965. A Prologemenon to the Forecasting of Transportation Development. Evanston, Ill.: Northwestern University, Transportation Center.

GREER-WOOTEN, B. 1968. The spatial structure of the urban field. Unpublished Ph.D. dissertation, Department of Geography, McGill University.

HUDSON, J. C. 1969. Diffusion in a central place system. Geographical Analysis 1:45-58.

MACKAY, J. R. 1958. The interactance hypothesis and boundaries in Canada: a preliminary study. Canadian Geographer 2:1-8.

NYSTUEN, J. D. and M. F. DACEY. 1961. A graph theory interpretation of nodal regions. Papers and Proceedings of the Regional Science Association 7:29-42.

OLSSON, G. 1965. Distance and Human Interaction: Review and Bibliography. Philadelphia: Regional Science Research Institute.

PEARSON, P. M. L. 1969. The planning and evaluation of intercity travel systems. Unpublished Ph.D. dissertation, Department of Geography, University of Waterloo.

RATCLIFFE, D. 1969. Passenger transportation and communication in the study area. Ottawa: Canadian Transportation Commission.

RIDDELL, J. 1965. Toward an understanding of the friction of distance: An analysis of long distance telephone traffic in Ontario. Unpublished M.A. thesis. Department of Geography, University of Toronto.

RUSSETT, B. M. 1967. International Regions and the International System. Chicago: Rand-McNally.

SIMMONS, J. W. 1968. Flǒws in an urban area: A synthesis. Research Paper No. 6, Centre for Urban and Community Studies, University of Toronto.

--------. 1970a. Interprovincial interaction patterns. Research Paper No. 24, Centre for Urban and Community Studies, University of Toronto.

-------- 1970b. Patterns of interaction within Ontario and Quebec. Research Paper No. 41, Centre for Urban and Community Studies, University of Toronto.

SMITH, R. H. T. 1970. Concepts and methods in commodity flow analysis. Economic Geography 46(Supplement):404-16.

TORNQUIST, G. 1968. Flows of information and the location of economic activities. Geografiska Annaler 50: Ser.B:99-107.

V

Implications of Urban System Growth in Rural Areas

16

Editors' comments

The trends and relationships in the growth of the urban system
of Ontario and Quebec documented in previous chapters hold wide
ramifications for urban and rural environments generally. Among
these are such obvious issues as the apparent increase in urban
and regional disparities resulting from the continued concentration of economic and social growth; the limited impact of past and
present policies in effectuating change in the basic pattern of urban growth; and the influence of increased metropolitanization on
the quality of urban life, on the environment in aesthetic terms,
on pollution levels, on agricultural production, on rural and
recreational landscapes. Two aspects of this complex array of
impacts are isolated from our broad environmental interest for
discussion in this section: first the implications of urbanization
and technological change for agricultural production; and second
the drastic changes in life styles of urban residents and their
expression in a new city form described as the urban field.

In the first paper, McDonald summarizes some of the recent
developments in Ontario agriculture and relates them to government regulatory and planning policies, urban growth and technological change. During the fifteen year study period, many
structural changes have taken place--i.e., changes in typical
farm sizes and total numbers of farms. In addition, agricultural
production has changed markedly in terms of magnitude, composition and spatial distribution. Finally, recent trends in farm

economies and in the role of agriculture generally in an urbanizing environment, are briefly described.

In the second paper, Hodge describes the changing images we have and have had of our cities. One of these images, previously suggested in the first section of this volume, is the urban field. This concept is designed to reflect the new life space which urban residents occupy. It is the area which urban dwellers utilize for such activities as daily outings or even less frequent weekend recreational trips. It is larger than the traditional metropolitan area, less obvious in its physical expression, but more accurate in describing the reality of the city as expressed through the broadening life style of its residents. Hodge describes the rationale of the concept, the factors which have generated this expanded life space, and the critical policy issues that this phenomenon presents in planning future cities.

There are of course many other implications which could not for lack of space be treated here. Some of these, in the Ontario and Quebec context, are presently being investigated in parallel studies and will be reported on in other publications.

17

Ontario agriculture in an urbanizing economy 1951-1966

G. T. McDonald

Changes in the nature of rural Ontario since 1951 may be summarized as "urbanization." However, not all the impetus derives from the urban centres; some of it originates within the agricultural sector as it takes its place in a rapidly expanding economy. These propositions are discussed with respect to the kinds of forces operating, structural and production responses, and the status of farm incomes.

Forces for Change in Agriculture

Over the period 1951-1966 Ontario has experienced large scale economic change. The total population of the province has increased by 51 per cent to seven million while the population living on farms decreased by 34 per cent to one-half million or from 15 per cent of the total population to 7.2 per cent. As a result of increasing labour productivity, higher incomes have favoured increasing consumption of manufactured goods and services. Only a small proportion of the increased personal income has been spent on food and other agricultural goods, and most of this increase has been in the demand for more 'luxury' foods and those with a higher level of processing and packaging. These changes in tastes have had a direct implication for agriculture and the overall effect has been to reduce even further the price elasticity of demand for products at the farm gate (Campbell 1966). Per capita incomes have risen from $1055 to $2200 over the period but this increase was by no means uniform over the region (Chernick 1966).

To maintain competitive incomes agriculture has had large increases in labour productivity, even greater than most other sectors. Agriculture has become less and less a way of life and more and more a business as more inputs are purchased from other sectors (seeds, fertilizers, buildings) rather than being produced on the farm, more outputs are produced for sale and less for use on the farm, and less processing occurs on the farm (e.g., dairy products) and more in the industrial sector. To a large extent the difference between rural and urban living is disappearing (Stewart 1958, Tremblay 1966).

Despite the changes in the farm structure, there are still many individual producers in a competitive environment. Improvements in farm technology have allowed rapid increases in production and in fact the continued adoption of these technologies has been necessary to ensure an acceptable standard of living for farmers. These steadily changing methods of production have favoured different regions; small stony plots may have been economic when tilled by a pair of horses, but the comparative advantage has moved in favour of large plots suitable for large machines.

The expansion of urban areas has consumed considerable amounts of agricultural land (Van der Linde 1969). The effect of urban growth and increased incomes on farm land does not stop merely with the loss of land for city expansion, but the

TABLE 17.1 PROJECTED LOSSES OF FARM LAND 1966 - 1981

	(acres in thousands)
Urban land	155
Urban oriented use	174
Highways, communications	38
Recreation	48
Forestry	457
TOTAL	872

SOURCE: Biggs (1969).

speculative mentality enlarges the area which comes under stress (Crerar 1962). The demand for recreation land similarly increases land prices as hobby farms, cottages and other facilities compete for land and in so doing place pressure on the prices of remaining farm land which are increasing at the rate of approximately 6 per cent per annum. These processes place many farms of the region in a position where their land investment is very substantial and has difficulty earning a satisfactory rate of return in agricultural use. In addition, the transfer of land into more economically sized holdings is hampered by the large capital costs involved.

At the other extreme, land which was initially and mistakenly put into agricultural use continues to revert to less intensive uses. See Table 17.1. This has influenced largely the marginal areas of the province and in fact a slight increase in the areas of improved land was recorded in southwestern Ontario.

During the 1950's and 1960's, the provincial and federal governments have assumed greater responsibility for the welfare of agriculture:

a) Trade in agricultural products has increasing government intervention at different levels such as quality control, product quotas, marketing boards' import and export policies including subsidies and excises (Perkin 1962).

224

b) The prices and availability of <u>inputs</u> to agriculture have been affected through such measures as the tax relief on a number of goods, transport subsidy to gasoline, seed certification, and particularly through the increased role played by government research into agricultural problems.

c) Regional planning carried out on a federal provincial level by organizations such as Agricultural Rehabilitation and Development Agency (A. R. D. A.) have attempted to provide some of the machinery (e.g., extension, education, land purchases, rented land) to make regional development more possible when combined with considerable financial support (Brewis 1969).

d) <u>Land Use Planning</u> on a more local level such as in the Toronto/Hamilton, Ottawa and the Niagara regions has attempted to direct and control the effects of urban growth on agricultural land. Reports such as the Design for Development (Ontario Department of Treasury 1971) if implemented will have a substantial effect.

e) <u>Transportation.</u> The most important single policy is known as the Freight Equalization Policy which originated during World War II to stabilize grain prices both for prairie producers and livestock operators in eastern Canada and British Columbia. While the terms of reference have changed considerably over time (Kerr 1966) the result has been to alter the regional competitive position of both groups of farmers. In addition, large scale highway building projects, government financed, have made all areas more accessible allowing farmers greater access to larger urban areas. The decline of the small service centre has been thus accelerated.

Structural Changes

Between 1951 and 1966, the total number of farms has declined from 149,000 to 109,000 (Russwurm 1951); MacDougall 1970; Putnam 1962). Several studies describe significant re-organization of the farm structure, shown in Tables 17.2 and 17.3. These might be summarized in the following way:

TABLE 17.2 FARMS CLASSIFIED BY GROSS REVENUE
1951 AND 1966 FOR REGIONAL AGGREGATIONS

Size in $	$15,000		10,000-14,999		7,500-9,999		5,000-7,499		3,750-4,999		2,500-3,749		1,200-2,499	
Ontario	1951	1966	1951	1966	1951	1966	1951	1966	1951	1966	1951	1966	1951	1966
Southwestern	2422	9540	2542	4595	9061	2201	4900	2301	6483	2525	7148	2948	2711	2742
Western	240	2332	489	2032	3634	4082	2917	1424	4195	1637	4464	1953	1666	1644
Niagara	266	1293	335	860	1717	1500	1113	544	1567	745	2204	1104	930	1322
South central	501	2628	766	1928	5088	4239	3662	1850	5516	2422	7249	3687	3126	3566
Northern	31	168	42	227	456	651	535	336	1118	52	2626	1064	1464	1528
Eastern	160	1025	296	1214	2428	3604	2499	1715	4750	2170	7506	2958	2889	2866

SOURCE: D.B.S. Census of Canada.

TABLE 17.3 NUMBER OF FARMS BY ACREAGE CLASS 1951 - 1966

	1951		1966	
Acreage	Number	Per Cent	Number	Per Cent
1-4	2704	1.8	3192	2.9
5-10	6332	4.2	3770	3.4
11-50	19702	13.1	13435	12.2
51-100	47642	31.8	28615	26.1
101-200	49757	33.2	35281	32.1
201-299	11716	7.8	11788	10.7
300-479	9490	6.3	10003	9.1
480-639	1579	1.1	2204	2.0
640+	998	0.7	1599	1.5

SOURCE: D.B.S. Census of Canada.

226

a) Related to economic size, or farm revenue:

    i) There is an increasing number of large farms.

    ii) The number of small farms has remained constant or increased.

    iii) The major declines have occurred in the medium size classes.

    iv) Significant regional trends are evident in these changes over the province, with the large farms becoming increasingly concentrated in the southwest. Retarded rates of change are evident in eastern and south-central Ontario.

If farms are to be viable full-time enterprises, scale increases are necessary. The persistence of small farms on the other hand may be explained by the ability of farmers to earn additional (urban) income and for urban dwellers to afford hobby farms.

b) A corollary of the reduced number of farms is an increase in average acreage from 139 to 162 from 1951 to 1966. The major reduction in farm numbers has been for farms in the range of 50-200 acres, with increases in the larger and very small farms. Facilitating these changes in the land/labour ratio in Ontario agriculture have been large increases in the use of machinery. Investment in machines of all types has increased threefold, particularly milking, combine and traction equipment (Campbell and Hill 1970). The latter innovations have allowed the release of the pastures consumed by some 190,000 horses for other uses. Apart from reducing the labour input per acre, an expansion of 900 per cent (Campbell and Hill 1970) in the use of fertilizers and the use of higher quality and hybrid seed varieties have increased output per acre.

Production Responses to Changing Conditions

Between 1951 and 1966 the total value of production has increased by 62 per cent, a change that can be apportioned into the 60 per cent increase in physical volume and 2 per cent due to price changes (D.B.S. catalogue 62-003). As shown in Table 17.4, only two subregions have increased at a rate faster than the province as a whole, southwestern and western Ontario. These two subregions together account for 71 per cent of the total

227

increase and by 1966 produced 64 per cent of the total output
(on only 50 per cent of the improved farmland).

The components of this change can be seen in Table 17.4
and Figure 17.1.

i) Virtually all of the increased production of grain and
fodder crops has occurred in the southwest and western
regions, the most dynamic crop being grain and fodder
corn, its acreage increasing from 623,000 to 1,160,000
and earnings from $40 to $107 million over the period.
Other regions have been static or declining in the sales

of these crops due to the increased competition from
suppliers in the U.S., prairies and southern Ontario.
Alternatively, these crops are grown for feed on the
farm and in total use 90 per cent of the province's
improved land. Determination of whether these crops
will be sold or consumed on the farm depends on relationships with the livestock industry and the joint cost
savings involved.

ii) The production of other field crops, largely tobacco,
sugar beets and potatoes, has increased significantly in
all regions except northern Ontario. Again southern
Ontario is predominant in this industry, particularly
for tobacco.

iii) Sales of fruit and vegetables have not grown rapidly and
one of the major producing areas, the Niagara Peninsula
(especially Lincoln county), actually recorded an absolute decrease, leading to a shift towards the south and
west and to Georgian Bay. The increasing importance
of contract canning for vegetables and the expansion of
urban areas on the Niagara Peninsula have influenced
this trend (Krueger 1959).

iv) Large increases in per capita consumption of poultry
meat, the feed price equalization policy and competitive
prices, made possible by increasingly large scale and
efficient production has made this one of the rapid growth
industries. Consistent expansion has been recorded
across the province except for northern Ontario.

v) The production of livestock is the most important of the
industry categories and it is locationally dependent on

TABLE 17.4 SHIFT RATIOS* AND TOTAL PERCENTAGE CHANGE OF AGRICULTURAL
PRODUCTION BY INDUSTRY AND REGION , ONTARIO 1951 - 1966

Industry	South-western	Western	Niagara Peninsula	Region South Central	Eastern	Northern	Total Per Cent Change
Grain and fodder	1.69	0.44	0.06	0.08	-0.24	-0.53	82.54
Other field crops	0.93	2.13	2.01	1.39	0.94	0.20	106.96
Fruit and vegetables	-4.75	0.54	-1.37	1.08	-0.62	-0.05	32.24
Poultry and eggs	1.11	1.01	1.53	0.68	1.08	-0.12	118.11
Livestock	1.57	1.24	1.08	0.62	0.00	0.11	81.48
Dairy products	1.12	1.65	1.16	0.68	0.88	0.58	66.88
Greenhouse and nursery	1.60	0.67	0.80	0.83	1.13	0.16	388.04
Total Production	1.38	1.16	0.77	0.71	0.42	0.16	86.60

✱ * per cent change in region/per cent change in industry

SOURCE: D.B.S. Census of Canada

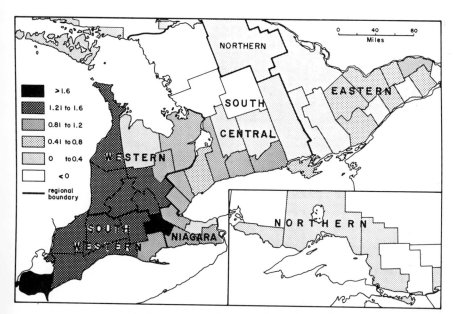

Figure 17.1   Shift ratios* of agricultural production,
Ontario 1951-1956
* per cent change in country/per cent change in province

229

its major input--feed. Accompanying the shift in grain
and forage production a major shift has occurred in livestock production to the southern and western regions and
the counties of Bruce, Huron, Kent, Middlesex, Perth,
Waterloo and Wellington have formed a region of livestock concentration. It is important to note that only
25 per cent of all livestock go directly to the consumer,
17 per cent is returned to agriculture, 9 per cent for
export and 50 per cent to the industrial sector (largely
packing). (Josling and Trant 1966). The location of
packing plants is reinforcing this regional concentration
which now supplies only 75 per cent of its own feed requirements.

vi) The dairy industry is more forage oriented than other
     livestock types and as far as fluid milk is concerned is
     highly market oriented. This industry is less region-
     ally concentrated than the others and the changes are
     more regionally dispersed. Expanding fluid milk sheds
     are partially responsible for the most rapid increases
     in the south and west.

vii) Production of very specialized greenhouse and nursery
     crops has expanded most rapidly of all industries and
     their demand for low quantity but high quality land, with
     the large inputs of capital, and market orientation has
     increased the regional concentration around the western
     shore of Lake Ontario.

Farm Incomes

Only large increases in output by a much reduced farm labour
force has enabled aggregate net income per farm to grow faster
than family living costs, thus providing an increase in real income. This has been very modest by comparison with real income changes in other sectors, the major factor mitigating
against a greater increase was the farmer's inability to pass
on the 50 per cent increase in the costs of production in the
form of higher prices (see Table 17.5). Not only has real income growth been retarded, but seasonal fluctuations in production and marketing conditions make incomes variable.

That serious income problems exist in agriculture can be
seen by comparing Tables 17.2 and 17.6. The estimated revenue levels for a reasonable net farm income of approximately

TABLE 17.5 NET FARM INCOME AND INDICES OF COSTS
AND PRICES IN ONTARIO AGRICULTURE 1951 - 1966

	1951	1954	1958	1962	1966
Total Net Income ($000,000)	448	293	356	337	414
Total net income	100	65	80	75	92
Number of operators	100	105	72	63	52
Net income per farm	100	62	111	120	181
Family living costs	100	103	105	116	127
Farm input costs	100	102	111	126	150
Farm price index	100	80	85	86	102

SOURCE: Lane (1967) p.2 .

TABLE 17.6 MINIMUM FARM REVENUE AND CAPITAL REQUIRED
FOR RETURN TO LABOUR AND MANAGEMENT OF $5,500 AND
7 PER CENT TO CAPITAL. (Family income approximately $6,800)

Type	Labour (Men)	Revenue ($000)	Capital ($000)
Cash grain	1	30	136
Beef (cow-calf)	1	26	92
Beef (feedlot)	1	31	100
Swine	1	37	78
Dairy	2	41	126
Laying hens	2	79	90

SOURCE: Biggs (1969) p.27.

$7000 are exceeded by less than 16 per cent of farms. This
highlights the fact that the distribution of income within agriculture is far from uniform. The largest 4 per cent of farms earn
34 per cent of gross income, while 75 per cent is earned by only

34 per cent of farms. Neither is this inequality distributed
evenly across the province. As indicated in Table 17.2, rural
poverty is much more prevalent in eastern and northern Ontario.
The physical difficulties of increasing output per acre in these
regions is only partially responsible.

Increasing employment in non-farm occupations is providing
additional income for farmers caught in this dilemma. The
availability of these opportunities is restricted to areas where
growing urban centres exist and to people with appropriate skills.
Particularly in the marginal areas, agencies such as A.R.D.A.,
Department of Manpower and Immigration and Economic Development have assisted on the one hand by attracting employers and
by providing job training, and on the other by financially and
technically assisting in the improvement of farm viability.

Conclusion

Since 1951 an estimated 450,000 farm people have either moved
to urban areas or become totally dependent on them for employment. This decline in the rural population together with increased mobility has resulted in the decline of the small village.
On the other hand, the increased orientation of agriculture
along business lines and its increasing ties with the cities for
inputs, marketing, goods, services and leisure activities have
increased the integration of farming within the urban environment. These changes have not been without side effects and
while agriculture is efficient and can meet most of the food
requirements of the province, there is need for continued concern with satisfactory farm prices and incomes and control of
the expansion of urban areas and their requirements for recreation space.

References

BIGGS, E. 1969. The Challenge of Abundance. Report of the Special Committee on
    Farm Income in Ontario. Toronto.

BREWIS, T. N. 1969. Regional Economic Policies in Canada. Toronto: MacMillan
    Co. of Canada.

CAMPBELL, A. and F. HILL. 1970. Changes in Ontario Agriculture. Ontario Department of Agriculture and Food. Toronto. Mimeographed.

CAMPBELL, D. R. 1966.* Overcoming the Canadian farm problem: theory and practice. Canadian Journal of Agricultural Economics 14:57-67.

CANADA DEPARTMENT OF REGIONAL ECONOMIC EXPANSION. 1970. Federal-Provincial Rural Development Agreement 1970-75. Ottawa.

CANADA DOMINION BUREAU OF STATISTICS. Index Numbers of Farm Prices of Agricultural Products, Monthly Catalogue 62-003.

CHERNIK, S. E. 1966. Interregional Disparities in Income. Economic Council of Canada, Staff Study 14. Ottawa.

CRERAR, A. D. 1962. The loss of farmland in the growth of the metropolitan regions of Canada. Resources for Tomorrow. Supplementary volume. Ottawa: Queen's Printer, pp. 181-95.

JOSLING, J. T. and G. I. TRANT. 1966. Interdependence Among Agriculture and Other Sectors. Agricultural Economic Research Council, Publication 2. Ottawa.

KERR, T. C. 1966. An Economic Analysis of the Feed Freight Assistance Policy. Agricultural Economic Research Council, Publication 7. Ottawa.

KRUEGER, R. 1959. Changing land use patterns in the Niagara Fruit Belt. Trans Royal Canadian Institute 32:39-140.

LANE, S. H. 1967. Input and output in Ontario agriculture. Regional Conference on Agriculture. Owen Sound, Ont.

MACDOUGALL, E. B. 1970. An analysis of recent changes in the number of farms in the north part of central Ontario. Canadian Geographer 14:125-37.

ONTARIO DEPARTMENT OF TREASURY AND ECONOMICS. 1970. Design for Development: The Toronto Centred Region. Toronto: Queen's Printer.

PERKIN, D. F. 1962. Marketing Milestones in Ontario 1935-1960. Toronto. Ontario Department of Agriculture and Food.

PUTNAM, R. G. 1962. Changes in rural land use patterns on the central Lake Ontario Plain. Canadian Geographer 6:60-68.

RUSSWURM, L. H. 1967. Expanding urbanization and selected agricultural elements: a case study, southwestern Ontario, 1941-1961. Land Economics 43:101-107.

STEWART, C. T. 1958. The urban-rural dichotomy: concepts and uses. American Journal of Sociology 44:152-58.

TREMBLAY, M. A. and W. J. ANDERSON, eds. 1966. Rural Canada in Transition. Agricultural Economic Research Council, Publication 6. Ottawa.

VAN DER LINDE, R. 1969. Urban-rural relationships: a survey of research and an empirical test. Research Paper No. 16, Centre for Urban and Community Studies, University of Toronto.

18

The emergence of the urban field[1]

G. Hodge

The city we have before us now is a different kind of city from those we have known. Most important, it is different from those we tend to associate with our ideals of urban life. Therefore, to try and solve the problems of the city that was is bound to be frustrating. We shall need to be tuned in to the city that is in order to plan new urban development effectively. And this will require us to acquire new modes of thought about the implications of urbanization and accept new concepts of urban form.

This paper is, essentially, a plea for a particularly promising concept of urban form--the Urban Field.[2] This concept may be of considerable help in understanding the issues and the options facing our urban areas today. It is a concept which is consistent with the turbulent, postindustrial society into which Canada is developing in the last one-third of the twentieth century.

In the body of this paper two sets of ideas are presented, first, the general dimensions of the urban field, and then, the issues and options raised by using this concept to view urban problems.

Changing Images of the City[3]
An image of the city which still persists in our ideals is one that corresponds closely to the Medieval City. That is, the image of the self-contained city in terms of places of residence, work, and play; the concentric city in terms of a focus on the

---

[1] An earlier draft of this paper was presented as a Brief to the Federal Task Force on Housing and Urban Development, Ottawa, 1968.

[2] The urban field concept originated with John Friedmann and John Miller of MIT, with whom the writer has been associated. Furthermore, the writer has been conducting research in this realm in the Toronto region for the past two years, including offering a Research Seminar in the Urban Field in the Department of Urban and Regional Planning at the Universtiy of Toronto with partial support from Bell Canada. Evidence and opinions derived from this research comprise the basis of this paper.

[3] An earlier version of the arguments in this section appeared in Hodge (1967).

cathedral, or the marketplace, or the transportation terminal; and the concentrated city in terms of large numbers of people and activities clustered closely to one another. This is the city of walking scale, of social cohesion, of neighbouring in neighbourhoods. Our Stratford's, Nanaimo's, Prince Albert's and Fredericton's are the Canadian counterparts of this kind of city.

Improved means of movement--the electric streecar followed closely by the commuter railroad--allowed the traditional city to expand greatly in both population size and area. Surrounding towns and villages were drawn into the orbit of the central city as places of residence for city workers. This was the metropolitan image: the "mother" city with its heartblood of commercial activities and job opportunities and its "brood" of dormitory towns or suburbs surrounding it and focused on the core by transportation.

Trends in urban development since World War Two have relegated both these traditional images of the city to the background. Two types of fundamental changes have been occurring in contemporary metropolitan areas. First, rapid growth at the sites of our largest cities has continued. The reasons for this are obvious--large cities are attractive for the great range of choice they offer in jobs, housing, and cultural outlets--they are the epitome in a society that is quickly becoming "urban." The large markets thus formed have revised the orientation of productive activities to the metropolis. Second, there have been equally striking shifts taking place within metropolitan areas, most notably the growing attractiveness of the periphery to metropolitan populations and industries. What was once the suburban residential ring around the core city is now attracting a rising share of the manufacturing and wholesale activities in the area. As automobile ownership increases, it has become possible for more and more people to join the exodus to outlying areas in search of space and privacy for residences. The area of the city has increased greatly.

The combination of the shifts in location of jobs and population has broken down the dominant pattern of movement to and from the central city. The journey to work is not just to downtown or to a few industrial areas. The fact that industrial plants are no longer tied to central locations, and indeed, demand larger sites than are normally available there, means a much more dispersed pattern of urban travel. Besides radial movements to the centre there are often equally large flows of workers laterally across the metropolitan area (Meyer 1962). Furthermore, as people have moved outward so have retail stores and personal service establishments; the journey to shop is now directed at regional shopping centres and shopping plazas as well as to downtown. Movements of people to and from outlying recreation areas on weekends, often at a higher volume than daily journey to work movements, are yet another indication of the dispersed locations of activities in which people in the modern metropolis participate.

The image of the present-day metropolis is, thus, much less concentrated, much less contained, and much less concentric than the traditional city or even the metropolis of pre-World War Two days. Almost universal large-scale growth is being accompanied by scattered development over a large area, possibly up to 100 miles from the core if summer residences of city dwellers are included in this portrait.

The changing scale of area over which city development now has a significant impact can be seen in the following figures. The city of Toronto and the older suburban towns, all largely built up 35 years ago encompass much less than 100 square miles. By the mid-1950's when the Municipality of Metropolitan Toronto was formed it was felt necessary to assign administrative jurisdiction to 230 square miles and planning jurisdiction to more than 700 square miles. Today, the Metropolitan Toronto Area Regional Transportation Study feels obliged to cover about 4000 square miles in order to encompass the full range of journeys of people and flows of goods important for this area's development. Summer cottagers in the Muskoka and Kawartha Lakes areas extend the area of interaction for Metropolitan Toronto to about 15,000 square miles.

The Forces for Change
As our metropolitan centres have grown, obviously they have had to grow outwards thereby generating a demand for space on the periphery. This growing demand for space for urban development in outlying areas has been stimulated largely by three forces: (1) incomes of higher levels available to metropolitan residents, (2) more leisure time for city dwellers, and (3) an expanded ability to travel afforded by the automobile.[4]

[4]See Friedmann and Miller (1965). This important paper has provided much of the stimulus for this study.

These are perhaps obvious explanations of the direction of city building in the past two decades, but it does not make them any less important. We must grasp, first, that it is these forces acting in combination --feedback and interchange--that makes the urban field significantly different; and second, that we seem to have crossed a threshold where the combinations of forces is articulating the much larger scale, much more complex, and much more diverse urban environment that the urban field is designed to represent.

Trends in these forces indicate that their strength and direction will continue. A brief examination of these trends will help show how the urban field will develop.

(1) Increasing Incomes . The general expectation is that personal incomes in Canada will rise nearly three times by the end of this century. This would mean average family income would be about $13,000 per year (in today's prices). If present consumption patterns are any guide, we can expect the new wealth to be used to purchase space (in the form, for example, of larger houses on larger lots, or two houses, or a summer cottage); privacy (interior and exterior space); travel (nearby and abroad); education (a demand for more and better facilities of all kinds); culture (both as active participant and as a patron in public ventures to secure cultural assets); and recreation (both private and public use).[5]

(2) Increasing Leisure Time . The prospects for leisure time at the end of this century are for both much more of it and many different forms by which it is organized. One likely dimension is the average 30-hour work week. Another is the 13-week annual vacation. In general, it seems that most people will have two-thirds of their waking hours free and unstructured (excluding meals).

Much of this added time will be articulated in terms of outdoor recreation activities. In the United States authorities expect a tripling of the demand for outdoor recreation by the end of the century (Outdoor Recreation Review Commission 1964). To indicate the scale of activities in recreation in the year 2000, we need only to look at the present levels of activity: there are just under 40 million boaters in the U.S. and already one million here in Ontario: the U.S. has 20 million campers (Ontario is forecasting

[5]The overtones of this are seen in Galbraith (1958) and other such books.

237

an increase of campers in provincial parks of 2.5 to 3.5 times by 1986)[6]; 7 million skiers (up by 600 per cent in the past decade, alone); and 7 million golfers.

This massive participation in outdoor recreation has its counterpart in amateur art activities -- 50 million Americans are currently involved in music, theatrè, painting, sculpture, and sketching. Furthermore, since 1950, the U.S. Government has reported new museums, aquariums, and zoos currently being established at the rate of one every three days. Analogous figures could doubtlessly be drawn together to reflect a similar picture for Canada over the past 15 years. Figures for Canada's Centennial year indicate that more than 500 parks, 500 recreation structures, 415 community centres, 136 libraries, and 64 museums were initiated across the country.

(3) Increasing Mobility. The effects of the combined trends in income and leisure are crystallized and their effects transmitted to land use patterns by our increasing mobility. The automobile has reduced the scale of distance by reducing the time required for most journeys and, thereby, has acted to extend the territory within which urban residents can maintain contact with their jobs and other activities. The motor truck has extended the area for industrial location. And both have made possible the regional shopping centre. Improved communcations by telephone, telex, computer circuitry and so forth continue to hold the city together functionally and allow it to expand spatially or, at least, open up a greater variety of locations for all urban activities (Mumford 1961).

Qualities of Human Life Space in the Urban Field
The above mentioned trends mean a much broader territory over which urban residents will seek the activities necessary for their personal fulfillment. The so-called "fringe" of urban areas must now be considered more than an incidental part of urban developmei Already towns like Newmarket, Brampton, and Oakville are integra parts of Metropolitan Toronto's pattern of life, even if outside its official planning area. And the plan prepared for the metropolitan region of Vancouver sees the necessity of considering towns 50-10(miles away as an important part of the picture there (Lower Mainland Regional Planning Board 1963).

It is not however, the spatial extension of metropolitan areas which is the most important implication of the urban field.

[6]See Ontario Department of Municipal Affairs (1966).

238

Urbanization is accompanied by new patterns of living as well as by physical changes. The urban field, therefore, should also be described in terms of the qualities which will characterize the life space of its residents. Three of the more significant ones are described below.

First, the geographic area within which one's life unfolds will be effectively much wider. That is, the area which includes one's home and its neighbourhood, places of work, schooling, and shopping, places for leisure and recreation, places for socializing with friends and relations will be much larger.[7] Higher speeds, greater versatility in means of movement, and lower per mile costs of transportation and communications will encourage the dispersion of people and activities. A 50 mile radius around one's home would be a common area of interaction for most urban residents.[8] Families and firms will make decisions to locate their premises less and less on economic grounds and more on other considerations. The additional mobility will help compensate for the changes in attitudes toward locations of houses and factories.

Second, with large areas being opened up for possible occupancy there is thus provided a wider choice of living environments. Within a radius of 100 miles from a metropolitan centre, i.e., two hours automobile travel time, which is the likely extent of the most intensive urban activities, families and firms will have available many different physical environments. Metropolitan cores, small towns, suburbs, satellite cities, agricultural lands, forests, shorelines on large water bodies within the approximately 30,000 square miles will be offered as living and working situations.[9] Alternatives for living environments include country and in-town living (perhaps combined in two houses), single-family homes and apartment towers, new towns (like Don Mills, Bramalea, and Ajax), old towns (like Newmarket, Georgetown and Uxbridge), and specialized communities (like Sheridan Park), using only the Toronto example.[10] And all will be relatively accessible to one another.

[7] See, for example, the wide-ranging travel patterns already existing for persons pursuing recreation in Ontario.

[8] A recent study shows that in the Outer Rural Ring, 20-50 miles around Toronto, the travel patterns and habits are much the same as for much closer-in areas.

[9] The impact of "cottaging" in the Toronto urban field is well documented in Hammer (1968).

[10] Another recent study has turned up the increasing prevalence of the large (10-25 acre) rural holding as a place of residence in the Toronto urban field.

Third, it appears that as urban dwellers have more variety in the choices they can make about work places, shopping places, homes, recreation areas, and cultural attractions the more they exercise these choices. Thus, we can expect that as the space around metropolitan centres increases in its effective access to all residents that they will experience a wider community of interests. Individual families, and individuals within families, will have interests in events and activities in a larger number of locations. The urban dweller of the future will tend to participate actively in different communities of interest -- cultural activities, sports, ethnic associations, charities -- scattered throughout the metropolitan region.[11] Moreover, he will likely participate in several at any one time.

The Options and the Issues

It is reasonable to assume that people in urban areas will want to exercise the increased range of choice they will have in living and working environments and in the other activities they can pursue. Similarly, as residents have a greater choice in where they locate there is a corresponding increase in the options open to those concerned about the form which the new urban environment will take. Epithets such as "urban sprawl," "scatteration" or "suburban chaos" will no longer be relevant in motivating people to consider the kind of community they would like to have. The new scale and diversity of urban development forces us to examine the new range of options open to us, the new constraints that might exist, and the new issues we must resolve in order to strive toward a bountiful urban environment. Let us conclude by examining some of the more urgent questions regarding our future cities and the implications of these questions by approaching them in terms of the urban field.

(1) What is the most desirable spatial distribution of population, job opportunities, and leisure time activities? It was once thought that the alternatives ranged only between the concentrated super-city and the grey formlessness of dispersed suburban development. Now we must include the distinct possibility of a constellation of diversified cities and towns (Wurster 1963). It must be remembered that very little of the area of the new metropolitan region will actually come under urban development, even if suburban densities were all that prevailed. Out of about 15,000 square miles that are within

[11]Household activity patterns are very revealing in this regard.

240

two hours of downtown Toronto only one-seventh, or 1,000 square miles, will be needed, at most, to accommodate the region's expected population in the year 2000. We have the possibility of structuring the built-up area in the region in a great variety of ways.

(2) Should there be an upper limit on population size of cities? Metropolitan Toronto expects to have a population of over 3 million people by 1985 and double the present size by the end of the century. Some say this is too many people. But how relevant is the question of the quantity of people when we are living in an urban field situation? Even now, we do not live in a homogeneous big city; we occupy many different kinds of community settings and housing types within the city. While the urban field promises that future populations will be linked to our present metropolitan centres, they may be physically distinct as people seek different environments. Rather, we should be concerned with distribution and quality of our population centres.

(3) Can "satellite cities" help control growth? If we conceive of the satellite city drawing off excess population from our present large cities, the answer is probably no. If we think that satellite cities can be new "self-sufficient" communities, the answer is definitely no. If we conceive of satellite cities connected by "transportation corridors" to facilitiate the movement of workers and shoppers to the metropolis, the answer is, again, no. We can no longer re-create either the self-contained city or the metropolitan satellite in our modern urban fields. The British and U.S. experience with new towns is instructive in this regard. But we can build new communities within the network of cities and towns of the urban field, if our aims are limited to providing alternate environments for living and to controlling the direction of urban development.

(4) Can we and should we continue to sustain a single strong centre? The process of dispersing historically centralized communities leaves in its wake tendencies to physical and economic deterioration. And as our investments in transportation facilities on the outskirts increase so does the dispersal of activities.[12] But can we afford to redress the balance with new transportation focused on the centre and costing considerably more to build? If so, what kind of activities should locate at the centre? Are our present administrative arrangements sufficient for the battle, or can they ever be? The automobile may already have won the contest and we may have to articulate our urban centres so that they are consistent with the emerging urban form encouraged by the automobile.

[12]The amount of people entering downtown Toronto every day has leveled off.

(5) <u>What standards should there be for public utilities</u>? There may be some areas which come under pressure for development which are costly to service with water and sewage. Still other areas, if not served at a high level, may affect the pollution levels of undeveloped areas. A related question is how to equalize geographica tax burdens given the possibility of a variety of bases upon which communities are founded?

(6) <u>What is the future of parks and open space</u>? One of the prime assets of the enlarging urban scope is its open space, scenic attractiveness, and traditional settings. It is essential that we do not destroy these assets in the process of urban development in the next 35 years. Conservation for human use as well as for safeguards for natural processes will have to become a focus of our urban regional planning. The maintenance of the historical qualities of older towns in the region which are sought as places of residence is important too... a rich environmenta experience, including the maintenance of agricultural lands, should be a chief objective of the development planning.

(7) <u>What are the likely effects on housing policy</u>? The urban field as we described it will not allow for any simply structured or homogenous housing policy. The large city containing the full array of housing types sufficient for purposes of "filtering down" will no longer be a valid model. The wide dispersal of jobs for all income levels will necessitate the wide dispersal of housing types, from public housing to affluent housing. The great diversity of environments which we can anticipate in the urban field calls for comparable diversity in our building regulations. And the relaxing of constraints on location due to our greater mobility argues strongly for land development control over the entire urban field -- possibly even nationalization of urban field land space.

References.

CHAPIN, F. S. and H. C. HIGHTOWER. 1965. Household activity patterns and land use. <u>Journal for the American Institute of Planners</u> 3(August):222-31.

GALBRAITH, J. K. 1958. <u>The Affluent Society.</u> Boston: Houghton Mifflin.

GRAVEL, R. 1968. Travel and trip patterns in the outer rural ring of Toronto. <u>Seminar Paper No. 4</u>, Centre for Urban and Community Studies, University of Toronto.

HAMMER, P. A. 1968. The distribution and impact of cottagers in Toronto's urban field. Seminar Paper No. 3, Centre for Urban and Community Studies, University of Toronto.

HODGE, G. 1967. Emerging bounds of urbanization. Community Planning Review 18:4-9.

FRIEDMANN, J. and J. MILLER. 1965. The urban field. Journal of the American Institute of Planners 31:312-19.

KUSNER, M. E. 1968. New parameters in rural land subdivision. Seminar Paper No. 2, Centre for Urban and Community Studies, University of Toronto.

LOWER MAINLAND PLANNING BOARD OF BRITISH COLUMBIA. 1963. Chance and Challenge. New Westminster, B.C.: LMPB

METROPOLITAN TORONTO AND REGION TRANSPORTATION STUDY. 1966. Growth and Travel Past and Present. Toronto: MTRTS

MEYER, J. R. 1962. Knocking down the straw men. Challenge 7-11.

MUMFORD, L. 1961. The City in History. New York: Harcourt, Brace.

ONTARIO DEPARTMENT OF MUNICIPAL AFFAIRS. 1966. Recreation Tomorrow. Toronto, Ont.

OUTDOOR RECREATIONS RESOURCES REVIEW COMMISSION. 1964. Action for Outdoor Recreation. Washington, D.C.: G.P.O.

WOLFE, R. I. 1966. Parameters of Recreational Travel in Ontario. DHO Report No. RB 111. Toronto: Ontario Department of Highways.

WURSTER, C. B. 1963. The form and structure of the future urban complex. In L. Wingo, Jr., ed. Cities and Space. Baltimore: Johns Hopkins, pp. 73-102.